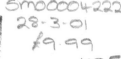

CONTENTS

0 415110939

Feminist Review is published three times a year by a London based collective.

The Collective: Avtar Brah, Ann Phoenix, Annie Whitehead, Catherine Hall, Clara Connolly, Dot Griffiths, Gail Lewis, Helen Crowley, Mary McIntosh, Sue O'Sullivan.

Guest editor this issue: Nel Druce

Corresponding editors: Kum-Kum Bhavnani, currently resident in the USA; Ann Marie Wolpe, currently resident in South Africa.

Correspondence and advertising
Contributions, books for review and editoral correspondence should be sent to:
Feminist Review, 52 Featherstone Street, London EC1Y 8RT.
For advertising please write to:
David Polley, Routledge, 11 New Fetter Lane, London EC4P 4EE

Subscriptions
Please write to: Subscriptions Department, Routledge Journals, Cheriton House, North Way, Andover, Hants SP10 5BE.

Contributions
Feminist Review needs copy to be presented in house style with references complete and in the right form. We can supply you with a style sheet. Please send in 3 copies plus the original (4 copies in all). In cases of hardship 2 copies will do. All papers are subject to peer review.

Bookshop distribution in the USA
Routledge, 29 West 35th Street, New York, NY10001, USA.

Typeset by Type Study, Scarborough
Printed in Great Britain
at the University Press, Cambridge

PHOTOCOPYING AND REPRINT PERMISSIONS

ISSN 0141-7789

The *Feminist Review* office has moved.
Please send all correspondence to:
Feminist Review
52 Featherstone Street
London EC1Y 8RT

EDITORIAL: The New Politics of Sex and the State

This issue of *Feminist Review* focuses on the new politics of sex and the state. The emphasis is on Britain, but we begin with an important overview from the Caribbean. Jacqui Alexander's account of recent legislation on sexual practices and sexuality considers ways in which postcolonial states attempt the public arbitration of private morality as a means of resolving crises of political legitimation. Powerful feelings about sexuality, femininity and masculinity are mobilized in the form of a claim by the state to embody and represent 'the nation'. One of the preconditions for this is the construction that the nation itself is in a process of disintegration – a notion reflected in popular discourses about moral decay. This disintegration manifests itself in part in a crisis of authority relations between men and women: state and civil society.

M. Jacqui Alexander's frame for reading recent changes in legislation in the Caribbean governing sexualities foregrounds the relationship between sexuality, legitimation and individual and national identity. Many aspects of contemporary British debates about sex and the state can be read using a similar frame, although there is an additional emphasis on ideological contestations about the family. In the eighteen months since we planned this issue of *Feminist Review*, Britain has seen an explosion of entanglements involving the sexual morality of politicians within the Tory government. Many of these cases graphically illustrate the changing nature of contemporary familial relations and sexual morality. These changes are at the same time being ignored and refused in a whole range of Tory policies and campaigning rhetoric which adversely affect women and young girls.

Nowhere is this more apparent than in the workings of the Child Support Agency. In the UK, this agency is attempting a major redistribution of resources in the form of reprivatizing income support for single mothers. Although this process is proving administratively and politically problematic, there is no doubt that the goal of these new sexual politics is to divest the state of other than minimal public and collective support for the families of single mothers. This policy of redistribution will secure a further extension of the feminization of poverty, an outcome which is being masked by the media attention on the complaints of fathers with second families. Divorce, marriage breakdown and subsequent 'second families' inevitably raise issues of equity in the living standards and life chances for all a man's children. They have been disguised by acceptance of the convention that children are the mother's responsibility, and a careless and conventional acceptance of women's 'state-subsidized' poverty. Whereas the government rhetoric is that the Child Support Agency precisely deals with these issues, the reality is that the vulnerability of single mothers has been exacerbated on all fronts. In her article, Jane Millar maps out the current predicaments faced by women – a reinstated dependence on absent fathers, pressure to enter the low-waged economy, and increasing, not decreasing, poverty.

These outcomes are inevitable because this particular child-support policy is monetarist in inspiration and driven by the politically imposed need to reduce public expenditure. Far from containing a new blueprint for family relations, the policy simply recycles an old ideal, embodied in the phrase 'the nuclear family'. It is the gender inequalities in this traditional family, which were themselves a source of female poverty, that women are seeking to escape in new family forms. As Millar shows, the Child Support Agency makes this less possible and not more.

Similar contradictions are apparent in relation to sex education and teenage pregnancies. Here the issue is not one of resources, but the complex ways in which these issues of private morality have been used in recent British political struggles. Rachel Thomson looks at the development of successive Tory interventions into sex education, the role of schools in inculcating values and at their links to the wider politics of education. She identifies the present moment as one in which values are to be imposed on young people in a climate of prescriptive moralism. As a result, careful programmes of progressive sex education centred on personal relations and sexual identity are being dismantled. The constraining and punitive nature of these interventions works in part through a process of self-censorship. Teachers feel exposed to the right-wing views of a minority of parents, who have been politically empowered by a series of legislative changes. This is part of the much wider Tory attack on an educational culture which still retains some sense of a progressive agenda. So, in spite of the growing evidence that there is an inverse relationship between teenage pregnancy and comprehensive progressive sex education, the Conservative Government offers only continence and chastity to teenagers facing difficult decisions about personal behaviour in an increasingly harsh world of sexuality and survival.

Susan Reinhold's article deals with an earlier moment in British politics when sex education took the centre stage in the battle for public support for the Tory Party. Before 1986 Tory Party discourses in sex education were about contraception, pregnancy, young people's sexual activity, marriage, divorce and single-parent families, but between 1986 and 1990, when Clause 28 was being put on the statute books, the discourses about sex education became centred on homosexuality. The positive-images campaigns planned by a few local councils, which aimed to reverse the negative stereotyping of homosexuality in schools, provided an ideological hostage for the wider programme of Tory Party assault on local government. The central element of this attack was a ferocious demonizing of homosexuality both in terms of its unnatural and abnormal sexual practices and the abnormality of its family structures and family values. Gay relationships were defined as in opposition to the family. The sustained and systematic attack on pretend families reveals an extraordinary ideological bankruptcy in relation to the reality of contemporary family relationships. Yet the rhetoric is completely empty. The gap is growing between the repressive state definitions of sexual identities and family forms and the complex negotiations of family, sex and sexuality in women's everyday lives. Clause 28 severely diminished the public spaces for these negotiations and secured a significant loss of personal freedom, which is again being challenged in the mobilization around the age of consent for gay men.

One issue which has been a sustained arena for struggles about personal freedom is that of abortion, dealt with here by Janet Hadley, who compares anti-abortion campaigns in Poland and the USA. In both cases, the strongest anti-abortion constituency has come from organized religion, Christian fundamentalists in the US and the Roman Catholic Church in Poland. In both cases, however, the particular trajectory of anti-abortion politics arises out of the ways in which these constituencies are taken up and used in wider political agendas. In Poland, abortion has become the flagship of a Catholic Church which paradoxically symbolizes the post-1989 democracy movement. In the US, the abortion issue, which has been a long-standing battleground between the moral right and liberalism, became central in the lead-up to the 1984 presidential election. By harnessing Christian fundamentalism, through the moral majority, Reagan reinvigorated a section of the increasingly dormant electoral population by refusing to condemn attacks on abortion clinics. British anti-abortionists, working in a much more secular national culture, have been blocked by a medicalization of access to abortion in which doctors exercise professional criteria in the decision to abort. While this has deprived anti-abortionists of an easier opponent (such as 'murdering mothers'), the recent developments in genetic screening open up a new set of issues around potential eugenicist technologies and their control and implementation.

Cheryl Overs makes the point that the state response to the issue of the sexual health of prostitutes in the context of the HIV epidemic varies from the highly repressive to 'softer' approaches. Some interventions take the form of funding for already existing prostitutes' rights organizations. Although she argues that some feminists have been on the same side as Christian fundamentalists against prostitution, she also points out that there are important potentials for alliances between these prostitutes' rights organizations and AIDS activists, including some feminists.

In the final section we turn to the questions of how and whether feminists can engage with the state to promote and represent women's interests. It is critical to examine the processes by which feminist agendas are incorporated and/or subverted when state institutions seemingly respond, but do so in the context of their own political, economic and organizational imperatives. As one example of this, Jeanne Gregory and Sue Lees examine the effect of changes in police practice which initially challenged the dominant sexist discourse about rape on the legal outcomes for North London women who have been raped. The fact that the state is not monolithic both provides feminists with opportunities to shift the agenda and contains these shifts. Women who have been raped still fail to secure justice because the positive response to feminist concerns is so very partial and the more powerful areas of the police and judiciary are as yet untouched.

Taken as a whole, this collection of essays suggests that feminist interventions in 'the state' must resolve the tension between the findings of such concrete empirically based studies and global or meta critiques. The clamour which seeks to reinstate repressive social orders, which in some cases has become hysterical, seems all pervasive, but analyses based on empirical studies provide some grounds for optimism. In them we see that postcolonial reality is everywhere challenging the post-colonial state's attempts to use discourses of sex and the family to retain power.

NOT JUST (ANY) *BODY* CAN BE A CITIZEN: The Politics of Law, Sexuality and Postcoloniality in Trinidad and Tobago and the Bahamas

M. Jacqui Alexander

I am an outlaw in my country of birth: a national; but not a citizen. Born in Trinidad and Tobago on the cusp of anti-colonial nationalist movements there, I was taught that once we pledged our lives to the new nation, 'every creed and race [had] an equal place.' I was taught to believe 'Massa Day Done', that there would be an imminent end to foreign domination. Subsequent governments have not only eclipsed these promises, they have revised the very terms of citizenship to exclude me. No longer equal, I can be brought up on charges of 'serious indecency' under the Sexual Offences Act of 1986, and if convicted, serve a prison term of five years. In the Bahamas, I can be found guilty of the *crime* of lesbianism and imprisoned for twenty years. In the United States of North America where I now live, I must constantly keep in my possession the immigrant (green) card given me by the American state, marking me 'legal' resident alien; non-national; non-citizen. If I traverse any of the borders of twenty-two states even *with* green card in hand, I may be convicted of crimes variously defined as 'lewd unnatural; lascivious conduct; deviate sexual intercourse; gross indecency; buggery or crimes against nature' (Robson, 1992: 58).

Why has the state marked these sexual inscriptions on my body? Why has the state focused such a repressive and regressive gaze on me and people like me? These are some of the questions I seek to understand in this paper. I wish to use this moment to look back at the state, to reverse, subvert and ultimately demystify that gaze by taking apart these racialized legislative gestures that have naturalized heterosexuality by criminalizing lesbian and other forms of non-procreative sex. It is crucial for us as feminists to understand the ways in which the state deploys power in this domain and the kinds of symbolic boundaries it draws around sexual difference, for these are the very boundaries around which its power coheres (Hall, 1994). Indeed, 'homosexual' difference is indispensable to the creation of the putative heterosexual norm. Located, then, within the very oppositional movements which the state has outlawed, I look back as part of the ongoing and complicated process of decolonization and reconstruction of the self, a project which has been seriously disrupted in most 'postcolonial' nation-states.

I want to suggest a way of thinking about state nationalism and its sexualization of particular bodies in Trinidad and Tobago and the Bahamas in order to determine whether such bodies are offered up, as it were, in an internal struggle for legitimation in which these post-colonial states are currently engulfed. What kinds of reassurances do these bodies provide, and for whom? The state's authority to rule is currently under siege; the ideological moorings of nationalism have been dislodged, partly because of major international political econ-omic incursions that have in turn provoked an internal crisis of auth-ority. I argue that in this context criminalization functions as a tech-nology of control, and much like other technologies of control becomes an important site for the production and reproduction of state power (Heng and Devan, 1992).

Although policing the sexual (stigmatizing and outlawing several kinds of non-procreative sex, particularly lesbian and gay sex and prostitution) has something to do with sex, it is also more than sex. Embedded here are powerful signifiers about appropriate sexuality, about the kind of sexuality that presumably imperils the nation and about the kind of sexuality that promotes citizenship. Not just (any) *body* can be a citizen any more, for *some* bodies have been marked by the state as non-procreative, in pursuit of sex only for pleasure, a sex that is non-productive of babies and of no economic gain. Having refused the heterosexual imperative of citizenship, *these* bodies, according to the state, pose a profound threat to the very survival of the nation. Thus, I argue that as the state moves to reconfigure the nation it simul-taneously resuscitates the nation as heterosexual.

Yet, the focus on state power is not to imply rationality or even internal coherence. In fact, what is evident in the legislation and in other contextual gestures surrounding it are paradoxical and contra-dictory ways in which the state exerts its will to power. Seemingly emancipatory practices such as legal 'protections' of women's interests or provisions which constrain violent domestic patriarchy are crafted in the same frame that disciplines and punishes people with HIV infection, and women who exercise erotic autonomy. In addition, the state moves to police the sexual and reinscribe inherited and more recently constructed meanings of masculinity and femininity, while simul-taneously mediating a political economy of desire in tourism that relies upon the sexualization and commodification of women's bodies. Further, the nationalist state mediates the massive entry of trans-national capital within national borders, but blames sexual decadence (lesbian and gay sex and prostitution) for the dissolution of the nation. It may no longer be possible to understand the state purely within the boundaries of the nation because these global processes are rapidly transforming the ways that nations constitute and imagine themselves. This is why methodologically I foreground the economic and political processes of transnationalization to better examine the processes of sexualization undertaken in the legal text. The role of the imperial in transforming the national is therefore crucial.

These paradoxes raise some perplexing questions for feminist theorizing and for oppositional movements. Clearly feminist mobilizations have been successful in wresting certain concessions from the state and in inaugurating vigorous public discussion about sexualized violence. They have also challenged the state on its meaning and definitions of crisis. Yet feminists are also caught in the paradoxical discursive parameters set up by the state and end up helping to devise and monitor the state's mechanisms that surveille criminalized women. On what basis then, would solidarity work among different women be possible? Further, when one examines the effects of these transformations, it becomes clear that some areas of patriarchy have been challenged while others have been resolidified. Citizenship, for instance, continues to be premised within heterosexuality and principally within heteromasculinity. In the absence of visible lesbian and gay movements, can feminist political struggles radically transform these historically repressive structures? How can women inscribe their own interests within fundamentally masculinist organizations (Irigaray, 1985).

I shall begin by reading the ways in which the heterosexual is naturalized in the legal text in order to isolate its importance to the state. In the section that follows, I analyse the ways in which naturalized heterosexuality shapes the definitions of respectability, Black masculinity and nationalism. We come full circle, then, as I argue that the effects of political economic international processes provoke a legitimation crisis for the state which moves to restore its legitimacy by recouping heterosexuality through legislation. I end by suggesting that the process of decolonization, which the nationalist state had claimed as its own, has been seriously disrupted and I draw out the implications for oppositional movements and analyses.

Naturalizing heterosexuality as law

In 1986, the Parliament of the Republic of Trinidad and Tobago scripted and passed the Sexual Offences Act: 'An Act to Repeal and Replace the Laws of the Country relating to Sexual Crimes, to the Procuration, Abduction and Prostitution of Persons and to Kindred Offences.' This gesture of consolidation was, in the words of law commissioners, an attempt 'to bring all laws dealing with sexual offences under one heading.' It was the first time the postcolonial state confronted earlier colonial practices which policed and scripted 'native' sexuality to help consolidate the myth of imperial authority.

Many of the thirty-five provisions of the legislation, then, had prior lives, and were being reconsolidated under a different schedule of punishments. Prohibitions regarding sexual violence within the family (incest), and against women who exchanged sex for money (prostitutes) and those who aided them (brothel-keepers), or those who exploited them (pimps) had long been established in the emendations to the Offences Against the Person Acts, that one-sided pivot of British jurisprudence. In keeping with its allegiance to hegemonic masculinity, the script upheld a prior provision that defined anal intercourse between men as buggery, outlawed it, and affixed a penalty of ten years imprisonment, if convicted. It moved, in addition, to criminalize new areas of sexual activity. Established were prohibitions against employers who took sexual advantage of their minor employees at the workplace, and against men who had sex with fourteen- to sixteen-year-old girls, who would now be guilty of a statutory offence. For the first time, a category called rape within marriage was established and criminalized: 'Any "husband" who had forceful intercourse with his "wife" without her consent' could be convicted and imprisoned for fifteen years under a new offence called sexual assault; and sex between women became punishable by five years under a new offence called '"serious indecency", if committed on or towards a person sixteen years or more.'

Three years later, the parliament of the Bahamas scripted and passed its own version of the Sexual Offences Act, cited as the 'Sexual Offences and Domestic Violence Act of 1989', *its* gesture of consolidation, formulated by law commissioners 'as an attempt to provide one comprehensive piece of legislation setting out sexual offences which are indictable', seeking, in its words, 'to make better provision in respect of the rights in the occupation of the matrimonial home.' As in the case of Trinidad and Tobago, it was the first attempt to impose a veiled sexual order on the chaotic legacy of colonialism. The commission had hoped to deal not only with this chaos, but also with the disruptions and violence of conjugal relations by reasserting the primacy of the matrimonial home and the rights of '*any* person' residing therein.

Its thirty-one provisions bore close resemblance to those of Trinidad and Tobago in terms of the injunctions, prohibitions and schedule of punishments against prostitution, incest, and sexual harassment and assault in the workplace. It too, conflated buggery, bestiality and criminality: 'If any two persons are guilty of the crime of buggery – an unnatural crime, or if any person is guilty of unnatural connection with any animal, every such person is guilty of an offence and liable to imprisonment for twenty years.' This definition resembles the first civil injunction against sodomy that was legislated in 1533 in Henry VIII's parliament (Cohen: 1989). In its injunction against sex between women, it abandoned the coyness of the Trinidad legislature in favour of an explicit approach that pronounced, criminalized and penalized a sexual activity in one single gesture: 'Any female who has sexual intercourse with another female, whether with or without the consent of that female, is guilty of the offence of lesbianism and is liable to imprisonment for twenty years.' Similarly, under restrictive stipulations that were an exact replication of those in Trinidad, it moved to criminalize violent marital sex, but fell short of calling it rape. The legislation asserted: 'Any person who has sexual intercourse with his spouse without the consent of the spouse is guilty of the offence of sexual assault and liable to imprisonment for fifteen years.' The law also moved to imprison (for five years) anyone with HIV infection who had consensual sex without disclosing their HIV status.

Its new provision, relating to domestic violence, made it possible for *any* party in the marriage to apply to the Supreme Court for an injunction that would restrain the other party from molestation and from using violence in the matrimonial home. What is remarkable about this act that calls itself a domestic violence act is that nowhere is there a definition of domestic violence. Rather the majority of the provisions focus upon the disposition of private property and on the minute distinctions among 'dwelling, estate, apartment', etc. These were not the terms on which the women's movement in the Bahamas had pushed for the criminalization of domestic violence. Over a five-year period, women held public rallies, campaigned door to door and gained more than 10,000 signatures and the knowledge from women's experiences of physical and sexual violence against themselves and their daughters. It would seem then, that even in the face of violent disruptions in marriage, conjugal heterosexuality is most concerned with the patrilineal transfer of private property.

Legislative gestures fix conjugal heterosexuality in several ways. Generally, they collapse identities into sexual bodies which, in the particular case of lesbian and gay people, serves to reinforce a fiction about promiscuity: that sex is all of what we do and consequently the slippage, it is all of who we are. Yet lesbian and gay sex, the 'pervert', the 'unnatural' are all indispensable to the formulation of the 'natural', the conjugal, the heterosexual. This dialectic must be made visible, for there is no absolute set of commonly understood or accepted principles called the 'natural' which can be invoked definitionally except as they relate to what is labelled 'unnatural'. Here is a remarkably circular definition of sexual intercourse that was attached as a supplementary note to the Trinidad and Tobago Act:

> [The Clauses] do not necessarily define 'sexual intercourse' but give a
> characteristic of it. 'Sexual intercourse' means natural sexual intercourse
> in the clauses relating to rape and other offences of sexual intercourse
> with women, whereas the clause concerned with buggery relates to
> unnatural sexual intercourse.

Heterosexual sex, even while dysfunctional (as in rape in marriage, domestic violence and incest), assumes the power of natural law only in relation to sex which is defined in negation to it (what natural sexual intercourse is not) and in those instances where desire presumably becomes so corrupt that it expresses itself as bestiality. In other words, heterosexual practices carry the weight of the natural only in relational terms and ultimately, one might argue, only in its power to designate as unnatural those practices which disrupt marriage and certain dominant notions of conjugal family. Beyond that, sexual intercourse remains necessarily, remarkably unclarified.

Conjugal heterosexuality is frozen within a very specific and narrow set of class relations between 'husband' and 'wife' in 'marriage', narrow because the majority of heterosexual relationships are in fact organized outside of this domain. Even while the Bahamian legislation might appear to address violence in all 'domestic' domains, its skewed emphasis on private property immediately renders it class specific. For working-class women who do not own property and are beaten by the men with whom they live, this legislation offers no protection. And even for middle-class and upper-middle-class women who are beaten by their husbands and might own property, the problem they face is how to disentangle the web of well-connected social relationships that protect *their* middle-class and upper-middle-class husbands from being prosecuted as criminals. For most women who stand outside of the legal definitions of 'parties to a marriage', they can make no claims for relief from the state. Thus, domestic violence works as a proxy for class and facilitates the reallocation of private property in disruptive conjugal marriage.

Both pieces of legislation systematically conflate violent hetero*sexual* domination, such as rape and incest, with same-sex relations, thereby establishing a continuum of criminality among same *sex* rape, domestic violence, adultery, fornication and dishonesty. On this continuum the psyche of homosexuality becomes the psyche of criminality. By criminalizing perverted heterosexual sex, the legislation aims to expunge criminal elements from the heterosexual so that it could return to its originary and superior moral position. However, homosexuality, inherently perverse, could only be cleansed by reverting to heterosexuality. And still, not all heterosexualities are permissible: not the prostitute with an irresponsible, 'non-productive' sexuality, and not young women whom the state defines as girls requiring its protection.

Outside the boundaries of the legislation, yet informing it, state managers generated a simultaneous discourse invoking nostalgia for a Bahamas and Trinidad and Tobago when there were ostensibly no lesbians, gay men and people with AIDS. In this move, heterosexuality becomes coterminus with and gives birth to the nation. Its antithesis can unravel the nation. The state has eroticized the dissolution of the nation, producing apocalyptic (mythic) visions of dread disease and destruction (paralleled in the destruction of Sodom and Gomorrah) brought about by prostitution and the practice of lesbian and gay sex. Yet, it simultaneously enacts the dissolution of the nation through a series of political-economic gestures (adherence to the narratives and practices of modernization through allegiance to multinational capital, tourism, etc.) that it ideologically recodes as natural, even supernatural, as the salvation of the people. In this equation, tourism, foreign multi-national capital production and imperialism are as integral and as necessary to the natural order as heterosexuality. But before examining these twin processes of sexualization and internationalization more closely, one would have to understand why conjugal heterosexuality is so important for nationalist state managers and the role it plays in constituting respectable masculinity. We would have to understand the sexual inheritances of nationalism as well as the new meanings of masculinity and femininity the nationalist state has invented.

State nationalism and respectability, Black masculinity come to power 1962, 1972

> Women, and all signs of the feminine, are by definition always already anti-national (Heng, 1992).

It would be difficult to map the minute and nuanced ways in which colonial hegemonic definitions of masculinity and femininity insinuated themselves throughout the variety of political, economic, social and cultural structures in history. We can, however, frame these definitions by examining what Kobena Mercer and Isaac Julien have called the 'hegemonic repertoire of images' which have been forged through the histories of slavery and colonization in order to identify the sexual inheritances of Black nationalism as well as its own inventions. (Mercer and Julien, 1988: 132–5). I am not suggesting that ideologies simply get foisted onto people (Burawoy, 1982), for there is always an ongoing struggle to redefine power. What is crucial for my argument, however, is the intransigence of dominance and, in this instance, the continuities and discontinuities between the practices of the colonial and the 'postcolonial' around those very images.

In the repertoire of images that developed during the organization of slave-plantation economy and in the consolidation of imperial rule, the English gentleman was given primacy. In Trinidad and Tobago white militarized masculinity had to concede the right to rule to the civilian who would displace the importance of war and the more visible signs of policing and terror. Similarly in the Bahamas, the pirate, the rogue and the wrecker (white predatory masculinity) were engaged in a protracted struggle with the English gentleman for cultural and economic authority until the latter was installed as representative of the crown in 1718. It marked the triumph of respectability and honour over the boorish, the disreputable (Saunders, 1990: 2).

Colonial rule simultaneously involved racializing and sexualizing the population, which also meant naturalizing whiteness. There could really be no psycho-social codices of sexuality that were not simultaneously raced. In general terms, these codices functioned as mythic meta-systems fixing polarities, contradictions and fictions while masked as truth about character. 'Laws for the governing of Negroes, Mulattoes and Indians' (Saunders, 1990:8; Goveia, 1970) made it possible for white masculinity to stand outside the law. As the invisible subject of the law, he was neither prosecuted nor persecuted within it. Since it was lawful to reinforce the ontological paradox of slave as chattel, Elizabethan statutes of rape operated to legitimize violent colonial masculinity which was never called rape, yet criminalized black masculinity for rape. This would solidify the cult of true womanhood and its correlates, the white madonna (untouchable) and the Black whore (promiscuous).

Here too, identities were collapsed into bodies. Black bodies, the economic pivot of slave-plantation economy, were sexualized. Black women's bodies evidenced an unruly sexuality, untamed and wild. Black male sexuality was to be feared as the hypersexualized stalker. These dominant constructions worked to erase indigenous (Lucayan, Carib and Arawak) sexualities. Indentured Indian femininity (in Trinidad and Tobago) was formulated as dread and desire, mysteriously wanton, inviting death and destruction, although it could also be domesticated. Indian manliness was unrestrained, violent and androgynous, the latter construction drawn from Britain's colonial experience in India. Free coloured women, who outnumbered Black women in the Bahamas, and their counterparts in Trinidad and Tobago who were believed anxious to 'acquire property and wealth by inheriting land for the natural white fathers', were also sexualized, but positioned as potential mates (Saunders, 1990:18, 19; McDaniel, 1986). Even with these differences in the construction of 'native' sexualities, however, colonized sexualities were essentially subordinated sexualities.

It would indeed require a complicated set of cognitive and ideological reversals for the British to turn the savage into the civilized, to turn those believed incapable of rule into reliable rulers. Herein lies the significance of socialization into British norms, British manners, British parliamentary modes of governance; into conjugal marriage and the 'science' of domesticity. This would operate in effect as socialization into respectability which George Mosse argues emerged in Europe at the end of the eighteenth century with the beginnings of modern nationalism. He argues that respectability emerged in alliance with sexuality and helped to shape middle-class beliefs about the body, sexual (mis)conduct, normality and abnormality, about virility and manly bearing. The control over sexuality evidenced in the triumph of the nuclear family was vital to respectability (Mosse, 1985:2–10). Whereas in Europe these processes were indigenous to the formation of the middle class, in the Caribbean it was imported through imperialism. The Black middle class would be schooled in the definitions of morality, civility and respectable citizenship in the metropolis, in the company of the British, while 'women of reduced means' and the working class would be trained at 'home'. Specialized training schools like the Dundas Civic Center in the Bahamas were established at the turn of this century to prepare cooks, general maids and hotel workers; and the Trinidad and Tobago Home Industries and Women's Self Help Organization and the Oleander Club of the Bahamas would train Black women in housewifery, cooking, sewing and knitting (Saunders, 1990; Reddock, 1984: 245).

It was the élites of the middle class who established the nationalist parties which later became part of the state apparatus. They mobilized consensus for nation building, moulded psychic expectations about citizenship and therefore consolidated their own internal power on the ideals of sovereignty, self-determination and autonomy from foreign mandates. Ostensibly this was a neutered invocation to citizenship; yet it was in the creation of the women's wing of these parties and in their organization of 'culture' that one begins to detect a gendered call to patriotic duty. Women were to fiercely defend the nation by protecting their honour, by guarding the nuclear, conjugal family, 'the fundamental institution of the society', by guarding 'culture' defined as the transmission of a fixed set of proper values to the children of the nation, and by mobilizing on the party's behalf into the far reaches of the country. She was expected to represent and uphold a respectable femininity and, in so doing, displace the figure of the white madonna. Patriotic duty for men, on the other hand, consisted in rendering public service to the country, and in adopting the mores of respectability. Thus, we can identify a certain trajectory in the establishment of nationalism which is grounded in notions of respectability, which like eighteenth-century European nationalism came to rely heavily upon sexual gestures that involved the *symbolic* triumph of the nuclear family over the extended family and other family forms.

In order to demonstrate that it had 'graduated from all schools of constitutional, economic and social philosophies' (Pindling, 1972), and that it could comport itself with 'discipline, dignity, and decorum, with the eyes of the world upon us' (Williams, 1962), Black nationalist masculinity needed to demonstrate that it was now capable of ruling, which is to say, it needed to demonstrate moral rectitude, particularly on questions of paternity. This required distancing itself from irresponsible Black working-class masculinity that spawned the 'bastard', the 'illegitimate', and that thus had to be criminalized for irresponsible fatherhood by the British. It also required distancing itself from, while simultaneously attempting to control, Black working-class femininity that ostensibly harboured a profligate sexuality: the 'Jezebel' and the whore who was not completely socialized into housewifery, but whose labour would be mobilized to help consolidate popular nationalism. Of significance is the fact that Black nationalist masculinity could aspire toward imperial masculinity and, if loyal enough, complicitous enough, could be knighted (Craton, 1986: 29), although it could never be enthroned. It could never become king.

If, as Toni Morrison has suggested, rescue and indebtedness

sometimes sediment as part of the psychic residue of the process of colonization, then respectability might well function as debt payment for rescue from incivility and from savagery (Morrison, 1992: vii–xxx). But a rescued masculinity is simultaneously an injured masculinity; a masculinity that does not emerge from the inherited conditions of class and race privilege. And it is injured in a space most vulnerable to colonial constructions of incivility. At one time subordinated, that masculinity now has to be earned, and then appropriately conferred. Acting through this psychic residue, Black masculinity continues the policing of sexualized bodies, drawing out the colonial fiction of locating subjectivity in the body (as a way of denying it), as if the colonial masters were still looking on, as if to convey legitimate claims to being civilized. Not having dismantled the underlying presuppositions of British law, Black nationalist men, now with some modicum of control over the state apparatus, continue to preside over and administer the same fictions.

To the extent that the sexual offences legislation polices non-procreative, 'non-productive' sex especially in relationship to women, the neutered invocation to citizenship becomes transparent. In fact we can read state practices as attempts to propagate fictions of feminine identity, to reconfigure women's desire and subjectivity and to link the terms of the nation's survival to women's sexual organs. This is what Geraldine Heng calls, in the specific case of Singapore, 'the development of a sexualised, separate species of nationalism, a nationalism gener-ated from the productive source of the womb.' To understand it in Heng's terms, the indictment of prostitutes and lesbians inscribes 'a tacit recognition that feminine reproductive sexuality refuses, and in re-fusing registers a suspicion of that sexuality as non-economic, in pursuit of its own pleasure, sexuality for its own sake, unproductive of babies, unproductive of social and economic efficiency' (Heng and Devan, 1992: 343–64). It registers a suspicion of an unruly sexuality, omnip-otent and omniscient enough to subvert the economic imperatives of the nation's interests. From the point of view of the state, it is a sexuality that has to be disciplined and regulated in order that it might become economically productive.

State claims of a non-productive femininity are deceptive in a number of different ways. Both the People's National Movement (PNM of Trinidad and Tobago) and the Progressive Liberal Party (PLP of the Bahamas) could not have consolidated their power or secured support for popular nationalism without women's labour, women who ironically would later have to struggle for citizenship. Yet once installed, state nationalism came to stand in an authorial relationship to women's interests and women's agency. The claim also works to mask women's labour in other areas of the economy, particularly in the tourist sector where women are the majority of a proletarianized and superexploited workforce. Capital accumulations from sex tourism and prostitution have been hidden, but given what we know about tourism and postcolonialism in South East Asia, it would be most plausible to assume that for the Bahamas in particular, there would be substantial (although now unacknowledged) accumulation from prostitutes' labour (Truong, 1990: 158–91). Further, women's unpaid labour compensates for the state's refusal to expand the social wage and for the disjunctures brought about by the adoption of structural adjustment programmes. It is to these questions I turn in the following section.

(Inter)national boundaries and strategies of legitimation

I wish to foreground the effects of international political economic processes in provoking the legitimacy crisis nationalist states are currently confronting, and argue that the sexual is pivotal in state orchestration of a new internal struggle whose contours are different now than they were at the moment of flag independence. In an almost ideal-typical sense, the nation had come to be shaped by what it had opposed (Anderson, 1983). Public opposition to the British had provided powerful ideological fodder for independence. We had all suffered colonial injustice together, and it was out of that experience of collective suffering that a collective vision of sovereignty could be built. Since 'independence', the state has colluded in adopting strategies that have locked these nations into a world economic and political system, the effect of which is re-colonization. The internal effects of internationaliz-ation blur the boundaries of the nation; they do not constitute anything unique anymore. Further, the reproduction of private accumulation by members of the indigenous bourgeoisie has been stifled (Gibbon, 1992), local patronage networks have been disrupted and people's material and communal lives have dramatically deteriorated. Paradoxically, these same states simultaneously preside over the transfer of substan-tial profits to metropolitan countries. All of these effects replicate the racialized colonial pattern of poverty, private ownership and lack of access to resources. These are the very grounds on which oppositional movements have challenged the state; it is the reason that its moral claim to leadership is unravelling.

But this is not how state managers see the crisis. Both in Trinidad and Tobago and the Bahamas they sound the danger of cultural contamination from the 'West' which they depict simultaneously as sexual intemperance, the importation of AIDS and the importation of feminism (read lesbianism). The Bahamian state has invoked an impending population crisis, positioned Haitian communities as 'immi-grants', 'refugees' and repositories of crime. It has vindicated its use of military and police force to expel Haitians from the nation's borders by claiming that they are no longer legitimate citizens; they imperil the nation. There are other strategies as well, ranging from policing oppositional movements and subtle, yet coercive ideological violence where Bahamian people, for instance, believe that the ballot is not a secret ballot and fear reprisals from the state. Individual state man-agers develop a patronage system to build their own authority in their own political interests, not necessarily consolidating support for nationalism, but for themselves and for their political parties.

State nationalism in Trinidad and Tobago and the Bahamas has neither reformulated nor transformed the fundamental premises upon which economic and material exchange is based. Its secular adherence to a linear definition of 'development' and progress has continued to imagine an (il)logic of a movement from 'tradition' to 'modernity' in which industrialization presumably serves as the motor for economic success. The contemporary version of development now called structural adjustment, finds expression in a powerful, yet unequal alliance among foreign multinational lending agencies such as the International Monetary Fund (IMF), the World Bank, United States Agency for International development (USAID), the American state and neo-colonial regimes. Their aim is to impose a set of lending arrangements that would ostensibly reduce the foreign debt through a combination of economic measures to accelerate foreign investment, boost foreign-exchange earnings through export, and reduce government deficits through cuts in spending (McAfee, 1991: 67–79). In particular, the programmes have been organized to reduce local consumption by devaluing currency, increasing personal taxes and reducing wages. The economy becomes privatized through state subsidies to private vendors, lowering taxes and providing tax holidays for foreign multinational corporations, expanding investments in tourism, dismantling state-owned enterprises, and curtailing the scope of state bureaucratic power by reducing the workforce and reducing the social wage – those expenditures for a range of social services for which the state had previously assumed some responsibility.

Although the Bahamas has not formalized 'structural adjustment' programmes (SAP), the continued subordination of its economy to the political and economic imperatives of the United States of North America has resulted in an economic infrastructure that bears all the marks of a country that has actually adopted structural adjustment. The most dramatic shift is evident in the displacement of capital and labour forces from agrarian production to service which now employs more than 50 per cent of the workforce, massive increases in the size of the food import bill (people are no longer able to feed themselves), the consolidation of foreign transnational capital in the tourist industry (hotels, airlines, services and tour operators, international finance capital, real estate), and the expansion of off-shore companies.

But perhaps the most significant and dramatic effect of SAP is that it has exacerbated the triple processes of proletarianization superexploitation and feminization of the workforce which began in the mid 1960s. By proletarianization I am referring not only to the influx, or even the magnitude of industrial capital, or the making of a gendered, racialized working class, but perhaps more importantly to the access that capital has in exploiting and even expelling relatively large percentages of the workforce. What makes this impact so profound for the nation in both Trinidad and Tobago and the Bahamas is the small size of the workforce (Rothenberg and Wishner, 1978). In the Bahamas, industrial capital has access to a sizeable portion of the workforce. More than 65% of the working population is employed in service with women comprising more than 73% of all workers, performing jobs such as housekeepers, cooks, maids, cleaners and laundresses. Two-thirds of these women earn incomes of $7,000 annually. Of the total workforce, 22% have never been employed. Women's unemployment, which has always been higher than men's, is 13%, and that of men is 11.7% and steadily increasing.

In Trinidad and Tobago, the process of proletarianization which began in the 1970s has had different, yet similar effects. Private capital employs roughly the same amount of the workforce as the state, 36% and 38% respectively. Areas such as construction, the impetus for proletarianization in the 1970s, have experienced severe retrenchment. This is particularly affecting women whose rate of unemployment in that sector is now 73%, compared to the national average of 46%. (Henry and Williams, 1991: 315). Like the Bahamas, there has been a signifi-cant growth in the service sector, but it has come from self-employment and within the state bureaucracy where women work as clerical workers, nurses, teachers and maids. State retrenchments under IMF restrictions have increased women's unemployment. The overall un-employment rate in Trinidad and Tobago is 19%; women's unemploy-ment rate is 23%.

Gendered superexploitation can best be assessed by the gap between workers' real wages and the profit which capital accrues and never returns to the workforce. Overall, the rate of return from the United States' investment in the Caribbean is considerably higher (31% to 14.3%) than the returns generated from investments in other parts of the world (Barry, 1984: 19). In the Bahamas, almost three-fourths of households (74%) live on an annual income of $10,000. Of these households, almost all (82%) are headed by women, at least half of whom are employed in the tourist industry. In contrast, earnings from tourism contributed 61% of the total export earnings of the Bahamian state (Rosensweig, 1988: 89–100). The limitations of tourism as a national economic strategy are immediately apparent with the recognition that 81 cents of every tourist dollar spent in the Bahamas finds its way back to the United States (Barry, 1984).

In the space between foreign- and state-controlled export has arisen a substantial informal economy that operates at different levels. Some elements of it are masculinized, particularly those in the drug trade that are linked to tourism. This marks another incursion on state control because people can make quick money and improve their standard of living. Drug lords can command authority and develop a horizontal patronage system that rivals that of state managers, while simul-taneously remaining outside the arm of state regulation. In fact, state managers have had to deal with an erosion of their own credibility because of their complicity in the drug trade – one of the many faces of the underside of respectability (Smith, Gomez and Willes, 1984). Not labelled an illegal activity by the state, the feminized informal economy is involved in trade and marketing, relying on kinship, long-established peer networks and communal ties. Much like farmers' co-operatives, these networks provide for people's everyday needs.

It is difficult to imagine that these massive economic disjunctures with corresponding deterioration in the quality of people's daily lives, precipitated by SAP, would not provoke a major political crisis for the state. Emerging within this crisis are serious contestations to the state's right to rule. The question is how do these movements frame their opposition to the state? Even with the importance of material struggles in people's lives, one of the more crucial elements uniting these varied constituencies is the urgency to move beyond questions of survival to, as Joan French has argued, 'creating, building community, deepening the understanding of oneself and of others, developing local, regional, and international structures for communication and participation' (McAfee, 1991: 188). The focus of the challenges, therefore, is to transform the nature and definition of development from profit and exploitation to holistic, participatory models, the maps of which are still being worked out (Antrobus in McAfee, 1991: 187). Not surprisingly, the most sustained, organized challenges have originated within non-governmental organizations, a loose affiliation of groups of trade unions, churches and grass-roots organizations. Farmers' co-operatives not only challenge the state with a model of collective agricultural production, very dissimilar to the corporate profit model, but also, under difficult conditions, they are doing what the state has refused to do: feed the population. A regional feminist movement in the Caribbean as a whole and specific movements in both countries have developed some of the most sustained critiques of the devastating effects of structural adjustment as state violence. They have argued that unemployment has destroyed the identity of the male 'provider' resulting in increased violence against women for which they hold the state accountable.

State nationalism, globalization and privatization

State-supported globalization of capital is crucial not only because of the internal political effects I outlined earlier, but also because these international processes help to refigure definitions of masculinity and femininity and simultaneously undermine the ideological bases upon which the state organizes, separates and draws from the 'public' and 'private' domains. International practices dovetail with state ideologies about masculinity and femininity, and in particular with ideological constructions of women's work. The most significant retrenchment with the adoption of SAP has taken place in those sectors which have been historically coded as women's work: health, clinic and hospital service, caring for the sick and elderly, social services and education. As women continue their work in the home and their work in the private or public service sector, they work, in addition, to care for the sick and elderly, and to continue the education of their children without state subsidies. The state relies upon and operates within these dominant constructions of a servile femininity, perennially willing and able to serve, a femininity that can automatically fill the gaps left by the state. Quite the opposite of a 'non-productive' femininity drawn in the legislation, these are women doing work, and ironically, state work.

International ideological registers are significant in another important regard that has to do with the presumed disjuncture between the 'public' and 'private' spheres. In one sense, one of the effects of a privatized state is that it becomes somewhat insulated from 'public' demands; what was 'public' responsibility is now shifted elsewhere, in this case on to women who compensate for retrenchment in both spheres. But there is also a paradoxical collapse of this dichotomy, for the state is now relying upon the private – private capital and private households to consolidate its own quest for economic and political power. We know that the household has been an important ideological instrument for the state. It has been indispensable in the creation of the 'public' against which it can be positioned. Because it has been an important space where a particular kind of hierarchical, patriarchal power has resided, the state must move to rehabilitate this sphere by specifically recoding women's experience of domestic violence and rape within it, and generally, by disallowing any household space for lesbians. Yet state economic practices are contributing to the demise of the 'male breadwinner' especially in working-class and working-poor households which are the ones hardest hit by SAP, and in a racialized context are actually intervening to fix racial polarities as well.

We can now return to one of the central paradoxes this paper raises, that of the nationalist state legislating against certain sexualities while relying upon women's sexualized body and a political economy of desire in private capital accumulation. Tourism is the arena in which the moves to privatize the economy through foreign investment, imperial constructions of masculinity and femininity and state constructions of sexualized woman all intersect.

The significance of tourism is that it foregrounds sexual pleasure as a commodity, based in the sexualization of land (through the old imperial trope woman-as-nation) and people. The sinister drama finds expression in commercial advertising and the production of certain fetishes that get signified as 'culture'. Bahama Mama, (there is no Bahama Papa) is a buxom, caricatured, hypersensualized figure that can be bought in the Bahamas; she can also be consumed as 'hot and spicy sausage' at any 'Nice and Easy' convenient store in the United States. Tourists upon their return home can continue to be intoxicated by the Bahamas, order Bloody Mary along with Bahama Mama, alterity as instrument of pleasure. European fantasies of colonial conquest, the exotic, the erotic, the dark, the primitive, of danger, dread and desire all converge here on virgin beaches and are traced back through the contours of imperial geography.

How does one prepare citizens for self-determination and for dependency on its antithesis, tourism, the practice of servility and serviceability, the production of maids, washers, cooks? Black women who must braid white women's hair in the market as they flirt with Blackness, for African styles can only be adopted far away from home. Difference is exotically and fleetingly adopted. These are a complicated set of psycho-sexual gestures converging in this (hetero)sexual playground; this arena which Caribbean state managers see as the economy of the future; where Black masculinity manages phantasmic constructions of Black femininity, satisfying white European desire for restless adventure, satisfying white European longing for what is 'rare and intangible' (hooks, 1992: 21–39).

Mobilizing heterosexuality: post-colonial states and practices of decolonization

My analysis suggests that the archetypal source of state legitimation is anchored in the heterosexual family, the form of family crucial in the state's view to the founding of the nation. This consolidation of domesticity in the very process of nation-building is the sphere in which a certain kind of instrumental legitimation is housed. There is an evident relationship among monogamous heterosexuality (organic representation of sexuality) nationhood and citizenship. Although presumably universal and falling on *every* body, we have seen that it is not just *every* and *any* body, for *some* bodies are not productive enough for the nation. The erosion of heterosexual conjugal monogamy is a perennial source of worry for state managers and so it is invoked and deployed particularly at moments when it is threatened with extinction. Nothing should threaten this sphere; not the single woman, the lesbian, the gay man, the prostitute, the person who is HIV infected. The state must simultaneously infiltrate this domain in order to recoup its original claim to it. It must continue to legislate its existence.

To whom do state managers believe they have access in mobilizing discourses around conservative, homophobic registers? Do they believe that a large number of citizens can be mobilized in its defence? Clearly, this mobilization serves to reassure different constituencies which historically have been important anchoring points for the state, but have currently lost political ground with feminist critiques of patriarchy. It serves to reassure men, for they are the archetypal citizen, conservative elements and religious constituencies in a context in which the religious provides important explanations for daily life, and in the case of the Bahamas, the potential tourist who presumably would not encounter diseased black bodies during his travels. With the globalization of specific definitions of morality, the state believes itself able to conform to the international, and in its view to widely accepted and respectable definitions of morality. Even with efforts to reinvoke patriarchal modes of behaviour and patterns of thinking that are familiar and secure, these nationalist states have not been able to solve their legitimation crisis.

Part of the difficulty we face as feminists doing this kind of analysis, and ironically one of the reasons the state can at least be partially successful in mobilizing heterosexuality, is the persistence of the belief in naturalized heterosexuality, the belief that it lies outside of the sphere of political and economic influence and therefore state influence. In the absence of any visible lesbian and gay movements in the Caribbean, state managers believe they can rely upon heterosexuality even more heavily. Our analyses and mobilizations of the naturalization of heterosexuality have perhaps lagged behind analyses of naturalization in other areas, like women's work, for example. We face a challenge to traverse inherited analytic boundaries that have kept us within discrete and narrow formulations. Radical lesbian and gay movements in metropolitan countries which have demystified heterosexuality, must now take on board analyses of colonization and imperialism, for the effects of these processes loop back to the centre from which they originated. These movements in metropolitan countries need to work assiduously, however, not to reproduce practices of imperialism. If feminists have analysed the masculinization of the state, it is imperative that we also analyse the heterosexualization of the state, for these are twin processes. The urgency of a research and political agenda that continues to make the processes of heterosexualization transparent, tying them to both national and international social interests cannot, therefore, be overstated. If sexualization and internationalization have been linked in the strategies of domination, *we* must link them in our strategies for liberation, although admittedly along different registers (Moraga, 1983). It might help to reduce the impulse to conflate capitalism with democracy and the more pervasive feminist theorizing of liberal *democratic* advanced capitalist states.

More work needs to be done in disentangling the state from the nation and in figuring out differing interests. If indeed our political mobilizations are located between the spaces of state and nation, even state and party, we would need to be clearer about our allegiances and the political bases of solidarity. The analysis should help point to the political responsibility feminists inside the state apparatus have to those on the outside. At the same time, we cannot diminish the intensity of our demands to make the state more accountable.

It is both analytically, and therefore politically necessary to disentangle the processes of decolonization and nation-building. In a real sense, the work of decolonization (the dismantling of the economic, political, psychic and sexual knowledges and practices that accompanied the first five hundred years of conquest) has been disrupted, especially in light of the map I have drawn of these new sexualized strategies of recolonization and the commodification of alienated sexual desire in tourism within nation-states that are infiltrated by corporate globalization politics. The work of decolonization consists as well in the decolonization of the body. Women's bodies have been ideologically dismembered within different discourses: the juridical; profit maximization; religious; and the popular.

How do we, in our alternative movements, construct a collectively imagined future that takes account of these dismemberments, fractures, migrations, exiles and displacements that have been part of these processes of domination? How do we construct home when home is not immediately understood nor instinctively accessible? Our challenge within oppositional movements is to invent home in different spaces that cross geography. We cannot afford to let the international be one-sidedly pernicious.

Notes

M. Jacqui Alexander is currently involved in researching questions relating to the historical construction of sexuality (particularly its legal production) in the Caribbean. An anti-racist worker, she is now at the New School for Social Research in New York City where she teaches courses grounded in feminist critiques of imperialism, colonialism and heterosexuality. An essay exploring the processes of sexualization in the Bahamas is forthcoming in a collection (co-edited with Chandra Talpade Mohanty, spring 1995) entitled *Histories, Movements, Identities: Genealogies of Third World Feminism*, New York: Routledge.

Projects like the one I have undertaken could only survive in an 'intellectual neighbourhood' (the phrase is Toni Morrison's). I am especially thankful to my neighbours Chandra Talpade Mohanty, Linda Carty, Honor Ford Smith, Jinny Chalmers and Mab Segrest for their keen insights, support and friendship. I also wish to thank David Trottman, Angela Robertson and the members of the *Feminist Review* Collective.

References

ANDERSON, Benedict (1983) *Imagined Communities: Reflections on the Origin and Spread of Nationalism* London: Verso.

BARRY, Tom *et al.* (1984) *The Other Side of Paradise: Foreign Control in the Caribbean* New York: Grove.

BRECHER, Jeremy *et al.* (1993) *Global Visions: Beyond the New World Order*, Boston: South End Press.

BURAWOY, Michael (1982) *Manufacturing Consent: Changes in the Labor Process Under Monopoly Capitalism* Chicago: University of Chicago Press.

COHEN, Ed (1989) 'Legislating the norm: from sodomy to gross indecency' *The South Atlantic Quarterly* 88(1): 181–218.

COMMISSION OF INQUIRY (1984) *Report of the Commission of Inquiry,* Bahamas: Bahamas Government Printing Department.

CRATON, Michael (1986) *A History of the Bahamas* Canada: San Salvador.

DEPARTMENT OF STATISTICS (1987) *A Collection of Statistics on Women in the Bahamas 1979–1985* Bahamas: Department of Statistics.

——(1991) *Labour Force and the Household Income Report 1989* Bahamas: Department of Statistics.

ENLOE, Cynthia (1990) *Bananas, Beaches and Bases: Making Feminist Sense of International Politics* Berkeley: University of California Press.

FANON, Frantz (1977) *The Wretched of the Earth*, New York: Grove.

GIBBON, Peter (1992) 'Population and poverty in the changing ideology of the World Bank' Stockholm: PROP Publication Series No. 2.

GOVEIA, Elsa (1970) 'The West Indian slave laws of the 18th century' Mona: University of the West Indies.

HALL, Stuart (1994) Paper presented at Conference, 'Race matters: Black Americans, U.S. Terrain' Princeton University.

HENRY, Ralph and WILLIAMS, Gwendolyn (1991) 'Structural adjustment and gender in Trinidad and Tobago' in Ryan, Selwyn (1991) *Social and Occupational Stratification in Contemporary Trinidad and Tobago* Jamaica: ISER.

hooks, bell (1992) *Black Looks Race and Representation* Boston: South End Press.

IRIGARAY, Luce (1985) *This Sex Which is Not One* New York: Cornell University Press.

LAWS OF TRINIDAD AND TOBAGO (1986) *The Sexual Offences Act*, Port-of-Spain: Government Printing Office.

McAFEE, Kathy (1991) *Storm Signals: Structural Adjustment and Development Alternatives in the Caribbean* Boston: South End.

McDANIEL, Lorna (1986) 'Madame Phillip-O: Reading the Returns of an 18th century 'Free Mulatto Woman' of Grenada' (unpublished manuscript).

MERCER, Kobena and JULIEN, Isaac (1988) 'Race, sexual politics and Black masculinity: a dossier,' in Chapman, Rowena and Rutherford, Jonathan (1988) *Male Order: Unwrapping Masculinity* London: Lawrence & Wishart.

MOHANTY, Chandra Talpade et al. (1991) *Third World Women and the Politics of Feminism* Bloomington: Indiana University.

MORAGA, Cherríe (1983) *Loving in the War Years* Boston: South End Press.

MORRISON, Toni (1992) *Race-ing Justice, En-gendering Power: Essays on Anita Hill, Clarence Thomas, and the Construction of Social Reality*, New York: Pantheon.

MOSSE, George L. (1985) *Nationalism and Sexuality: Middle-Class Morality and Sexual Norms in Modern Europe* Madison: The University of Wisconsin Press.

PARKER, Andrew et al. (1992) *Nationalisms and Sexualities* New York: Routledge.

PARLIAMENT OF THE BAHAMAS (1991) *The Sexual Offences and Domestic Violence Act* Nassau.

PINDLING, L. O. Hon. (1972) 'Speech at the opening session of the Bahamas Independence Conference,' London: Her Majesty's Stationery Office.

REDDOCK, Rhoda (1984) 'Women, labour and struggle in 20th Century Trinidad and Tobago: 1898–1960' Amsterdam (Ph.D dissertation).

ROBSON Ruthann (1992) *Lesbian (Out)law: Survival Under the Rule of Law* Ithaca: Firebrand.

ROSENSWEIG, Jeffrey A. (1988) 'Elasticities of Substitution in Caribbean tourism' *Journal of Development Economics* 29(2): 89–100.

ROTHENBERG, Jane and WISHNER, Amy (1978) 'Focus on Trinidad' *NACLA* (July, August): 16–29.

SAUNDERS, Gail (1985) *Slavery in The Bahamas* Bahamas: The Nassau Guardian.

TRUONG, Thanh-Dam (1990) *Sex, Money and Morality* London: Zed Press.

WILLIAMS, Eric (1960) 'We are Independent,' in Sutton, Paul K. *Forged From the Love of Liberty: Selected Speeches of Dr. Eric Williams* (1981) Longman: Caribbean.

STATE, FAMILY AND PERSONAL RESPONSIBILITY: The Changing Balance for Lone Mothers in the United Kingdom

Jane Millar

In the UK there are about 1¼ million lone-parent families, making up 19 per cent of all families with children. The numbers of lone parents have almost doubled since the early 1970s and this increase is part of wider patterns of change in family structure. These are the result, for example, of the rise in extramarital births (now accounting for over a quarter of all births), the increase in cohabitation (half of women have cohabited prior to marriage), the rise in divorce (one in three marriages currently contracted will end in divorce), and the extent of remarriage and cohabitation after divorce (about a quarter of all marriages are second marriages for one or both partners). Kiernan and Wicks (1990) suggest that by the year 2000 it may be that as few as half of all children in Britain will have spent all their lives in a conventional two-parent family with both their natural parents.

These changing family structures present something of a challenge for social policy, especially in relation to the issue of state financial support for families. The British post-war social security system was founded on three important assumptions: full employment, male breadwinners and stable families. Thus the main form of family support is male wages, which the state will replace under certain conditions (for example, in the case of involuntary unemployment, sickness, disability and death). The state will also supplement male wages with child benefit for all families, and more recently with means-tested benefits for families with low wages. Otherwise the financial arrangements of families are considered to be essentially private. This has two particular consequences. First decisions about how families allocate and spend their money are seen as the responsibility of the family and not the business of the state. Secondly, because male wages are perceived as the main element of family support, decisions about whether or not the woman should work outside the home are also seen as private family decisions.

But separation and divorce, and unmarried motherhood, do not fit easily into this model. The financial arrangements of the 'family' are not private because the state becomes involved in deciding the allocation of resources between the two new households: the lone parent and the children on the one side; and the absent parent, usually the father, on the other side. The state must also take responsibility for enforcing the financial arrangements made and, if the absent parent is unwilling or unable to pay, must either replace his contribution or expect the lone mother to support herself and her children through employment. Thus the mother's decisions about employment are no longer simply private, but are influenced,or even determined, by state policy.

The rising numbers of lone-parent families therefore raise funda-mental issues about the balance between family, state and individual financial responsibilities; and about the roles of men and women as parents and as workers. The 1991 Child Support Act, implemented from 1993, represents an attempt to change this balance by introducing new mechanisms for setting and enforcing maintenance payments for children. It is similar to the 'child support' schemes recently introduced in some other countries, notably parts of the USA (Kahn and Kamer-man, 1988; Garfinkel and Wong, 1990) and Australia (Harrison *et al.* 1990, 1991). This article examines these policy developments in the UK and their implications for separated couples and their children. The first section provides the background, describing recent trends in lone parenthood and the financial circumstances of lone parents in the UK. The second section looks at the context in which recent policy has been developed. The third section looks at the provisions of the Child Support Act in more detail, and the final section concludes by considering some of the wider implications for family and gender roles.

Background

In 1974 the Finer Committee on One-Parent Families (Finer, 1974) reported, in two large volumes, on the circumstances of lone parents in the UK. The Committee had been set up in response to concerns about the increasing numbers of lone parents, who were very often reliant upon state benefits and at risk of poverty. In the early 1970s there were about half a million lone-parent families. Today that number has more than doubled and lone parents are once again the subject of policy concern. The reasons are similar.

First there has been a significant rise in the numbers of lone-parent families. Table 1 shows the increase in the numbers of lone-parent families since the early 1970s, when the 1969 Divorce Reform Act came into operation. This made divorce much more widely available and lead to a substantial increase in the number of divorcing couples. Between 1971 and 1990 the number of divorced and separated women with

Table 1 Numbers of lone-parent families, Great Britain 1971 and 1990

	1971	*1990*
Single mothers	90,000	390,000
Divorced/Separated	290,000	650,000
Widowed mothers	120,000	75,000
All mothers	500,000	1,115,000
Lone fathers	70,000	110,000
Lone parents	570,000	1,225,000
As a proportion of all families with		
children	8%	19%

Source: Haskey (1993), Figure 2.

children rose from 290,000 to 650,000; the number of single mothers rose from 90,000 to 390,000. The numbers of lone fathers have also increased (from 70,000 to 110,000) but they remain very much in the minority, at about 10 per cent of all lone parents. Thus most lone parents are women and just over half are women who are divorced or separated from their former husbands. Black families are slightly more likely than white families to be headed by a lone parent (18 per cent and 15 per cent respectively in 1988) with particularly high rates of lone parenthood (about half of all families) among West Indian families (Haskey, 1991).

Many other countries have also seen significant increases in the number and proportion of lone-parent families, again mainly as a consequence of marital breakdown (Ermisch, 1990). It is difficult to get estimates for the number of lone-parent families which compare different countries on exactly the same basis because different countries define and count lone parents in different ways (Roll, 1992). However, Table 2 shows some recent estimates for the proportion of lone-parent families in other countries. The UK has a relatively high proportion of families headed by a lone parent in relation to other European Community countries (at about 17 per cent compared with an EC average of about 10 per cent), but many other countries have at least as many, or more, lone-parent families as the UK.

The increase in the numbers of lone parents would not, by itself, necessarily give rise to policy concern. However, alongside the increase in overall numbers there has been a substantial rise in both the number and proportion of lone parents in receipt of state benefits, especially social assistance benefits (supplementary benefit, or as it is now known, income support). In 1979 there were about 310,000 lone mothers on supplementary benefit, equivalent to about 45 per cent of all lone mothers. By 1989 this had risen to about 740,000 lone mothers on income support, or about 72 per cent of the total (DSS, 1991). In all, about 30 per cent of people of working age receiving income support are lone parents, and over 60 per cent of the children living in families on income support live in lone-parent families.

Table 2 Proportion of families headed by a lone parent, various countries, late 1980s

European Community countries	%	OECD Countries	%
UK	17	USA	21
Denmark	15	Sweden	15
France, Germany	11–13	Australia, Austria, Canada	
Belgium, Luxembourg, Ireland, Portugal, The Netherlands	9–11	Finland	13
Greece, Spain, Italy	5–6		

Sources: European Community from Roll (1992); OECD from OECD (1993).
Note: refers to families with children aged under 18.

The main reason for the increased reliance on state benefits has been a fall in employment rates, especially in full-time employment. In the late 1970s just about half (47 per cent) of lone mothers were employed, 22 per cent full time and 24 per cent part time. By the late 1980s less than two-fifths (39 per cent) of lone mothers were employed, 17 per cent full time and 22 per cent part time (OPCS, 1990). Lone mothers are now less likely to be employed than married mothers, of whom 56 per cent are employed (18 per cent full time and 38 per cent part time).

Falling employment and increased reliance on state benefits have in turn meant that the incomes of lone mothers have fallen, both relatively (compared with other families) and absolutely (compared with prices). In 1979 lone parents had incomes which were on average equivalent to about 57 per cent of the incomes of couples with two children, but by 1989 this had fallen to about 40 per cent. Over the same period the average incomes of lone parents rose by less than the Retail Price Index (DE, 1980; 1990; see also Roll, 1988). Thus lone mothers are increasingly at risk of poverty, as shown in both official statistics (DSS, 1993) and independent research studies (Frayman, 1991; Bradshaw and Millar, 1991). According to the official statistics, the proportion of lone parents with disposable incomes of less than half of the average (taking into account family size) rose from 19 to 60 per cent between 1979 and 1990/1.

In recent years, therefore, the number of lone parents in the UK has been increasing, their reliance on state benefits has been rising and their employment rates have been falling. Poverty has increased and most lone parents live on incomes substantially lower than the average for other families with children. However, during this time policy for lone parents has been, as Bradshaw (1989) puts it, 'in the doldrums'. The Finer Committee recommendations were not taken up and such policy developments as there have been have consisted of fairly minor modifications to existing benefits rather than any fundamental review (Millar, 1989).

Changing policy

In the late 1980s, however, lone parents came under more detailed scrutiny from the government. The social security system as a whole had been reviewed in the mid 1980s and legislation introduced in 1986. Lone parents were not particularly targeted in that review although they were, of course, affected by the changes introduced (Millar, 1992). However, after that review was completed, policy attention turned specifically towards lone parents. One of the most important reasons for this was financial. As described above, the number of lone parents on income support had been rising rapidly throughout the 1980s and so therefore had the costs – in real terms social security spending on lone parents increased threefold between 1981 and 1988 (DSS, 1990). The control of public expenditure was a key economic objective for Conservative governments in the 1980s and so these rising costs were bound to cause concern.

However, although the pressure for policy change may have been primarily financial, it was ideological factors which largely determined the direction of the policy response. These ideological factors included a number of related threads, tied in various ways to ideas and ideals about the 'family' and family obligations. First, there was the long-standing and generalized concern that lone parenthood *per se* is bad for both the families themselves and for society in general and the state, therefore, should seek to discourage the formation of such families or, at the very least, not encourage them. This is a view which, despite the lack of evidence to support it, has gained even more ground recently with a series of speeches from government ministers – including Peter Lilley as Secretary of State at the Department of Social Security – critical of lone parents. Dennis and Erdos (1992) and Dennis (1993) have gained significant publicity for their argument that 'families without fatherhood' are destroying communities and society.

Secondly, one of the central tenets of Conservative social policy in the 1980s was that the state had become too supportive, providing too much welfare, and this meant that individuals and families were no longer taking responsibility for themselves. This, it was argued, meant that a 'culture of dependency' had grown up in which people had lost the motivation to help themselves and instead relied on the state to meet all their needs. Separated, or unmarried, parents provided two prime examples of this abdication of personal responsibility. On the one hand there is the father, walking away from his family responsibilities and expecting the state to carry the cost. On the other hand there is the lone mother, increasingly relying on the state to provide an income. Receipt of benefits, or 'dependency' as such receipt was pejoratively termed, was thus increasingly defined as a matter of personal choice rather than external constraint.

These ideas are linked in the concept of the 'underclass' as it was developed in the US (most influentially for British social policy by Murray, 1984, 1990). According to these accounts the underclass is mainly composed of unemployed men and single mothers, who have no incentive to work or to marry, and no motivation either to support their families or to help themselves out of dependency on the state. They are thus excluded from the labour market and excluded from the values of society as a whole (Smith, 1992). The US debate has had very strong racial overtones that are largely lacking in the UK context (Morris, 1994) but, that aside, these sorts of ideas have been influential in policy, especially towards unemployed people. Unemployment has been increasingly defined as a problem of unemployed people not wanting to work rather than a problem of lack of jobs, and this has led to a very harsh benefit regime for unemployed people in the 1980s, with cuts in benefit and restrictions on benefit entitlement (Atkinson and Mickelwright, 1989; McLaughlin, 1992).

However, for lone parents – especially lone mothers – the solution to the 'culture of dependency' is not so straightforward. This is because there is considerable ambiguity over the way in which the 'personal obligations and duties' of lone mothers should be defined. On the one hand, because they are mothers, their primary role and responsibility is defined as being the care of their children. This means that they should not necessarily be expected to work outside the home and indeed current policy does not require lone parents to work if they have dependent children under 16 years of age. On the other hand, however, many mothers are now employed and nearly all the recent, and predicted future, employment growth has been among women (NEDO, 1989). The question of mothers and employment thus raise some difficult issues for conservative values and the situation of lone mothers brings these very clearly into focus (Brown, 1989). Should lone mothers be expected, or even compelled, to reduce their 'benefit dependency' through employment? Or should they, as mothers, be expected to stay at home and care for their children? Are they, as Lewis (1988) has put it, mothers or workers?

Directly confronting the issue of whether lone mothers should or should not be expected to take paid work therefore raises much wider issues about the state's role in relation to women's employment. If lone mothers were to be required to work outside the home the state would almost certainly have to make much more provision for child care, or accept that children might not be properly cared for while their mothers were at work. Providing, or subsidizing, such child care would not only be expensive but would also raise the issue of the child-care demands of married mothers. In comparison with other EC countries the UK has very low levels of child-care provision (Moss, 1990) and, as employment rates of married mothers have risen, there has been increasing pressure on the government to reconsider child-care policy (Cohen and Fraser,

1992). This has so far largely been resisted but if child care were to be provided for lone mothers this would undoubtedly raise the pressure from employed married mothers for more help with their pressing child-care problems. Thus the current policy – that the state is neutral with regard to employment among lone mothers, neither encouraging nor discouraging paid work (NAO, 1990) – is important in maintaining the notion that for mothers paid employment is a private choice and the needs that arise out of it, such as the need for child care, are not the responsibility of the state.

However, if lone mothers cannot be rescued from benefit dependency by their own employment, then what other alternatives are there? Fortunately for the government, a potential solution to this dilemma can be found by turning to the 'personal obligations and duties' of the absent parent, which is usually the father. Here the obligations and duties can apparently be much more easily and unambiguously defined: 'parenthood is for life . . . Legislation cannot make irresponsible parents responsible. But it can and must ensure that absent fathers pay maintenance for their children' (Margaret Thatcher, reported in *The Independent*, 19.7.90). The role of fathers is to financially support their families through employment and so enforcing this obligation for separated couples would seem to provide the required alternative to either open-ended state financial support or to a positive employment policy for lone mothers. Enforcing maintenance obligations thus has the potential to kill as many as three birds with one stone – it increases the 'responsibility' of the absent father (who would no longer simply be able to walk away from his financial obligations to his family); it reduces the 'dependency' of the lone mother on the state (if child support can replace income support); and it saves state money. Policy-makers therefore started to look towards the issue of maintenance and this led to the 1991 Child Support Act.

The 1991 Child Support Act

In theory children are already entitled to financial support from both parents following family breakdown. In practice many children in lone-parent families receive little or no financial support from their absent parent. Table 3, drawn from a recent national survey of lone-parent families, shows that only about three in ten of the families were receiving maintenance. Separated and divorced families were more likely to receive maintenance than those who had never been married. For those receiving maintenance the payments contributed, on average, about a fifth of net income. For all lone parents maintenance contributed only about 7 per cent of total net income.

Prior to the introduction of the Child Support Act the courts had responsibility for setting and enforcing maintenance obligations. The White Paper introducing the Child Support proposals (DSS, 1990: para 1.5) identified a number of problems with these existing procedures:

Table 3 Receipt of maintenance among lone mothers, UK 1989

	% in receipt	*(base)*
All lone parents	29	(1420)
Divorced	40	(622)
Separated	32	(279)
Single	14	(519)

Source: Bradshaw and Millar (1991), Table 7.1.

- discretionary decisions and hence inconsistent and inequitable treatment;
- the levels of maintenance awarded are often low;
- there is no automatic review of awards;
- many awards are not paid or not paid regularly;
- the system takes too long; and
- requires considerable effort on the part of the lone parent to pursue maintenance.

The Child Support Act aims to solve these problems by establishing an Agency to take responsibility for setting and enforcing maintenance payments for children; and by determining levels of maintenance according to a fixed formula. Thus the Act has shifted child maintenance away from a system of judicial discretion to a system of administrative procedures, with the aim of producing 'consistent and predictable results' and enabling 'maintenance to be decided in a fair and reasonable way' (DSS, 1990: para 2.1). However it should be noted that only child maintenance is included in this, all other financial matters (e.g., property settlements) are left to the courts; as are all issues of child custody and access.

Alongside the Agency and the formula the Act also introduced a major change to the eligibility criteria for claiming income support and family credit. This relates to the hours of paid work that are allowed for each benefit. Prior to 1992 the dividing line between these two benefits was set at 24 hours – only those working for less than 24 hours could claim income support while those working for 24 or more hours (and with low wages) could claim family credit. Now the cross-over point comes at 16 hours so anyone working 16 hours or more per week cannot claim income support but may be able to claim family credit. At first sight this might seem a little out of place in this legislation, given that the main concern is with child maintenance. In fact it is an integral part of the philosophy behind the Act because the aim of these rules is to encourage more part-time work among lone mothers. As we have seen, part-time work is relatively uncommon among lone mothers, although for married mothers it is more common than full-time work. Part-time work is expanding and has the advantage of reducing the need for child care but, for lone mothers, it has the serious disadvantage of not providing an adequate income. Part-time earnings tend to be low and cannot provide lone mothers with enough money to support themselves and their children (Bradshaw and Millar, 1991). The Child Support Act aims to get round this by encouraging lone mothers to work part time to supplement their earnings with child support and with in-work benefits such as family credit. So, instead of relying on one source of income (earnings or benefits or maintenance) total income can be made up as a 'package' of all three. The rules are intended to encourage this – any child support received by lone mothers on income support is deducted from their benefit, so there is no financial gain from child support for those receiving income support. But, for those who take jobs and claim family credit, the first £15 of any child support received is ignored. (The subsequent announcement in the 1993 budget of a 'child-care disregard' for family credit also relates to this policy objective.) The three parts of the Act – the Agency, the formula, and the changed benefit rules – all work together to encourage more *private* as opposed to *public* financial support for lone parents.

When the Act went through Parliament there were two issues in particular that caused the most controversy. The first concerns the point mentioned above that lone mothers on income support gain nothing financially from any child maintenance collected. About three-quarters of lone parents are on income support so unless they can get off income-support benefits and into employment they will be no better off financially, no matter how much child support is collected. Thus it was argued that these proposals would increase rather than reduce family poverty, because second families could be struggling to make child-support payments which do not even financially benefit the first families (Millar, 1992). Secondly the Act requires all lone parents who claim means-tested benefits (income support, family credit, housing benefits) to register with the Agency and to comply by giving details of the absent parent. Those who refuse to do so will in effect be fined by having their income-support personal allowance reduced unless they have 'good cause' not to name the absent parent. The government have been reluctant to define 'good cause' but have indicated that this includes rape, incest and fear of violence. Critics have argued that this measure penalizes lone mothers and allows violent partners to escape making payments.

These two features of the legislation lead some commentators to suggest that the White Paper that introduced these changes should have been called 'Treasury Comes First' rather than 'Children Come First' since it seems that saving money was the main policy objective. This view is strongly reinforced by the fact that registration with the Child Support Agency will be compulsory for benefit recipients but only voluntary for other separating couples. But alongside this drive to reduce public expenditure the Child Support Act also reflects a particular response to changing family structures and gender roles.

Family structure and gender roles

The UK is not alone in either the problems with the 'old' maintenance system or in the proposed solutions. Studies in other countries (for example USA, Australia, Canada, Ireland, France) find the same sorts of difficulties – low and variable awards, irregular or non-existent payments – and so maintenance rarely contributes much to the incomes of lone-parent families (Griffiths *et al.*, 1986; Millar, 1989; Maclean, 1990; Millar *et al.* 1992). In a recent review of child-support measures in the OECD countries, Garfinkel and Wong (1990: 112) conclude that there has been movement towards 'standardization and administrative enforcement across countries' and that many countries are looking at ways to strengthen and enforce the financial obligations of non-custodial parents. Thus Britain is far from alone in responding to the increasing numbers of lone-parent families by trying to ensure more private as opposed to public support. However, as a response to changing family structures, the measures introduced in the UK seem to be aimed at *containing* change rather than *adapting* to it. There are several aspects to this.

First, what these proposals do is to try and reproduce traditional family and gender relationships after couples have separated. The separated family is treated almost as if the relationship had not broken down at all. Thus the men are to fulfil their traditional role as financial provider and the women are to fulfil their traditional role as mother. These days the acceptable role for mothers includes some part-time work, so lone mothers are also to have improved access to part-time employment. In a way the government is trying to 'turn back the clock' and make policy on the assumption that the traditional gender division of labour within the family can continue even when other aspects of the family, such as marriage, have begun to disappear.

For lone mothers there are likely to be a number of negative consequences of this fixation on traditional gender roles. In the first place the women's ability to improve their incomes much above basic levels will be very limited. The income 'package' of part-time (low-paid) work, child support and means-tested benefits creates a very long 'poverty trap' since increases in either earnings or child support will simply mean reductions in benefit so that total income changes very little. Furthermore, if lone mothers do try to achieve this package they will continue to be financially dependent on their former partners, and their incomes will to some extent depend on the circumstances and choices that he makes. The child maintenance is not guaranteed by the state (as it is in some countries) and so the women will continue to be dependent on the willingness and ability of the men to pay. Finally the focus on part-time work means that the question of state responsibility for child-care can continue to be side-stepped. Lack of child care is the largest single barrier to employment for lone mothers and nothing in these proposals is going to increase child-care provision. Thus it could be argued that lone mothers will suffer the disadvantages of marriage – the double burden of paid and unpaid work, the financial dependency on men, the responsibility for arranging child-care – but with none of the advantages.

Secondly the child-support proposals centre on reinforcing the financial obligation of the 'natural' or 'biological' parents. Fathers (and mothers) remain responsible for 'their' children, no matter what happens. So, for example, if a man remarries, his maintenance bill will be reassessed if he has children with his second wife but not if she already has children for whom he becomes a stepfather. About a million children live in stepfamilies (Kiernan and Wicks, 1990) but these measures imply that step-parents are not financially responsible for their stepchildren, who always remain the financial responsibility of their 'natural' parents. Given current patterns of marriage and remarriage the outcome of the strict application of this principle would be that money would have to pass between and through several households. Even a fairly simple example – two divorced people each with children who marry and have more children – produces quite a complicated set of financial obligations across a number of households.

In addition, all children do not have two 'natural' parents – 'family formation can be as diverse as assisted reproduction, surrogacy, substitute parents, serial marriage or cohabitation and single parenthood, as well as the normal (*sic*) situation of blood parents married to each other' (Craven-Griffiths, 1991: 326). Such families are difficult to fit into the current provisions and will tend to remain so in the future.

Thirdly the provisions are based on the principle that the obligations of natural parents are absolutely unconditional. As the opening words of the White Paper setting out the changes put it:

> Every child has a right to care from his or her parents. Parents generally
> have a legal and moral obligation to care for their children until the
> children are old enough to look after themselves. The parents of a child
> may separate. In some instances the parents may not have lived together
> as a family at all. Although events may change the relationship between
> the parents – for example, when they divorce – those events *cannot in any
> way* change their responsibilities towards their children. (DSS, 1990:
> Foreword; emphasis added)

But, as the response to this legislation has shown, not everyone agrees that there is such an unconditional responsibility. Clearly many men do not think so and have been very active in their opposition to the Act and indeed instrumental in having changes made to the formula since the Act was introduced (Social Security Committee, 1993). Criticisms of the Act from pressure groups such as Families Need Fathers (and the many other groups that have been formed to oppose the legislation) have focused on issues such as the retrospective nature of the Act (such as that previous 'clean break' arrangements can be overturned); the failure to adequately recognize the needs of second families; the failure to take into account the costs of being an absent parent (costs to visit children, etc.); the introduction of higher payments without any phasing-in period; the way in which the formula includes an amount of money for the lone parent (intended to reflect her role as carer of the child but perceived by many as spouse maintenance). In addition the way in which the Act was implemented – apparently focusing on extracting higher payments from those already paying rather than on enforcing payments among non-payers – has led to criticisms of inequity and injustice (Social Security Committee, 1993).

The groups representing absent parents have given much less attention to the issues of principle raised by the Act, which is not surprising given that they have sought to stress their 'responsibility' towards their children. However, the issue of contact with children has been stressed and it has been argued that, if fathers are not allowed access to their children, they should not have to pay child maintenance. Burgoyne and Millar (1994), on the basis of in-depth interviews with a small group of absent fathers, argue that the obligation to maintain children is not seen as an unconditional obligation but rather depends on a number of factors including the men's views of their own, and their former partner's, situations. If former partners had remarried then very often the view was taken that maintenance obligations should be reduced or even cancelled, and evidence from the 1990 *British Social Attitudes Survey* found the population in general ambivalent about this. Half (51 per cent) of the respondents said maintenance payments should continue if the woman remarried, 13 per cent said they should stop, and 33 per cent that it would depend on the new husband's income (Kiernan, 1992). The absolutely unconditional obligation that underpins the White Paper does not seem to command widespread support.

From the point of view of the women there are also many reasons why some will be reluctant to receive maintenance. For some there is a fear of violence and Bradshaw and Millar (1991) found that violence was reported by 20 per cent of the lone mothers as a factor in the breakdown of their relationship. Others might have had no substantive relationship with the child's father. Others might want the relationship to end completely and not want to be financially dependent on their former partners. Others might be trying to maintain a relationship between the father and the children and fear that this would be more difficult if financial matters were introduced. Among lone mothers on income support both the women and the men might consider that there is little point in the man having to make payments which reduce his income quite substantially while doing nothing to increase hers or that of the children. The lone mothers interviewed in depth by Clarke *et al.* (1993) were thus rather uncertain about the value of the Act to them in practice:

> There was a marked contrast between the lone mothers' beliefs about the
> principles underpinning fathers' continuing financial obligations to their
> families, and the realities surrounding such payments . . . [there was] a
> profound ambivalence surrounding the receipt of maintenance by these

lone mothers. On the one hand, they felt that fathers did have a
continuing obligation to make a financial contribution to their children.
But on the other hand, the giving of that support enmeshed them in the
very same patterns of obligation and control from which they had tried to
escape in the course of rebuilding their lives as single parents.

The response of the government to these sorts of points has been that it
is right to enforce child support because the obligation to support children *is* unconditional and that neither the mother nor the father has the
right to abrogate this responsibility, either for themselves or for the
other person. Thus the mother cannot refuse to co-operate in finding the
father and the father cannot refuse to pay. But in practice enforcing a
particular definition of family responsibilities requires at least some degree of acceptance that the definition is fair or just (Finch, 1990), and it
is by no means clear that these child-support provisions will be seen in
this way – indeed quite the reverse seems to be the case.

Finally these measures do little or nothing to tackle the underlying
issues of gender inequality that are apparent in the breakdown of marriage. When couples separate the extent to which the costs of caring for
children fall on women and not on men becomes very clear. The women's
access to employment is limited and so current income tends to be low,
making it difficult for them to support themselves. Their future income
security is reduced because they lose access to the pension entitlements
derived from their partners. The distribution of property, including pension rights, after divorce does not fully take into account the unpaid contribution of women's work to the marriage. The child-support scheme
focuses mainly on the direct costs of children, attempting to share these
more equally between the mother and the father. The indirect costs are
partially recognized in that the maintenance bill includes an assess-
ment for the 'mother as carer' but this relates to the caring costs incurred after separation and does not compensate for the costs incurred
during marriage.

Allocating the direct and indirect costs of children between the
mother, the father and the state raises many difficult issues. The child-
support approach analysed here for the UK and also adopted, in broadly
similar ways, by several other countries in what have been called the
'liberal' welfare state regimes (Esping-Anderson, 1990) provides one response to these issues. An alternative approach can be seen in the 'advanced maintenance schemes' adopted in many of the 'social democratic'
welfare regimes, notably Sweden. The key features of this approach are
that it provides an assured child-support benefit, payable to all lone
parents regardless of income or employment status, and recouped by the
state from the absent parent. In Sweden the children receive a payment
set at 40 per cent of the officially determined basic needs of a child and
the absent parents pay a standardized amount (Garfinkel and Wong,
1990; Kamerman and Kahn, 1983). Thus advanced maintenance payments seem to 'provide something of a bridge between the private and
the public systems of income support, providing the custodial parent

with guaranteed support without entirely undermining the obligation of the absent parent to provide support' (Millar, 1989: 150).

As Joshi has written:

> The price a man pays for parenthood is generally being expected to support his children and their mother. The price a woman pays is that of continuing economic handicap and an increased risk of poverty. One of the many advantages of being male is that it is easier to opt out of the obligation to maintain than it is to opt out of the unwritten obligation to care. (1987: 131)

Whether measures such as these are enough to prevent men from 'opting out' remains to be seen. But also legislation such as this arguably starts in the wrong place – in order to reduce inequalities *after* marriage (or relationship) breakdown we also need to find ways to reduce inequalities between women and men *within* marriage. Women and children will continue to be poor as lone-parent families until women in general are able to achieve a more substantial degree of equality and independence.

Note

Jane Millar is Professor of Social Policy at the University of Bath. An earlier version of this article was given at a seminar on 'Gender and Family Change in Industrialised Countries' organized by the International Union for the Scientific Study of Population in Rome, January 1992.

References

ATKINSON, A. B. and MICKELWRIGHT, J. (1989) 'Turning the screw: benefits for the unemployed 1978–1988' in Atkinson, A. B., *Poverty and Social Security* Brighton: Harvester Wheatsheaf.

BRADSHAW, J. 1989 *Policy in the Doldrums* London: Family Policy Studies Centre.

BRADSHAW, J. and MILLAR, J. (1991) *Lone-parent Families in the UK* London: HMSO.

BROWN, J. (1989) *Why Don't They Go to Work?* London: HMSO.

BURGOYNE, C. and MILLAR, J. (1994) 'Child Support: the views of separated fathers' *Policy and Politics* 22, 2, 95–104.

CLARKE, K., CRAIG, G. and GLENDINNING, C. (1993) *Children Come First? The Child Support Act and Lone Parent Families* Manchester: The Children's Society/NSPCC/NCH/Save the Children/Barnados.

CRAVEN-GRIFFITHS, J. (1991) 'New families for old: have the statutes caught up with reality?' *Family Law* August: 326–30.

COHEN, B. and FRASER, N. (1992) *Childcare in a Modern Welfare State* London: Institute for Public Policy Research.

DENNIS, N. (1993) *Rising Crime and the Dismembered Family* London: Institute of Economic Affairs.

DENNIS, N. and ERDOS, G. (1992) *Families Without Fatherhood* London: Institute of Economic Affairs.

DEPARTMENT OF EMPLOYMENT (DE) (1980) *Family Expenditure Survey 1979* London: HMSO.

—— (1990) *Family Expenditure Survey 1989* London: HMSO.

DEPARTMENT OF SOCIAL SECURITY (DSS) (1990) *Children Come First* Cm 1263 London: HMSO.

—— (1991) *Social Security Statistics 1990* London: HMSO.

—— (1993) *Households Below Average Income: 1979–1990/91* London: HMSO.

DUSKIN, E. (1990) editor, *Lone-parent Families: The Economic Challenge* Paris: OECD.

ERMISCH, J. (1990) 'Demographic aspects of the growing number of lone-parent families' in DUSKIN (1990).

ESPING-ANDERSON, G. (1990) *The Three Worlds of Welfare Capitalism* Oxford: Polity Press.

FINCH, J. (1990) *Family Obligations and Social Change* Oxford: Polity Press.

FINER, M. (1974) *Report of the Committee on One Parent Families* London: HMSO.

FRAYMAN, H. (1991) *Breadline Britain in the 1990s* London: Domino Films/LWT.

GARFINKEL, I. and WONG, P. (1990) 'Child support and public policy' in DUSKIN (1990).

GLENDINNING, C. and MILLAR, J. (1992) editors, *Women and Poverty in Britain* Brighton: Harvester Wheatsheaf.

GRIFFITHS, B., COOPER, S. and McVICAR, N. (1986) *Overseas countries maintenance provisions* Canberra, Australia: Dept. of Social Security.

HARRISON, M., SNIDER, G. and MERLO, R. (1990) *Who Pays for the Children?* Melbourne: Australian Institute of Family Studies.

HARRISON, M., SNIDER, G., MERLO, R. and LUCCHESI, V. (1991) *Paying for the Children* Melbourne: Australian Institute of Family Studies.

HASKEY, J. (1991) 'Estimated numbers and demographic characteristics of one-parent families in Great Britain' *Population Trends* Vol. 65: 35–49.

—— (1993) 'Trends in the number of one-parent families in Britain' *Population Trends* Vol. 67: 26–33.

JOSHI, H. (1987) 'The cost of caring' in GLENDINNING and MILLAR (1992).

KAHN, A. J. and KAMERMAN, S. B. (1988) *Child Support* New York: Sage.

KAMERMAN, A. J. and KAHN, S. B. (1983) 'Income transfers and mother-only families in eight countries' *Social Service Review* 57: 448–64.

KIERNAN, K. (1992) 'Men and women at work and at home' in Jowell, R., editor, *British Social Attitudes: The Ninth Report* London: Social and Community Planning Research.

KIERNAN, K. and WICKS, M.(1990) *Family Change and Future Policy* London: Family Policy Studies Centre.

LEWIS, J. (1988) 'Lone-parent families: politics & economics' *Journal of Social Policy* 18(4): 595–600.

MACLEAN, M. (1990) 'Lone-parent families: family law & income transfers' in DUSKIN (1990).

McLAUGHLIN, E. (1992) *Understanding Unemployment* London: Routledge.

MILLAR, J. (1989) *Poverty and the Lone-parent Family: The Challenge to Social Policy* Avebury: Gower.

—— (1992) 'Lone mothers and poverty' in GLENDINNING and MILLAR (1992).

MILLAR, J., LEEPER, S. and DAVIES, C. (1992) *Lone Parents, Poverty and Public Policy in Ireland: A Comparative Study* Dublin: Combat Poverty Agency.

MILLAR, J. and WHITEFORD, P. (1993) 'Child Support and lone-parent families: policies in Australia and the UK' *Policy and Politics* 21(1): 59–72.

MORRIS, L. (1994) *Dangerous Classes: The Underclass and Social Citizenship* London: Routledge.

MOSS, P. (1990) *Childcare in the European Community* Brussels: European Commission Child Care Network.

MURRAY, C. (1984) *Losing Ground* New York: Basic Books.

—— (1990) *The Emerging British Underclass* London: Institute for Economic Affairs.

NATIONAL AUDIT OFFICE (NAO) (1990) *Department of Social Security: Support for Lone-Parent Families* London: HMSO.

NATIONAL ECONOMIC DEVELOPMENT OFFICE (NEDO) (1989) *Defusing the Demographic Time-Bomb* London: NEDO.

OFFICE OF POPULATION CENSUSES AND SURVEYS (OPCS) (1990) *General Household Survey 1988* London: HMSO.

ORGANISATION FOR ECONOMIC COOPERATION AND DEVELOPMENT (OECD) (1993) *Breadwinners or Carers? Lone Mothers and Employment* Paris: OECD.

ROLL, J. (1988) *Family Fortunes: Parents' Incomes in the 1980s* London: Family Policy Studies Centre.

—— (1992) *Lone-parent Families in the European Community: The 1992 Report* London: Family Policy Studies Centre.

SMITH, D. (1992) editor, *Understanding the Underclass* London: Policy Studies Institute.

SOCIAL SECURITY COMMITTEE (1993) *The Operation of the Child Support Act* London: HMSO.

MORAL RHETORIC AND PUBLIC HEALTH PRAGMATISM: The Recent Politics of Sex Education

Rachel Thomson

Sex education seems to be an inherently problematic area of social policy, highlighting as it does tensions both within and between political traditions. The controversy that surrounds the development of policy in this area is testament to the complex interplay of political ideologies that signifies the boundaries of state intervention. School sex education, along with law on abortion and censorship, mark the political front line between the personal and the public. For libertarians this line falls between the individual and the state, for moralists, between the state and the family and for paternalists between the individual and the public good.

Yet sex education is not only about the boundaries of state intervention, it is also a gendered debate. The political tensions that have shaped the development of sex education policy are rooted in the ways in which governments have responded or refused to respond to changes in the structure of the family and sexual relations. Sex education is potentially a vehicle for social engineering par excellence, be it progressive or traditional. Yet paradoxically, in an age of socio-sexual change and life-threatening sexually transmitted diseases, it is also a right and an entitlement. Sex education not only brings into focus tensions around gender, but also tensions around generation and the public acknowledgement of adolescent sexuality. Current debates around the age of consent for gay men and access to contraceptive advice for under-16s illustrate the ambiguity of the role of the law in this area.

In this essay I will trace the evolution of contemporary sex education policy in England and Wales, focusing on the recent development of sex education policy from Thatcherism to the 1993 Education Act. In particular I will explore how tensions between education and health, between central and delegated control and between social authoritarianism and public health pragmatism have interacted to thwart the development of a co-ordinated national programme in schools. I will reflect on how progressive sexual politics have influenced this agenda and consider the opportunities and constraints that are likely to shape its future direction in terms of both policy and practice.

Sex education: cultural specificity

International comparison suggests that the fate of school sex education is dependent on the degree to which national governments secure a consensus within and outside government. The potential for such consensus is related to how the aims of sex education are formulated and the relative dominance of medical and moral discourses within this formulation. Where medical discourses dominate, the aims of sex education are defined in terms of limiting unplanned pregnancy and the spread of STDs. Where moral discourses hold ascendancy, the role of sex education is formulated in terms of the legitimacy of adolescent sexual activity and concerns over the sexual exploitation of women and children.

On the international stage the effectiveness of sex education is currently measured in terms of low levels of teenage pregnancy and abortion (Baldo *et al.*, 1993; Jones *et al.*, 1985). On the basis of these criteria Holland and Sweden lead the way. Although they have achieved this position through very different routes they share a pragmatic public consensus regarding the legitimacy of adolescent sexuality and the role of sex education, reflected in low ages of consent and easily accessed contraceptive services (Meredith, 1989). In Holland sex education has only recently been formulated into a national curriculum, although there is a long-established tradition of sexual health services for the young. In Sweden there has been a national curriculum for sex education for thirty years. Through successive national commissions they have developed an accountable and democratically formulated programme described as 'a long and systematic public analysis of the psyche of its inhabitants and the ways in which what are perceived as negative traits might be corrected through the state educational apparatus' (Meredith, 1989: 101).

The United States and Britain, both of which have comparatively high rates of teenage pregnancy and abortion (Jones *et al.*, 1985) have yet to establish a political consensus as to the role of school sex education. In the United States this is aggravated by structural and legislative factors. Political decision-making about sex education is delegated to state legislatures and local school boards. An established system of challenging legislation on the basis of constitutional and first amendment rights and a tradition of well-funded moral lobbies has led to sex education being a highly politicized issue. The politicization has revolved primarily around the aims of sex education. Proponents of abstinence programmes, promoting an agenda focusing on sexual abuse, the threat of HIV/AIDS and date rape, are clashing with those who support sex-positive curricula and who wish to make contraception and condoms available to young people through school-based clinics (Hafner, 1992).

The divisions that dog the US system are those between the public good and the defence of the family (does the state have a right to intervene?) and between liberal and authoritarian interventionism, (should interventions aim to limit the sexual activity of the young or to promote sexual health?). The way in which a society deals with the challenge of sex education is inevitably culturally specific; the size and heterogeneity of the population is crucial, the degree to which there is a tradition of consensus welfare politics is significant, as is the relationship and relative power of health and education discourses within government and public life. Significantly, both Holland and Sweden have small, relatively homogenous populations, have been relatively stable and experienced late industrialization. The development of policy consensus in this area is related to broader historical dimensions of political development and social and political stability. In Britain its political genesis was tied to political and social responses to the development of a working-class and questions of suffrage (Mort, 1987).

The origins and evolution of sex education policy in England and Wales

Despite widespread public concerns about the nation's sexual and moral health (Bland, 1982; Mort, 1987) it was not until 1943 that the British Board of Education officially addressed sex education in the secondary curriculum. Neither of the popular social movements that marked the beginning of the century, the social purity movement and subsequently the social hygiene movement, resulted in an official national government response. The medico-moral alliance that led to the imposition of the Contagious Diseases Act in 1864 was halted in its tracks by the development of a moralist/feminist opposition, leading to the Act's repeal in 1883 and the emergence of the populist social purity movement. Social purity opposed the authority of medical expertise, countering it with voluntary 'rescue work' with women and the reform of male sexuality through public meetings and coercive legislation, resulting in the Criminal Amendment Act of 1885.

The medico-moral alliance reappeared with the social hygiene movement which was to supersede social purity, replacing a language of overtly religious moralism with a eugenic concern for racial purity. Social hygiene regarded prevention rather than punishment as the means to counter moral decay, placing great emphasis on the development of sexual hygiene through education. Yet social hygiene did not succeed in establishing an official consensus as to the role of sex education in schools. The movement was divided as to the appropriate role of state involvement and whether the family or the school should take the lead. A London County Council Inquiry in 1914 came out strongly against formal sex education instruction in schools and confirmed the government's reluctance to formally address the issue (Mort, 1987). Social hygiene led instead to a tradition of voluntary and local interventions.

Historically, the British state has shown a marked reluctance to legislate in this area and even less willingness to develop a national or co-ordinated response to questions of public sexual health and personal morality. Where the state did act it was often as a result of pressure from popular political movements. In terms of sex education the government tended to restrict its role to defining the scope for action of local or independent interventions. This combination of legislative restriction and a *laissez-faire* approach to curriculum development characterizes much of the history of sex-education policy in Britain that was to follow.

In the early 1920s the National Birth Rate Commission, a leading eugenics body, put out a model syllabus for elementary schools on personal hygiene, preparing the ground for education in sexual hygiene. The government eventually delegated to independent voluntary agencies, primarily the National Council for the Prevention of Venereal Disease (NCPVD), the responsibility for public education on sexually transmitted diseases and contraception, including education at schools. Local authorities, voluntary agencies and individual schools worked to develop interventions and programmes within general guidelines from central government. A Board of Education *Handbook of Suggestions on Health Education* first issued in 1928 and revised over thirty years, provided general guidelines on content and moral code.

The ethos of social hygiene and its concern with sexually transmitted diseases, sexual hygiene and personal morality dominated the nature of pre-war interventions. (Sex education for girls focused primarily on preparation for motherhood.) There was general agreement that prohibition and moral warning were inadequate and a discourse developed allowing positive aspects of the 'sexual instinct' to be explored within the confines of marriage and the family. It was a highly gendered discourse and 'social hygiene perpetuated the double-standard by insisting that male self-control, though possible, was problematic, and that girls should help men to act responsibly by watching their own behaviour' (Mort, 1987: 191).

In the post-war years social hygiene became embodied in the emerging welfare state. With a new legislative framework for state education the authority of educational philosophy grew. Initially pronatalist, this philosophy drew upon an increasingly non-medical discourse embodied in successive influential reports concerned with the development of the family and social cohesion (Crowther Report, 1959; Newsom Report, 1963, Cohen Report, 1964). Over time the form of school sex education was influenced by a growing partnership between the educational and health establishments and the development of holistic notions of healthy sex roles, healthy lifestyles and healthy families. The task of sex education was relatively uncontested, aiming to expose young people to the 'facts of life' and 'a range of instructional activities aimed to encourage a healthier way of life' (Meredith, 1989: 75).

Social, political and technological changes during the 1960s, including the oral contraceptive pill, changes in the social attitudes of adolescents and the 1967 Abortion and Sexual Offences Acts, led to a re-evaluation. Sex education came to be seen as more complex than had previously been thought, demanding expertise beyond that on offer from medical experts, and 'bona fide' voluntary organizations received government funding to train and resource teachers. These included the National Marriage Guidance Council (NMGC) and the Family Planning Association (FPA). Eventually the NMGC passed full responsibility in this area to the FPA. While neither were established to fulfil the role of training in sex education specifically, it was felt that the FPA's expertise in this area, due to its role in training health professionals, was more significant and appropriate.

In 1968 the Central Council on Health Education (previously the NCPVD) was replaced by the Health Education Council, later the Health Education Authority. While the aims of sex education continued to be framed by preventative imperatives of public health, the form of such interventions in school was increasingly influenced by progressive educational pedagogies and the development of holistic approaches to personal health in the form of Personal and Social Education (PSE) programmes (Doggett in Allen, 1987; Reid, 1982). Sexual responsibility was addressed through the development of self-esteem and contraceptive awareness, inevitably perpetuating a gendered, information based, and reproductively oriented approach.

During the late 1970s and early 1980s, feminism, anti-racism and gay liberation began to make an impact on local government and education in the form of equal opportunities and anti-racist philosophies (Haringey Council, 1988). In the area of sex education this marked a tentative move beyond the reproductively oriented model of sex education to social or rights-based interventions which attempted to educate against prejudice. Local initiatives included the ILEA sexuality project, and a number of positive-image exercises in the area of lesbian and gay sexuality such as the video *A Different Story*. Research undertaken at this time by the London Lesbian and Gay Teenage Group for the first time made visible the experiences of lesbian and gay pupils at school. Within voluntary agencies such as the FPA, experiential models of education, influenced by consciousness raising and therapeutic discourses, gained authority, leading to a model of teacher training in sex education that could be characterized as 'sexual responsibility through personal growth'.

Throughout this period there was no formal curriculum framework within which sex education was taught (Farrell, 1978; Allen 1987). Local education authorities had the responsibility for providing curriculum guidance to schools in this and other areas. While the provision of and approach to sex and health education was inconsistent across the country, pockets of progressive practice emerged and a growing consensus about the value of developing young people's – particularly young women's – critical abilities and communication skills emerged in educational practice and philosophy (Burchell, 1989; Weiner, 1985). The influence of anti-sexist strategies in education and girls work in the youth sector encouraged a critical approach to sex education. The gendered nature of sex education, previously unquestioned, was recognized and progressive local education authorities such as the ILEA Sexuality Unit developed strategies for teaching sex education which questioned gender roles, sexual identity, sexual stereotyping and issues of control and consent in sexual relationships. Yet, 'Whether by accident or design, the political structure governing sex education turned out to be a series of sub-contracting operations which has served to remove responsibility from any one single body' (Meredith, 1987: 82).

Subcontracting the responsibility for curriculum development to education authorities and independent bodies may have served the short-term political ends of government, enabling it to avoid publicly confronting questions concerning the aims of school sex education. Yet it also meant that the developments in aims and practice that took place were not subject to public debate (Meredith, 1989). While there was a growing professional consensus between education, health and voluntary agencies, this was not reflected in Parliament, within the media or within public opinion. As such the consensus was vulnerable to attack.

Thatcherism and the politicization of sex education

A debate in the House of Lords in 1976, over government funding of the FPA, marked the beginning of the end of this consensus. Throughout the late 1960s and early 1970s, in response to wide-ranging social and cultural changes within society, there had been a growth in independent interest groups taking both traditionalist and progressive stances. These interests coincided with ideological tensions between government departments and exploited the absence of a clearly defined rationale and code of practice for sex education. It is significant that during the Lords debate, the Department of Health was left to defend the ethos and practices of the FPA single-handedly, without the support of the Department of Education. Tensions between these two government departments have played an increasingly important part in the politics of sex education in recent years.

The growing polarization of progressive and traditional responses to social and sexual change provided one of the key focuses of the philosophy of Thatcherism. At an ideological level Thatcherism effectively reformulated the definition of the 'public good' from benevolent state intervention to a libertarian self-sufficiency, epitomized by Margaret Thatcher's phrase 'there is no such thing as society, just individuals and families'. During the Thatcher years sex education became the focus of a populist discourse of family values, which raised

anxieties about the potentially corrupting influence of state intervention into the sphere of the intimate, undermining the exercise of
authority within the family.

Yet despite an explicit discourse of personal morality and 'Victorian
values' the Thatcher Government was in practice reluctant to legislate in
this area. In his review of the moral politics of Thatcherism, Martin
Durham argues that the Thatcher years did not signal the development of
a British moral majority, similar to that which arose in the United States
under Reagan. Rather, the ideological tensions between economic
liberalism and moral authoritarianism in fact served to temper the
practice of the administration. While the government met moralist
demands on sex education (teaching about homosexuality and censorship) it did not fall to them on abortion, under-16s contraception and
embryo research (Durham, 1991). It can be argued that Thatcherism
employed moral politics in an instrumental way, in order to rally populist
fears and gain support for other, often radical structural reforms.

Where medical, health or scientific research was involved, then the
Thatcher government was likely to harken to the advice of its civil
servants, the BMA or scientific bodies. But on other, more populist issues,
where it believed expertise was a guise for sexual liberalism and where
there was a chance to lambast the Labour Party, then the government
took up some of the hopes of the moral majority. (Durham, 1991: 140)

The case of sex education is an example of a coincidence of interests
between moral lobbies such as The Responsible Society, Family and
Youth Concern and CARE (Christian Action for Research in Education)
and the broader Thatcherite mission to revolutionize the structure of
education. The two campaign focuses of these moral groupings were to
establish a parental right of withdrawal from sex education and to
curtail the freedom of schools to teach about lesbian and gay issues in
the classroom. While neither of these objectives were fully achieved,
changes to the provision of sex education within the 1986 Education Act
and restrictions as to how homosexuality could be presented in the
classroom in Section 28 of the Local Government Act had a significant
impact on the framework and climate within which school sex education
was and is taught. They also played an important role in fueling the
attacks on local education authorities and the professional integrity of
teachers necessary for the major reorganization of control within
education policy that was to follow.

Irrespective of the rhetoric of 'parent power' and local control, the
Thatcherite revolution in education led to a centralization of power and
the destruction of the accountable structures of local education authorities. To achieve this objective it was necessary to discredit the
authorities and to undermine parental trust in the expertise and advice
of the teaching profession. Alongside anti-racist education, sex education played the role of the 'trojan horse' through which public support
for these wider changes was rallied. Appeals to popular racism and
homophobia were key elements in the process by which some local
education authorities acquired the stigma of 'loony left' and teachers
were villified for progressive educational practices. The label of 'loony
left' stuck and in turn played a critical role in galvanizing public support
for a generalized attack on the education system. Media ridicule of the
progressive methods of 'trendy' teachers meant that their warnings and
protests went largely unheeded. The press and the government together
succeeded in convincing the public that the enemy within lay in the
schools and the local education authorities, and that political indoctrination if not sexual corruption was taking place in the classroom
(Scruton *et al.*, 1985).

The 1986 Education Act – governor control

The events that led to the transfer of control over sex education from
local education authorities to school governing bodies and the introduction of a moral framework for sex education in the 1986 Education Act

are typical of the interplay between moral lobbies and government that have characterized the politics of sex education in recent years. Amendments calling for the establishment of a parental right of withdrawal were introduced late in the passage of the Education Bill through Parliament. The amendments were introduced by backbench Tory MPs supported by small but vociferous moral lobbies which laid claims to the government's stance of traditional family values. The government made a compromise between the imperatives of public health and their own moral rhetoric. The result was a government amendment which devolved control of sex education (including whether it was taught at all) to school governors, imposed the requirement to consult with parents, and the power to grant parents discretionary withdrawal rights from sex-education classes. Most significantly it established in primary legislation the requirement that sex education must be taught within a moral framework. 'Where sex education is given . . . it is given in a manner as to encourage those pupils to have due regard to moral considerations and the value of family life.' The parental right of withdrawal, which would potentially undermine public health interests, was not conceded. Nor was funding withdrawn from key voluntary sector bodies such as the FPA or Brook Advisory Centres, as campaigned for by the moral lobbies. However the legislation did mark the dismantling of the subcontracting arrangements that had characterized the political control of sex education in the past.

In 1987 the Department For Education issued guidance to school governors on their new responsibilities for sex education, which more forcibly pushed a prescriptive and moralistic framework within which sex education should be taught:

> teaching about the physical aspects of sexual behaviour should be set
> within a clear moral framework in which pupils are encouraged to
> consider the importance of self-restraint, dignity and respect for
> themselves and others, and are helped to recognise the physical,
> emotional and moral risks of casual and promiscuous sexual behaviour.
> Schools should foster a recognition that both sexes should behave
> responsibly in sexual matters. Pupils should be helped to appreciate the
> benefits of stable married life and the responsibilities of parenthood.
> (DOE, 1987: 4)

This guidance went further than the requirement to encourage pupils to have 'due regard to moral considerations' laid out in the 1986 Act.

> Good teachers have always taken a pastoral interest in the welfare and
> well-being of pupils. But this function should never trespass on the proper
> exercise of parental rights and responsibilities. On the specific question of
> the provision of contraceptive advice to girls under 16, the general rule
> must be that giving an individual pupil advice on such matters without
> parental knowledge or consent, would be an inappropriate exercise of a

teacher's professional responsibilities, and could, depending on the circumstances, amount to a criminal offence. (5)

Speaking of homosexuality the guidance notes:

> There is no place in any school in any circumstances for teaching which advocates homosexual behaviour, which presents it as the 'norm' or which encourages homosexual experimentation by pupils. Indeed, encouraging or procuring homosexual acts by pupils who are under the age of consent is a criminal offence. It must also be recognised that for many people, including members of religious faiths, homosexual practice is not morally acceptable, and deep offence may be caused to them if the subject is not handled with sensitivity by teachers if discussed in the classroom. (4)

Although the guidance did not have statutory status, in the absence of alternative interpretations this circular had a significant impact on the way in which school sex education was and continues to be perceived.

Section 28 of the Local Government Act

Following the successes surrounding the 1986 Education Act, the attention of the moral lobbies moved on to 'homosexuality'. During the local elections of May 1986 controversy arose over the activities of Haringey Council's positive-images initiative. A Private Member's Bill was introduced into the Lords calling for a ban on local authorities 'promoting homosexuality as a pretended family relationship'. This amendment did not itself receive government support, but was followed by a government amendment to the Local Government Bill which became the infamous Section 28 legislation which prohibits LEAs from 'promoting homosexuality'. While this legislation had the desired effect of placating the moral right and reinforcing the dominance of a traditional model of sexual relations in sex education, it did not in fact prohibit the discussion of lesbian and gay issues in the classroom. A Department of Environment circular issued in 1988 clarified that Section 28 applied to the activities of local authorities, not to schools, and that it should not hinder objective discussions of homosexuality in the classroom, in particular that it should not hinder education about HIV and AIDS.

Sex education and the National Curriculum

The public health agenda within education was given renewed impetus in the late 1980s by the threat of HIV/AIDS. The changes brought about to sex education in the form of the 1986 Education Act took place before widespread public acknowledgement of the threat of HIV and AIDS. AIDS was considered to be a serious threat by the government, which established a cabinet task group and undertook an unprecedented public education campaign through the Health Education Authority (Berridge, 1992). Although this public education campaign, conducted primarily through television and popular newspapers and magazines, had a significant impact on public opinion and awareness of HIV/AIDS, it was not immediately translated into educational policy.

The changes to sex education effected by the 1986 Education Act, and the moral lobbies whose confidence and influence had been strengthened by their successes, were to complicate and thwart renewed attempts to address sexual health within schools. With the introduction of the National Curriculum from 1988 onwards, some aspects of sex education, particularly the reproductive and disease components, were included in the science curriculum, Significantly, a fuller holistic curriculum for sex education was not included in the core National Curriculum, but as non-statutory guidance.[1]

Schools were given a contradictory framework which embodied the growing tensions between the interest of public health and the moral right. Although school governors supposedly had control over whether and what kind of sex education was taught in schools, their powers in this area were compromised. Governors could not decide that the school would not teach sex education (as aspects of it were included in the National Curriculum), nor could they allow parents to withdraw pupils from sex education included in the National Curriculum. It was clearly felt that irrespective of rhetoric about parental and governor control of the sex-education curriculum it was necessary to provide a safety net in the interests of public health. In 1991 the National Curriculum Science orders were revised to include HIV/AIDS at Key Stage 3 (11–14 years) ensuring that all pupils would receive some education about HIV and AIDS while at school.

In the same year the government published *The Health of the Nation* which identified five key areas for public health intervention. One of these five key areas was sexual health for which targets were set, including the reduction of under-16s pregnancies by 50 per cent by the year 2000. School sex education was identified as a central means by which these targets could be achieved and by which Britain's standing at the top of the European league for teenage pregnancies could be addressed (Babb, 1993). Yet while *The Health of the Nation* was a government document, tensions were evident between the Department of Health and other key government offices, in particular the Department for Education.

As the government published *The Health of the Nation*, the Department for Education, under the leadership of self-avowed moralists John Patten and Baroness Emily Blatch, produced the white paper (now Education Act) *Choice and Diversity: A New Framework for Education*. This identified the reduction of truancy and the spiritual and moral development of students as the future direction of educational policy. It is worth noting that *Choice and Diversity* selectively aims to promote students' spiritual and moral development, and fails to

It is my interpretation of the 'Moral Framework' Sir!

address the full entitlement to 'spiritual, moral, social and cultural development'. Significantly this document did not mention sex or health education but instead emphasized the development of moral values. The document effectively posed a challenge to the health-education consensus. Where the development of moral autonomy, decision-making and social skill had previously been the territory of the part of the curriculum known as PSE, the white paper alongside NCC guidance on 'spiritual and moral development' placed the development of morality within an increasingly religious framework. This rise of religious moralism in sex education has been paralleled by moves to 'reclaim' religious education from multiculturalists. The requirement of the 1988 Education Act for RE to be broadly Christian in character was won by the same moral lobby that has campaigned around sex education and has found an ally in Baroness Blatch who has vigorously pursued its implementation.

The direction and stewardship of education policy gave renewed confidence to the moral right. The inclusion of HIV in the National Curriculum was picked up by the moral lobbies who again began a concerted campaign for the right of parents to remove their children from National Curriculum classes. Arguments were couched in the government's own rhetoric of parent power and family values:

In my view the order is yet another erosion of parental rights. It is the sacrifice of a parent's rights to guide the moral well-being of their children and it is sacrificing it to the newest politically correct attitude. Members of this House and another place then wonder why parents want to slough off their responsibilities when the state tells them they may not have a conscience about what is taught to their children in our schools on matters of sex and sexual morality. As I say it is little wonder that parents are becoming concerned about the state's attitude towards their ability to bring up their own children. (Stoddard, 1992)

The government found itself performing a political juggling act in attempting to balance the conflicting imperatives of public health pragmatism, parent power and moral authoritarianism.

There will occasionally be areas where those two interests, the secular and the religious, to some extent overlap. The current case is one. There are strongly held and irreconcilable views. After careful consideration of the issues, the Government have taken the line that they should follow the broad principles that parliament agreed should be enshrined in the 1988 Education Reform Act: that the curriculum should fully prepare all pupils for the challenges and problems, as well as the opportunities, which their adult lives will present; and that to this end all pupils are entitled to receive a broad, comprehensive curriculum. To create rights of exemption from the secular curriculum would not in my view be in the interests of securing an effective, broad education for every child. That must be our first concern. However I must repeat that the teaching of sex education and HIV within national curriculum science must, and I repeat must, have due regard to moral considerations and the value and promotion of family life. (Blatch, 1992, replying for the Government)

The instrumental deployment of moral politics under Thatcherism helped to strengthen a political alliance of the moral right both within and outside government. It also effectively dismantled the subcontracting arrangements that had previously characterized the political control of sex education. Consequently, unresolved underlying tensions between education and health over the aims of sex education became evident. With the growing public health crisis of HIV/AIDS these contradictions were exposed within a government increasingly at the mercy of an unrepresentative moral lobby which now had a voice within both government and Parliament. It is this same moral lobby that the government is having to reckon with in the fight for control over the definition of 'back to basics' and it was this lobby that pushed the government into again legislating on sex education in the 1993 Education Act.

The 1993 Education Act: the parental right of withdrawal

In the summer of 1993 the Department For Education issued draft guidelines on sex education for consultation. The guidelines replaced the previous circular and would clarify the confusion between governor control of sex education and the place of sex and HIV/AIDS education within the National Curriculum. Yet before the end of the consultation period, the guidelines were to be rendered redundant by a parliamentary ambush in the House of Lords.

Amendments to the Education Bill were introduced in the House of Lords calling for a parental right of withdrawal from sex education. A combination of an absent Secretary of State for Education, the support of Baroness Emily Blatch, the complicity of the Department of Health and the temerity of the Labour Party, led to the introduction of a government amendment to the Act at third reading. This amendment called for all non-biological aspects of sex education (including education about contraception, STDs and HIV) to be removed from the National Curriculum, for sex education to become a compulsory requirement of secondary education and the establishment of a parental right of withdrawal. Despite widespread opposition from educationalists and the voluntary sector the amendment was passed without debate in the Commons in July 1993, to become effective from August 1994. The Department of Education has again issued guidelines to schools, they no longer contain threatening references to Section 28, yet urge teachers to inform parents of 'precocious' questions and suspicions that pupils may be in breach of the law or at 'moral risk' (DOE, 1994).

The present policy framework for sex education is a complicated compromise position, which attempts to resolve previous inconsistency yet opens sex education to further politicization in the form of local activism to encourage parental withdrawal. Sex education is now a distinct subject, set apart with religious education from the rest of the National Curriculum. All secondary school students will receive some sex education, unless they are withdrawn by their parents. Governors are responsible for developing the schools approach to sex education in consultation with parents and must ensure that the approach and resources used in the school are consistent with the moral framework defined ambiguously in statutory legislation, and more restrictively in government circulars.[2] The parental right of withdrawal from sex education mirrors that for religious education and, as is the case with RE, it is expected to be exercised primarily by religious minorities. Two recent initiatives have been undertaken to ensure that schools are aware of religious and cultural diversity in their sex education teaching (Lenderyou, 1994; Sex Education Forum, 1993). Young people have no right to sex education at school nor to confidentiality concerning their sexual practice from their teachers.

Practice

Developments in practice in the area of PSE and sex education have taken place in spite, rather than because of government policy. Under the system of delegated control notions of good practice in sex education were pioneered by independent bodies such as the FPA, institutes of higher education and specialist local education authority units. Given that these bodies primarily had responsibility for the training of professionals, good practice was seen to be rooted in methodology and the skills of the teacher. The dismantling of LEAs and the cessation of funding to local specialist advisory teachers has undermined the authority of such bodies and has reopened the debate about the aims of sex education and definitions of good practice.[3] Unresolved tensions between medical and moralist perspectives return to question whether sex education should aim to promote abstinence or informed decision-making and the relative worth of didactic and child-centred methodologies.

The innovations which have taken place in sexual-health education in recent years have been mainly through public health and community education. The advent of HIV/AIDS created a close relationship between public health, the voluntary sector and academic research (both epidemiological and sociological). This resulted in the development of a range of progressive health education initiatives promoting client-centred approaches and empowerment strategies (such as MES-MAC, 1992). Innovations in this area have been encouraged by the contribution of social research into sexual behaviour and HIV/AIDS. Such research serves to challenge the increasingly idealized public discourse of sexual moralism, and by bringing evidence of the rules and conduct of intimate relations into the public sphere encourages the 'personal to be made political' in a pragmatic way (Watney, 1991). In the same way that the social purity movement's strategy of 'speaking out' challenged the silence and assumed naturalness of the sexual status quo (Mort, 1987), social research has helped to open up the possibility of speaking about sex within the public arena. The identification in research of a gap between the knowledge of sexual risks, intentions and actual behaviour has placed issues of power, control, masculinity, femininity and sexual identity tentatively on the public health agenda (Holland *et al.*, 1991; Weatherburn *et al.*, 1992, among others). Research that demonstrates a disparity between stated sexual identities or orientation and sexual practices again complicates and challenges common-sense notions of sexual identity and the sexual safety of supposedly monogamous married relationships (Boulton *et al.*, 1992). Qualitative research that has explored the ways in which young men and young women understand sex and sexuality and the way in which they relate to dominant ideals of masculinity and femininity provides an alternative empirical basis from which educational initiatives can develop.

Influencing the agenda

Ironically, the opportunity for progressively influencing the agenda in education may now lie in turning moral rhetoric into educational practice. Although the moral right has effectively influenced the official moral framework for sex education, it has so far been unable to translate this hegemony of rhetoric into educational practice. The production of the first 'abstinence' video on sex education by CARE launched in 1994, marks the beginning of the involvement of the moral lobbies in curriculum matters. While education ministers may call upon schools to teach young people the difference between 'right' and 'wrong', such a prescriptive approach is educationally limited. If schools did attempt to engage young people creatively in an exploration of values and morality they would find that young people hold strong opinions about what is fair and what is unfair, and that these opinions differ significantly from those envisaged by the politicians: environmental issues, sexism, racism and bullying rather than sexual moralism and a respect for property. A recent discussion document produced by OFSTED, the new school inspectorate, on pupils' spiritual, moral, cultural and social development, suggests that movement in this area could have progressive potential, avoiding moralism and indoctrination.

However uncomfortable progressive sexual politics feels with the language of morality, it may be precisely this area which it is best equipped to address. The gap between knowledge and behaviour, between social and sexual identity, is also the arena of moral autonomy and empowerment. For sex education to be meaningful it needs to address and develop moral autonomy and to do this it needs to address power and interconnecting relationships of power (Thomson and Scott, 1991). As turn-of-the-century feminist campaigners discovered, the language of morality can provide a discourse within which to express outrage, resistance and oppression. It can also legitimize the extension of individual and personal experience into the broader public and political spheres. In a society where ethnicity is increasingly defined in terms of religion, such an agenda also opens the possibility of an exploration of questions of cultural diversity (Lenderyou, 1994; Sex Education Forum, 1993).

The development of 'abstinence programmes' for sex education that swept the United States in the 1980s have not yet been mirrored in this country and evidence on the effectiveness of such interventions makes it unlikely that such an approach will make a great impression.[4] Morality cannot simply be taught or imposed and changes in the structure of the family, sexual relations and expectations cannot simply be denied or reversed. Participatory and empowerment methodologies which creatively engage young people are being recognized as having greater and more lasting impact than those which are morally prescriptive. Learner-centred methodologies such as role play, theatre and peer education, where young people define and address their own agendas around sexual health, are beginning to be adopted enabling educators to circumvent some of the political problems constraining sex education.

Yet there continues to be a gulf between the public agenda of sex education, as defined by 'gatekeepers' and policy-makers and the needs and opinions of young people. Research into young people's attitudes and behaviour in relation to HIV/AIDS has uncovered widespread dissatisfaction with the approach and emphasis of school sex education.

Young people's criticisms of sex education complain that the biological and reproductive focus bears no relation to the real-life world of adolescent sexuality, pays too little attention to emotions and relationships and avoids questions of sexual identity (Thomson and Scott, 1991; Mori, 1991). Initiatives involving young people have found them to be forceful critics of policy-makers in their own right and that they are aware of the difficulties that teachers have in delivering the curriculum in a confident manner (National AIDS Trust, 1991). The emergent discourse of children's rights in social policy offers a possible way forward in the argument for sex education in that it challenges the paternalistic character of the current sex-education agenda, and disrupts both the dominant discourses of public health and moral authoritarianism.[5]

The impact of the reproductive focus on sex education for girls and boys is significant and enduring. In the absence of other positive representations of embodied female sexuality it serves to reinforce the absence of sexual self-interest among girls and notions of natural sexual self-interest among boys (Thomson and Scott, 1991; Holland *et al.*, 1993). Both official and informal sex education continues to focus on girls who receive more sex education in school, from parents and from friends, than do boys (Allen, 1987). The sex education that girls and boys receive within the home is significantly different. Girls tend to be educated within a protective discourse emphasizing the dangers of boys, pregnancy and being 'caught out' while boys are more likely to be teased and encouraged in the development of their sexuality. It is clear that the way in which young people learn about sex has implications for how they understand themselves as sexual people. School sex education is only one small part of this process, yet is has an important role, potentially both positive and negative.

By mapping the political tensions and alliances that have influenced the contemporary sex education policy I hope to have also uncovered an emergent strategy for the future – primarily that it is necessary to act strategically. For parents this means realizing local accountability and engaging in the consultations required for the development of individual schools sex-education policies. For schools it means involving young people and recognizing and respecting the reality, diversity and cultural specificity of their experience. Politically it entails engaging in the growing moral discourse, while challenging the authoritarianism that constructs sex education around the twin poles of 'just say yes' or 'just say no'. American commentators conclude that the key to the success of the moral right in controlling the sexual politics of social policy is the 'failure of traditional liberalism to provide an adequate alternative to an authoritarian social logic which advocates increased surveillance and regulation of bodies in ways that support and reproduce hegemonic relationships of dominance' (Singer, 1993). An ethos that is both child-centred and celebrating of diversity would effectively challenge the authoritarian tendencies of both the moral right and public health.

Finally, issues of gender need to be kept on the agenda of school sex education, both politically and at the level of practice. Feminist positions on school sex education have traditionally been ambiguous; while feminists have been in the forefront of campaigning for state intervention in this area they have also been forceful critics of the role that the state has played through education and health in defining and constraining the female sexuality and the family (Mort, 1987: 180). The feminist axiom that the 'personal is political' continues to provide an important and disruptive critique of the natural order of both the private sphere and the public good. Neither medical nor moralist discourses are without their dangers. Nevertheless, strategically both must be engaged with, developing their respective potential of pragmatism and empowerment, and resisting their respective dangers of surveillance and illiberality. Feminism must also be careful to recognize its own weaknesses in this area. The involvement of feminists in campaigns for sex education at the turn of the century are instructive in that their contribution resulted in the private world of bourgeois womanhood being brought to bear on the public world of social and moral problems. Feminist perspectives need to include an understanding of the way in which class, ethnicity and diversity should lead us to reformulate the question of sex education and other social and moral issues.

Notes

Rachel Thomson is the Senior Development Officer for the Sex Education Forum, an umbrella body bringing together thirty organizations involved in supporting school sex education. She is a member of the Women Risk and Aids Project team (WRAP) and has contributed to the Men Risk and AIDS Project.

Contact address for the Sex Education Forum: The National Children's Bureau, 8 Wakley Street, London EC1V 7QE.

1 Sex education also appears in the National Curriculum as part of health education, a non-statutory cross-curricular theme, i. e., it is not tested and does not have to be taught by law. This curriculum encourages the use of participatory models of learning and although information-based also includes debate and discussion and positive messages about sex and social aspects of sexuality. Due to the non-statutory nature of cross-curricular themes it is questionable whether it will be taught (National Curriculum Council, 1990).

2 A new circular on sex education is out for consultation at the time of writing, and will be issued to schools with accompanying models of 'good practice' in August 1994.

3 A recent attempt to define a consensus position on the aims of sex education can be found in Sex Education Forum (1992).

4 A recent WHO review of 19 studies on the effectiveness of sex education concludes that sex education neither increases nor encourages sexual activity and that programmes that combined an emphasis on delay of sexual activity

as well as promoting safe sex among the sexually active are more effective than those that promote abstinence alone (Baldo *et al.*, 1993).
5   Article 13 of the UN Convention of the Rights of the Child establishes children's right of access to education about health. See Newell (1991). The Children Act (1989) also requires that young people are consulted and involved in decisions that affect their lives. There is growing concern that much of the recent education legislation is in contradiction to the ethos of the Children Act.

References

AGGLETON, Peter, HART, Graham and DAVIES, Peter (1991) editors, AIDS: *Responses, Interventions and Care* London: Falmer.

ALLEN, Isobel (1987) *Education in Sex and Personal Relationships* London: Policy Studies Institute.

BALDO, M., AGGLETON, P and SLUTKIN, G. (1993) *Does Sex Education Lead to Earlier or Increased Sexual Activity in Youth?* Report PO-DO2-3444, Geneva: WHO.

BABB, Penny (1993) 'Teenage conceptions and fertility in England and Wales 1971–91' *Population Trends* No. 74, Winter.

BERRIDGE, Virginia (1992) 'AIDS, the media and health policy' in Aggleton, Peter, Davies, Peter and Hart, Graham *AIDS, Rights, Risk and Reason* London: Falmer Press.

BLAND, Lucy (1982) 'Guardians of the race or vampires on the nation's health? Female sexuality and its regulation in twentieth-century Britain' in Whitelegg, E. *et al.*, editors, *The Changing Experience of Women* Oxford: Martin Robinson.

BLATCH, Baroness (1992) *Hansard* 11 June.

BOULTON, Mary, HART, Graham and FITZPATRICK, R. (1992) *The Sexual Behaviour of Bisexual Men in Relation to HIV Transmission AIDS Care* Vol. 4, No. 2.

BURCHELL, H. and MILLMAN, V. (1989) editors, *Changing Perspectives on Gender: New Initiatives in Secondary Education* Milton Keynes, OUP.

DOE (1987) 'Sex education at school', Department of Education and Science Circular 11/87.

DOGGETT, Marie-Anne in ALLEN (1987)

DURHAM, Martin (1991) *Sex and Politics: The Family and Morality in the Thatcher Years* London: Macmillan.

FARRELL, Christine (1978) *My Mother Said . . . The Way Young People Learned About Sex and Birth* London: Routledge & Kegan Paul.

HAFNER, Debra (1992) 'Sexuality education in policy and practice' in Stears, James *Sexuality and the Curriculum: The Politics and Practice of Sexuality Education* New York: Teachers College Press.

HAMILTON, Val and LYNCH, Frankie (1992) 'Educating young people about HIV/AIDS' in Aggleton, Peter, editor, *Young People and HIV/AIDS: Papers from an ESRC Sponsored Seminar* London: ESRC/University of London.

HARINGEY COUNCIL (1988) *Equal Opportunities: The Lesbian and Gay Perspective.*

HMSO (1992) *Choice and Diversity: A New Framework For Schools.*

—— (1994) Education Act 1993: Sex Education Schools. Circular 5/94.

HOLLAND, Janet, RAMAZANOGLU, Caroline, SCOTT, Sue, SHARPE, Sue and THOMSON,

Rachel. (1991a) *Pressure, Resistance and Empowerment: Young Women and the Negotiation of Safe Sex* London: Tufnell Press.

HOLLAND, Janet, RAMAZANOGLU, Caroline, SCOTT, Sue, SHARPE, Sue and THOMSON, Rachel (1991b) 'Between embarrassment and trust: young women and the diversity of condom use' in AGGLETON, HART and DAVIES (1991).

HOLLAND, Janet, RAMAZANOGLU, Caroline and SHARPE, Sue (1993) *Wimp or Gladiator: Contradictions in Acquiring Masculine Sexual Identity* London: Tufnell Press.

INDEPENDENT (1994) *AIDS Campaign Falls Victim to Back to Basics* 29 January.

JEFFREYS, Sheila (1985) *The Spinster and her Enemies: Feminism and Sexuality 1880–1930* London: Pandora.

JONES, Elise *et al.* (1985) 'Teenage pregnancy in developed countries: determinants and policy implications' in *Family Planning Perspectives* Vol. 17, No. 2.

LENDERYOU, Gill (1994) *Sex Education, Values and Morality* London: Health Education Authority.

MCKEGNAY, Neil and WARNER, Marina (1992) *AIDS, Drugs and Sexual Risks: Lives in the Balance* Buckingham: OUP.

MEREDITH, Philip (1989) *Sex Education: Political Issues in Britain and Europe* London: Routledge.

MESMAC (1992) *The MESMAC Guide to Good Practice* London: Health Education Authority.

MORI (1991) *Young Adults: Health and Lifestyles* London: Health Education Authority.

MORT, Frank (1987) *Dangerous Sexualities: Medico-moral Politics in England Since 1830* London: Routledge & Kegan Paul.

NATIONAL AIDS TRUST (1991) *Living for Tomorrow: the National AIDS Trust Youth Initiative* London: NAT.

NATIONAL CURRICULUM COUNCIL (1990) *Curriculum Guidance 5: Health Education* York: NCC.

NEWELL, Peter (1991) *The UN Convention and Children's Rights in the UK* London: National Children's Bureau.

REID, Dorothy (1982) 'School sex education and the causes of unintended pregnancy: a review' *Health Education Journal* Vol. 41, No. 1: 4–10.

RHODES, Tim and HARTNOLL, Richard (1991) 'Reaching the hard to reach: models of HIV outreach health education' in AGGLETON, HART and DAVIES (1991).

SEX EDUCATION FORUM (1992) *A Framework For School Sex Education* London: National Children's Bureau.

—— (1993) *Religion, Ethnicity and Sex Education: Exploring the Issues* London: National Children's Bureau.

SCRUTON, Roger, ELLIS-JONES, A. and O'KEEFE, D. (1985) *Education and Indoctrination: An Attempt at Definition and a Review of Social and Political Implications*.

SINGER, Linda (1993) *Erotic Welfare: Sexual Theory and Politics in the Age of Epidemic* New York: Routledge.

THOMSON, Rachel (1993) *Unholy Alliances: The Recent Politics of Sex Education* London: Lawrence & Wishart.

THOMSON, Rachel and SCOTT, Sue (1991) *Learning About Sex: Young Women and the Social Construction of Sexual Identity* London: Tufnell Press.

STODDARD OF SWINDON, LORD (1992) *Hansard* 11 June.

WATNEY, S. (1991) 'AIDS: The second decade' in AGGLETON, HART and DAVIES (1991).

WEATHERBURN, Peter, HUNT, Anthony, HICKSON, Ford and DAVIES, Peter (1992) *The Sexual Lifestyles of Gay and Bisexual Men in England and Wales* London: HMSO.

WEEKS, Jeffrey (1981) *Sex, Politics and Society* London: Longmans.

WEINER, Gaby (1985) editor, *Just a Bunch of Girls: Feminist Approaches to Schooling* Milton Keynes, OUP.

WIGHT, Daniel (1992) 'Impediments to safer heterosexual sex: a review of research with young people' *AIDS Care* Vol. 41, No. 1.

THROUGH THE PARLIAMENTARY LOOKING GLASS: 'Real' and 'Pretend' Families in Contemporary British Politics

Susan Reinhold

A local government shall not intentionally promote homosexuality . . . as a pretended family relationship. (From Section 28 of the Local Government Act 1988)

Here I am interested in family not so much as an institution, but as a contested concept, implicated in the relations of power that permeate societies. (Weston, 1991: 3)

Due to a series of scandals involving the sexual and affectional behaviour of its own ministers and MPs, the Major Government has fallen short of its recent campaign to return 'back to basics' with an emphasis on 'family values'. This recent furore has in fact been only a more sensational episode in the ongoing negotiation of the meaning of family in British society.

The argument implicit in the 'back to basics' campaign and in much of the construction and theorization of families in Conservative discourse exhorts the truth and importance of the nuclear family form, with its concomitant claim that this family form is under attack and must be defended at all costs. This was certainly the case during the period encompassed by a conflict over a policy that endorsed the promotion of 'positive images' of homosexuality in schools in Haringey, north London, that ran its course between 1986 and 1990.

In 1986, prompted by the urgings of local activists, the Labour Party in the London borough of Haringey adopted a plank in its election manifesto that called for the 'promotion of positive images of homosexuality' in local schools. This was more an attempt to show its electorate general support for lesbian and gay rights and less an indication of a real plan for the implementation of 'positive images', a term that remained undefined for two years. Local opponents of this education policy soon attacked the plan as, among other things, 'turning abnormal normal and normal abnormal'. Labour won the Borough elections, and its opponents accused the newly elected Council and other supporters of 'positive images' of corrupting children, destroying the family, spreading AIDS, and contributing to social revolution. The local conflict ran its course over the following two years. Although the conflict was polarized and violent, it did not change the long-term political composition – in terms of electoral representation – of the borough.

One might think that this was merely a local political issue. However, the local conflict opened up a window of opportunity for a Conservative Party hostile to local government, especially when that government was controlled by the left wing of the Labour Party. Immediately following the Labour Party's victory in the local elections of 1986 and these local campaign attacks, the issue was picked up by the nationally dominant Conservative Party.

During the following two-year period, the Conservative-controlled British Parliament used this very issue to force regressive legislative changes to sex education provision and limit local government's control over local education. In the spring of 1988, after an earlier 1986 attempt, Parliament passed, as part of its local government bill, a law now known as Section 28, which prohibits the 'promotion of homosexuality' by local authorities. The London Borough of Haringey's paper policy was the prime piece of 'evidence' used to argue the need for this prohibition on the 'promotion of homosexuality'. This was the first and only time that a sexual *identity* – in this case homosexuality – as distinct from a sexual *act* had been promulgated as part of British law. Most surprisingly, the only definition of homosexuality offered in the legislation itself was that of a 'pretended family relationship'.

I wish here to address the concept of 'the family' in its idealized form – as a Haringey Conservative councillor put it – the 'normal family unit of husband, wife, and children' – as it is writ large across the British political and ideological landscape. More specifically, I will examine how it was that in this particular historical instance, the family was defined more in relation to what it was not – homosexuality – than in relation to what it ostensibly was. In doing so, I will illustrate why and how it is that homosexuality is constructed as a threat to both the family and the state. I also will show that the demonization and exclusion of homosexuality as the opposite of family, while the result of extraordinary political effort, is at best a tenuous proposition. Like the more contemporary furore over 'family values', single parenthood, and 'deadbeat dads', the meaning and structure of the family and the role of the state in relation to it is constantly being contested. Overall, this paper will provide an historical example of the state's continuing struggle to prescribe and regulate both family forms and sexual behaviour.

The concept of the family: attack, reality, ideology

The contest over 'positive images' of homosexuality and debates over sex education and the supposed 'promotion' of homosexuality raged in Haringey and then at the national level during a two-year period. It is surprising that only a few actors who participated in this conflict, both at the local and national levels, explicitly defined the term 'family'. The great majority did not. Specific and positive definitions of family – definitions that were made through stating what family was and definitions that invoked specific relationships – were few and far between during this conflict over homosexuality. In parliamentary debate on the subjects of 'positive images' and the 'promotion' of homosexuality, that traversed two years, family was invoked a total of 230 times. It was only positively defined twice.[1] During this period, family was, in effect, only defined in opposition to homosexuality, and so an easy polarity developed.

Regardless of how family was defined, Conservatives who took part in these 1980s debates agreed on one issue: the family was threatened by Haringey's policy, and the family was 'under attack'. A group of Conservative councillors thought that 'positive images' constituted a 'vicious attack by the Labour Party on the family'. In Parliament, Dame Jill Knight, who spearheaded backbenchers' drive for the legislation that became Section 28, argued: 'The family unit is under attack: there is no doubt of that.' A supporter of the legislation in the House of Lords also claimed that 'teaching homosexuality' 'undermines the concept of family life'. Here the concentration is on the *concept* of family life as distinct from *actual* family life. This distinction is critical to my analysis.

This reification of an ideal yet endangered family form took place, of course, against a backdrop of continuous changes in British family structures that are by no means sudden nor new. Changes in three central elements of family structure – children born to married and unmarried women, the number of parents in families, and rates of divorce – point to an ongoing process as opposed to a sudden danger or attack from an invader such as 'positive images' of homosexuality (HMSO, 1990). Indeed, the contemporary British family form is often a far cry from the 'normal family unit of husband, wife, children'. However, this idealized family form, which originally took hold as an ideology in the nineteenth century, is firmly lodged in place as a naturalized element of British life (Davidoff and Hall 1987; Barrett and McIntosh 1982; Williams 1983; Weeks 1985; Mosse 1985). The ideologically potent category of family, mobilized as a natural, normal relation, is not a primordial cultural given, but an ongoing site of struggle.

The abnormal normal and the unnatural natural

During this period, the family was invoked as both a 'normal' entity and a 'natural' unit. In addition, heterosexuality, marriage and family were

FightBack

NUMBER 27

CONSERVATIVE
Campaign HQ

5 Bruce Grove, N 17
01- 808 5074

****

" OUTRAGE "
HOMOSEXUAL & LESBIAN
EDUCATION

MOTHERS PLAN BOYCOTT

Many Tottenham mothers have decided already to take thier children out of school if these plans go ahead. Many more are looking to schools outside the borough as the only answer.   **" THOUSANDS SIGN PETITION AGAINST "**

" FROM NURSERY "ONWARDS

This is the order from the Homosexual Unit - "Children must be educated from nursery to secondary education in a manner designed to "promote" Lesbians and Homosexuals.

QUOTES

LABOUR MANIFESTO

"Heterosexual is pernicious"
"We are not born normal"
"We will campaign against normal sex"

SIGN THE PETITION   TURNING NORMAL **ABNORMAL** & **ABNORMAL** NORMAL   SIGN THE PETITION

CHURCH SCHOOLS THREATENED

ALL CONSERVATIVE GOVERNORS SACKED Quote "We will move towards the elimination of religious instruction and acts of worship."

AIDS the KILLER

American AIDS victims are found to average 1100 "contacts".

YOU CAN HELP

1. Sign our petition.

2. Talk to other parents, explain what is happening.

3. Ask teachers for their views.

4. Talk to Church and Community Leaders, enlist their support.

Conservative Health Warning AIDS CAN KILL YOU

TO: Tottenham Conservative Association   5 Bruce Grove N.17 Tel 8085074

I wish to help with petition and/or enclose £.......... For information pack.

Name   Tel

Address

P & P by T.C.A., 5 Bruce Grove, N.17.

Leaflet produced by Tottenham Conservative Association and handed out in 1986 local elections in Haringey

alluded to interchangeably, and all three ideas contiguously slipped into the domain of the 'natural' and 'normal'. Overall, both Haringey anti-'positive images' activists and Conservative MPs and peers emphasized not actuality or practice, but values and beliefs. A local campaign group called for a 'return to normal family values'. Another activist argued that it is 'natural that people should be heterosexual'. A Conservative peer who was in contact with Haringey activists argued

"My name is Betty Sheridan.

I live in Haringey.

I'm married with two children.

And I'm scared.

If you vote LABOUR they'll
go on teaching my kids about
GAYS & LESBIANS instead of
giving them proper lessons."

E Sheridan

Committee for a Free Britain

Advert paid for by Committee for a Free Britain and placed in the Sun *and* Evening Standard *on 8 June 1987*

that 'the balance' had 'swung to . . . outright attacks on the normality of heterosexuality'.

The use of the terms normal and natural, of course, allow the concept of the unnatural and abnormal. Homosexuality was roundly and almost hysterically decried as unnatural and abnormal during the furore over 'positive images'. A local Conservative Party contended: 'A CHILD OF 3 BEING TAUGHT THAT HOMOSEXUALISM IS NORMAL IS TURNING THE WORLD UPSIDE DOWN.' In Parliament, Tory MPs and ministers made similar albeit less extreme statements.

Even government policy during this period declared: 'There is no place in any school in any circumstances for teaching which advocates homosexual behaviour, which presents it as the "norm"' (HMSO, 1987).

The arguments about 'positive images' and other local-government policies included assertion after assertion by local and national opponents that homosexuality could not be treated as 'equally valid' as heterosexuality, family and marriage. At certain instances, the outrage of the gathered activists, MPs and peers reached a point where they claimed that Haringey and other boroughs were positing homosexuality as superior to heterosexuality. This claim was far off the mark in terms of the facts of the borough's policy, but the claims are instructive as elements of a political and ideological mobilization.

These discussions of homosexuality illustrate a significant definition of family and heterosexuality through the description of homosexuality as its unnatural and abnormal opposite. As such, this mirrors the dynamic that Metcalfe (1990) describes: a social group can be dehumanized with much care and detail in order to define the moral character of those engaged in a struggle for dominance. In fact, the references to the persecution of heterosexuals on the local and national levels equal the creation of the ideological equivalent to Gilroy's assertion that, in the 1980s, the opponents of anti-racism constructed anti-racists and Black people as the 'real' racists (1987: 229). Similar to Douglas Hurd's assertion, following the violence at Broadwater Farm in 1985, that Haringey Council leader Bernie Grant was a 'high priest of race hatred' (*Guardian*, 5 October 1985), Haringey Council's policy *for* 'positive images' was construed as discrimination *against* heterosexuals, marriage and families.

I think it is significant that opponents of 'positive images' spent so much time and energy in Haringey and in Parliament claiming, over and over to a point almost approaching absurdity, that homosexuality was not normal and not natural. This begs an obvious question: if the family and heterosexuality are that natural and that normal, and that much a part of the dominant social fabric of the country, then why did these people have to stand up in the Haringey Council chamber and in the Houses of Parliament and elsewhere to state and shout time and time again that it was? Why did it need to be protected and defended? Quite simply, by admitting a need to battle against 'positive images', the response of local opponents of the policy and their contemporaries in Parliament – open opposition to the policy – had lost them part of the war: they had to publicly contest that which had once been hegemonic. The vehement and repeated opposition between homosexuality and heterosexuality/family/marriage also indicates a clear instance of ideological fracture and contestation. Although the concept 'family' may be naturalized, it is not so naturalized that it is not, as Weston puts it, 'a contested concept' (1991: 3).

Shifting boundaries of 'the' family

The contestation of 'family', however, signified far more than the construction of an easy polarity and consequent dismissal or exclusion of the unnatural and abnormal. As the conflict progressed, two important shifts occurred. First, the special condemnation of other family forms historically singled out by Conservatives, such as single-parent families, diminished considerably. Contiguously, as the matter was debated in Parliament, gay relationships – especially those that were part of a partnership in raising children – were singled out for special censure. This constituted a significant shift in the overall politicized meaning of family.

In June 1986, before Haringey's policy became so problematic, the government, in response to pressures from Conservative peers, drafted an amendment that would command local education authorities to change the ethos of sex education. This amendment, part of the 1986 Lords Education Bill, stated that 'where sex education is given to any registered pupils in the school it is given in such a manner as to encourage those pupils to have due regard to moral considerations and the value of family life'. In this earlier debate on sex education and family, peers and MPs expressed a predominant concern with contraception, pregnancy, young people's sexual activity, marriage, divorce, and single-parent families. Clearly, then, the issue of sex education at this time was seen as being connected to a variety of social ills, and not only to homosexuality.

The government's sudden endorsement of the teaching of the 'value of family life' came under some attack from their opponents during debates. Many MPs opposed the legislation on the grounds that the government were attempting to reify a family form that was increasingly on the wane. At this time, Labour and Liberal MPs worried publicly that the government were trying to sanction a 'class' system of families. In this context, the appearance of 'positive images' was a sort of gift to the Tory Party. Faced with a battle about the reification of an ideal but demographically shrinking family form, the government now pointed to the 'promotion of "positive images"' of homosexuality as a reason for reinforcing 'family life'.

After 'positive images' and other stories came to the attention of those backing this sex-education amendment, discussions of the breakdown of family life and 'permissive' sex education became irrevocably tied to homosexuality. The first questions about Haringey's policy were tabled in the House in the middle of the sex-education amendment's progression through the House of Commons. At this time, all earlier concerns about marriage, divorce, single-parent families, contraception and 'permissive sex education' simply disappeared. Instead, supporters of the sex-education amendment, and then of Section 28, addressed the question of 'the family' exclusively through the rubric of the threat posed to the family by homosexuality and the need to exclude homosexuality from any consideration of the largely undefined 'family' and 'family life'.

In contrast, the 'pretended family' – homosexuality – was described eloquently and extensively, in prurient and rather perverse detail. The ensuing definition of homosexuality as 'pretend family' was the definitive movement into what Watney calls the 'use' of homosexuality to pose the state as the 'supreme guarantor of "family values"' (1989: 27).

This special condemnation of homosexuality and a move away from earlier concerns about marriage, divorce, single-parent families and other elements of changing family forms shifted the boundary between 'family' and 'not family'. The new attack on homosexuals as not-families constituted a shift in the boundary of what constituted an acceptable family. I do not wish to imply here that these family forms – single-parent families, families that include remarriage and stepchildren, families in which siblings or grandparents act as heads of households – still do not experience material and ideological exclusion as a result of their departure from the ideal family relationship. However, the singular definition of 'not family' that developed during this period constituted a new definition of family that now included these less than ideal families by default.

In a more practical legislative mode, the government had indeed previously defined family in a very wide way. I think it is important to note this previous legislative definition at length because it allows a clear idea of what a government promulgating the idea of a 'pretended family relationship' might, in different circumstances, classify as 'real' family. During the initial Committee discussion of Clause 28, Labour MP Allan Roberts took the government to task for its naming of homosexual relationships as 'pretend family' by reading out the government's definition of 'family' in the 1980 Housing Act, which enabled citizens – and their families – to buy council-owned houses:

> A person is a member of another's family within the meaning of this Chapter if he is his spouse, parent, grandparent, child, grandchild, brother, sister, uncle, aunt, nephew or niece, treating –
> (a) any relationship by marriage as a relationship by blood, any relationship of the half blood as a relationship of the whole blood and the stepchild of any person as his child; and
> (b) an illegitimate person as the legitimate child of his mother and reputed father; or if they live together as husband and wife.

This broad definition of family that *includes* remarriage, illegitimacy, and common-law households was noted by Roberts, who added: 'That includes everyone but the goldfish and the budgie. Do the Government mean that two people of the same sex who live together cannot be classed as a family, and should not be discussed?' The minister present for the government, as in other instances, did not answer Roberts's question, nor did he respond to his comments. As I will show below, Roberts's criticism of the government's definition of 'family' is right on the mark. 'Family' now potentially included everyone but the goldfish, the budgie, and lesbians and gay men.

Exiles from 'real' kinship

Weston contends that lesbians and gay men are conceived of as 'exiles from kinship' (1991: 21). This was certainly the case in the later discussions of the sex-education amendments and in the case of Section 28. Weston, following Watney, comments on contemporary processes informing the idea that there is an 'absolute divide between the two domains of "gay life" and "the family"' (Watney, 1987: 22):

> Two suppositions lend a dubious credence to such imagery: the belief that gay men and lesbians do not have children or establish lasting relationships, and the belief that they invariably alienate adoptive and blood kin once their sexual identities become known. (Weston, 1991: 22)

In the debates on the meaning of 'family' and 'pretend family' these concepts – predominantly the one about children and lasting relationships – were present not as suppositions, but as assertions. Again, this phenomenon of prolonged outrage and comparisons of the meaning and import of the categories 'gay' and 'family' was a signal of the process of ideological fracture and an attempt to alter or halt such a process.

During the debates at the parliamentary level, relationships or partnerships between members of the same sex and lesbians and gay men with children were singled out for special comparison with the (largely undefined) 'family'. Some considered these relationships as almost like family, but others condemned them for their approximation or imitation of relationships that speakers wished to preserve for 'true' family. In the House of Lords, Baroness Cox conceded that the phrase 'pretended family relationship' might 'be taken as derogatory of stable homosexual relationships, where partners live together discreetly for many years'. Lord Monson also argued that the phrase might imply that 'promiscuous homosexual relationships . . . are in some way preferable to stable, quasi-family homosexual relationships', and at another juncture said that if homosexuality was not taught as a pretended family relationship, there was the danger that it might be promoted as a 'genuine family relationship'. These two peers, who were directly involved in the local dispute in Haringey, thus espoused a somewhat contradictory stance: homosexual relationships should ideally approximate the ideal family form, but they can only constitute, at best, a 'quasi-family' relationship.

Other supporters of Section 28 in Parliament were not so concerned with the subtlety of the legislation's phrasing, but took special care to censure homosexual relationships that might approximate family relationships. Lord Mason of Barnsley, who had been sympathetic to opponents of Haringey Council's policy, revealed some of the reasoning behind this preoccupation with family appearances:

> Indeed I am totally opposed to spending public money on promoting and encouraging homosexual and lesbian [sic] relationships, particularly as

happy family units, thereby in the eyes of our young people making our proper established family institution look odd or queer.

The implicit reasoning behind this Lord's statement is that he would rather have the subject of homosexuality addressed in schools and local authorities around the rubric of unhappiness and completely removed from the concept of family. If this is not the case, families will start to look queer, and 'queers' will start to look like families.

This concern over the confusion of queer and family was illustrated by statements made by the government spokesman in the House of Lords during the Section 28 debates in the peers' extensive discussion of the meaning and import of the term 'pretended family'. The Earl of Caithness, in a very informative twist of phrases, defended his government's definition of homosexuality as 'pretend family': 'In our view the term "pretended family relationship" is preferable to the term "normal family relationships" because we do not wish to use the word "normal" for the one case to imply abnormality in the other.'

Evidently, then, the supporters of Section 28 here have definitively thrown out the concept of the 'normal' and the 'abnormal' – terms used predominantly at the local level – for something decidedly murkier: families are designated real, although the government and the legislation's main supporters freely admit that families are not what they wished they might be. Alternatively, taken with the peers' comments above, gay relationships are designated pretend, but they can seem to be family relationships – or, rather, quasi-family relationships.

Indeed, the glaring contradictions and ironies inherent in these discussions of homosexuality and family do help to illustrate how tenuous the ideological logic of family actually is. This contradiction also clearly reveals the process of the mystification of the ideal family form: when pressed, some of those in favour of Section 28 in fact agreed that lesbian and gay couples indeed lived in family relationships – or something quite close to them. However, this extremely reluctant acknowledgement of 'gay families' perhaps provides some indication of precisely why these families were defined as something 'pretended': they seemed so very real.

Exiles from 'real' kinship II: gender and reproduction

Those fighting against 'positive images' of homosexuality in Haringey and for Section 28 in Parliament were concerned with the actual order and structure of ideal families and the relation they held to their understandings of homosexuality and homosexual relationships. They linked the order of the family and the disorder – and threat – of homosexuality to the three main areas of gender differentiation, physical reproduction and social reproduction. In the end, it was not only appearances that were important: the reality of what happens *in* families was also of concern.

The key to understanding the fundamental opposition between homosexuality and the family is through an understanding of the way in which a gendered order – or disorder – is integral to the dominant configurations of both entities. Indeed, the late nineteenth-century clinical definition of homosexuality was based on an understanding of two opposite genders. The original – and still present – definition of homosexuality is closely linked to an idea of a person's supposed attraction to characteristics of the opposite gender in the same sex, and the presence of differently gendered characteristics present in the same person – the homosexual (Krafft-Ebing, 1896). This construction of homosexuality as a mutation of gender characteristics ascribed to men and women was recognized during the conflict at the local and the national level. A Haringey activist opposed to 'positive images' made this link between gender and homosexuality when speaking of the variability of gendered attributes in all people:

> You can't get away from the fact that there are feminine men just as there are masculine women. But when you look at the way their bodies are made . . . a man knows what he's got, a woman knows what she's got. So of course they can't be completely converted [to homosexuality], can they?

The activist admits to fluidity of the quality of gender, but also refutes homosexuality and contiguously naturalizes human sexuality as heterosexual at the level of biological characteristics: 'the way their bodies are made'. At the national level, Lord-Rhys-Williams also commented on this phenomenon, with much the same conclusion:

> But it is an obvious fact that a man's physique shows rudimentary female characteristics . . . Few women, I think, would wish to be entirely without any element of manliness . . . [but] it is repugnant to the majority of people to see the endowments of our bodies, which enable us to recreate our own likeness and to perpetuate human life, turned into useless or unnatural channels.

Lord Rhys-Williams thus sees gender and its relation to homosexuality in much the same manner as the Haringey activist. Although there is some acceptable variability between the two genders within a person of one sex, there is a clear imperative. However fluid gender might be, those concerned with family forms demonstrate a clear conception of homosexuality as crossing a final and forbidden boundary beyond proper gender differentiation. The existence of homosexuality literally calls into question what it means to be a man or a woman, and this has important implications for the organization of families.

Of course, the organization of the stated 'ideal' or 'traditional' family – heterosexual wage-earning man married to heterosexual woman working in the home raising children – depends on strict gender differentiation, and, in fact, on gender subordination. The family and heterosexuality, acting as organizing concepts and institutions for both physical and social reproduction, are crucial linchpins in the oppression of women. During debates on the topics of sex education and homosexuality, MPs and peers recognized the link between the normative family and the subordination of women.

Speaking of his original insertion of the term 'family' in his earlier bill that became Section 28, the Earl of Halsbury thus defended his use of the term: 'I want only to say that I attach some importance to retaining the word "family" because it is part of homosexual propaganda that the family is a form of male chauvinism, which is not something I believe should be said.' The Earl links and disapproves of gay and feminist critiques of the family, but his dismissal is informative: the family as a 'form of male chauvinism' – or, rather, as a form of subordination of women – is not something the Earl believes should be said. Considering the debates as an ideological mobilization, this particular point of debate by the Earl seems to be made rather weakly. Moreover, weak attacks on gay critiques of the family were made in two other ways during the debates on the earlier Halsbury Bill and on Section 28, both in relation to a 1973 document authored by the Gay Liberation Front. Lord Bellwin read out from the Gay Liberation Front Manifesto: 'we . . . must aim at the abolition of the family. The end of the family will benefit all women and gay people.' He concluded: 'I feel very much that this is the kernel of the whole argument. It is naive in the extreme to suppose that the homosexual community wants only to be allowed to go its way.' Here, similar to the Earl, he does not engage with the argument that the dominant family structure, or ideal, oppresses women, and he asserts that if the 'homosexual community' has its way, it might not only end the family, but, implicitly, end the oppression of women.

Dame Jill Knight also offered a hint of fear at the idea of gay liberation transforming the lives of women in families. Offering the same citation from the Gay Liberation Front about the 'abolition of the family' and consequent 'benefit' for 'all women and gays', she stated: 'We could argue for some time about how true it is that the abolition of the family would help women, but it is debatable whether it would be anything other than a disaster for the country.' Again, Knight offers no argument to the Gay Liberation Front's assertion, but instead admits that a debate over the oppression of women in the family is indeed possible. However, she reaches the same conclusion as Lord Bellwin: any such change would result in 'disaster for the country'. Even supporters of Section 28 implicitly admitted that the ideal family form was one that oppressed women.

Fitzgerald points out that other family forms, such as single-parent family forms and 'communal forms of household' 'came to be seen as deviant' because they 'can subvert the thesis of the complementary heterosexual relation as the basis for the household's division of labour' (1983: 49). 'Gay family' is certainly included in this grouping of 'deviant' family forms. Moroever, gay family forms, unlike their more 'traditional' heterosexual counterparts, does not necessarily include the oppression of women and the usual division of labour. Weston's discovery of a lack of hierarchical structure in gay family organization in the United States points toward a possible transformation of the ideal family form in the creation of gay families (1991: 206). Although only a tentative indication in the context of this British discourse, gay families could represent a movement away from 'gendered divisions of labor' and 'relations stratified by age and gender'.[2]

Another area in which homosexuality was contrasted to the 'family', of course, was in the area of physical reproduction. Overall, during this period, such reproduction was seen as the exclusive province not of 'humans', but of 'families' – heterosexual families. Baroness Blatch states quite directly that 'the future of our society depends upon the relationship between man and woman and the product of man and woman – the child . . . there is no future for society in women with women and men with men'. This concern with the 'product of man and woman' and the future of society brings out clearly the importance of physical reproduction as a product of heterosexual relations.

There is an almost obsessional theme running through these debates of the endorsement of homosexuality leading to the end of human life due to a lack of reproduction. An anti-'positive images' activist stated: 'you naturally wonder where the next generation is coming from, if everybody's a homosexual'. The Duke of Norfolk also endorsed the 'nuclear unit of mankind to reproduce our species of mother and father', and stated that this was the 'ideal unit for man to go on breeding', concluding that 'it would be trite to add that otherwise our human race would tend to become extinct'. The Duke exhibits the same concern about homosexuality leading to human extinction, underlining the reproductive imperative, but also does so within the rubric of the heterosexual family being the only producers of children.

In contrast to the ideal family as the proper domain of physical reproduction, gay people or gay relationships were addressed as existing completely outside this domain. In late January 1987, Bernie Grant, the leader of Haringey Council, stated that he thought that gay people could competently parent children. This prompted a flurry of letters to a local paper, the *Hornsey Journal*, on the subject of gay people bearing and rearing children. One letter-writer commented:

> If God had wanted people of the same sex to have children he would have made it possible . . . How could Bernie Grant know if gay people would make good parents? No one has tried, to my knowledge. If anyone had been raised this way would they admit to the fact?

The absolute divide between actual physical reproduction and gay existence is clear: heterosexuals reproduce, while homosexuals do not. The writer's comment that if anyone had been raised 'this way', they would be ashamed to admit to it relates closely to the rubric of shame and discretion with which the opponents of 'positive images' thought homosexuality – and now, it seems, homosexual parenting – should be treated. Another letter prompted by Bernie Grant's statement did not even admit to this possibility, and emphasized, like Baroness Blatch, the role of physical reproduction in the ideal family:

> Parentage, as defined in the dictionary, is the relation of parent to child, the producer to the produced. As gays and lesbians are unable to produce it follows that they cannot be parents and can have no knowledge of how it feels to be a parent.

Again, the child as product of the *heterosexual* family relation is writ large, and, quite simply, 'gays and lesbians are unable to produce'.

The inability of homosexuals to produce was also put quite clearly in the House of Lords. The Earl of Longford, discussing Haringey Council's plans, argued that 'the tragedy of such [homosexual] people is that they cannot enjoy family life and they cannot have children'. Of course, the Earl of Longford's statement and these other concerns about physical reproduction defies logic: lesbians, of course, can actually physically give birth and raise children, and gay men can both father and raise children. These supporters of the legislation instituting the notion of the 'pretend family', however, chose not to see reproduction in these terms, but in the terms of the reproduction that occurred within their vision of family. This ideal, or 'real' family unit, then, is organized not only around 'marriage and childrearing', as Weston puts it, but also clearly around child*bearing*, or the potential of childbearing, within a closed unit of mother and father or potential mother and father. As a consequence, lesbian and gay couples, even those who might actually have children, are still 'pretend'.

In the House of Lords, supporters of Section 28 were faced with a contemporary example that appeared to contravene the absolute exclusion of the possibility of gay parenting – both bearing and rearing children – within the rubric of the 'real' family. During the discussions of the last Lords amendments to the Section, Lord Rea moved to delete everything from the Clause except for the one phrase: 'A local government shall not intentionally promote homosexuality.' He gave a specific reason for deleting the phrase 'pretend family':

> I have added my name to the amendment put down . . . because it gives us another opportunity to look at that odd phrase 'pretended family relationship' . . . I personally find this phrase particularly offensive . . . I say this because from the age of seven, after my parents separated, I was brought up by two women, one of them my mother, in an actual family relationship. There was no pretence there. Quite frankly, I cannot see why this should be considered in any way objectionable. It was a good family, and I maintain that there is nothing intrinsically wrong with a homosexual couple bringing up a child. I consider that I had as rich and as happy a childhood as most children who are reared by heterosexual couples, and far better than many I see in my daily practice as a doctor. I do not think any of the defects of my character, of which I have an average

number, have arisen from my being brought up by two women. My sexual orientation is, I am told, pretty average and so is that of my children.

Rea provided supporters of Section 28 with an example of a living, breathing well-socialized professional heterosexual man, with hetero-sexual children – thus a normal traditional family man who was also a peer – who had been raised by his lesbian mother and her lover. And, unlike the supposition of the Haringey resident who thought that 'no one has tried' to raise children in a gay household and 'if anyone had been raised this way' they would not 'admit to the fact', Lord Rea was not afraid, at least in this instance, to admit this fact as a matter of public debate. This admission, at least in the place where he uttered it, might have begun to blur the long-distinct line between family and homosexu-ality, as well as the clear place of homosexuality in the iconography of deviance. Unfortunately, supporters of the Section did not engage with his argument, offering a fine example of one of the ways that Seidel describes as a majority reaction when they are 'disconcerted' by 'minority discourse': they 'frequently ignore, ridicule or marginalize them, and the "periphery" from which they come' (1988: 9). When faced with the living, real example of one of their colleagues, the peers arguing so vehemently about the 'disquiet' prompted by the thought of gay families chose to ignore him.

'Pretend' as a modifier for homosexual relationships and lesbian and gay families thus seems still to have applied to those who supported Section 28 in the House of Lords, even when presented with contrary evidence in the form of Lord Rea. The example of a single peer in the debate did not appear to affect the predominant configuration of homosexuality being opposed to family on the grounds of opposing processes of gender differentiation, the subordination of women in 'ideal' family households, and the difference between the types of physical and social reproduction that might occur in heterosexual as opposed to homosexual families. In the eyes of those involved on this side of the dispute, particularly at the national level, lesbians and gay men appear to be and truly are 'exiles from kinship'.

'The' family and society

What possible threat did Lord Rea and his family – or a thousand or even a million families like his – pose to the country to the point that the government became so determined to define them as 'pretend', prohibit local authorities from recognizing or serving them, and use the law to single them out for special censure? In short, this 'pretend' family, with its fluid relation to sex, physical and social reproduction, and a gendered division of labour in the household threatened the social order. Connell writes that 'conservative sexual ideology reifies the family as *the* basis of society' (1987: 159). Contrary to those who firmly held to the belief that only a certain form of family is the 'building block' that creates society, gay families threaten to change the shape of such blocks, potentially creating not only new families, but also a different kind of family structure.

The family was seen in these debates as the strength – or potential weakness – of the nation. The Conservative councillor who defined family as 'the husband, wife, and children unit' concluded that this unit 'should be maintained', for 'the family unit is important to the well-being of the nation'. Viscount Massereene and Ferrard agreed during the early debates on sex education, stating, that 'stability in family life is one of the foundations of the state'. The well-being of family – the 'husband, wife, and children unit' is essential to the well-being of nation, and, oppositely, homosexuality – even homosexual relationships that appear to be family relationships – threaten the nation.[3]

Following the 1987 election victory in which the Conservative Party placed the 'gay issue' in their manifesto and used it in their campaign, Margaret Thatcher made a similar statement in her speech to the Conservative Party Conference:

> And we must draw on the moral energy of society. And we must draw on the values of family life. For the family is the first place where we learn those habits of mutual love, tolerance and service on which every healthy nation depends for its survival. (Conservative Party News Service Release 664/87)

Here, too, the survival of the nation depends directly on the health of the family, through the attributes of 'mutual love, tolerance and service'. Given the context of the national debate over 'positive images' and homosexuality in which this statement was fashioned and made, it is not too far-reaching to assume that the Prime Minister too thought that 'the family' precluded the existence of homosexual relationships within it, no matter how loving, tolerant or giving these relationships might be. Indeed, the Prime Minister invoked this family and nation metaphor several times during her career, and at least twice posited the nation not as dependent on the family, but as a family. At the 1979 Conservative Party Conference following her first election victory, Margaret Thatcher implored her audience to 'let us remember we are a nation, and a nation is an extended family' (cited in Fitzgerald, 1983: 51). Using one of her favourite metaphors eight years later, weeks before Section 28 was tabled with the support of her government, she made another direct comment in an interview to a woman's magazine: 'A nation of free people will only continue to be great if family life continues and the structure of that nation is a family one.' (*Woman's Own*, 31 October 1987) In that same interview, she made the spectacular comment on society and family: 'You know, there is no such thing as society. There are individual men and women, and there are families.'

The final Prime Ministerial statement documented here provoked massive comment, and much has been written about it. I do not wish here to concentrate only on that statement, but to consider it with the entirety of statements uttered about nation and society and family in relation to a discussion of homosexual relationships, or 'pretended family relationships'. These comments, taken as a whole, demonstrate an ideological compression of family, nation and society: one constitutes the other. Barrett and McIntosh argue that 'just as the family has been socially constructed, so society has been familized' (1982: 31). Although the proponents of Section 28 would perhaps have not wished to admit the point about the social construction of family, they certainly constructed an outright familization of both society and nation through their comments on family and against homosexuality. Following the logic of these statements in the context of the Thatcher Government's legislation on homosexuality as a 'pretended family relationship', one can conclude that homosexuals are a threat to the life and health of the nation and the life and health of society – or perhaps, at best, considered 'individual men and women'. The Prime Minister's comment regarding the 'nation of free people' continuing 'if family life continues' is instructive: those who are free are in families, and family is elevated to a status similar to the individual as a primary element of social organization. Writing a critique of this configuration before this statement was made, Caplan could none the less have been addressing this ministerial contention. Calling the conservative project 'an argu-ment for an extreme individualism of existence, property, values and action', she contends: 'In this the family figures as the true and natural unit of freedom . . . Attack the family, and it is freedom itself that bleeds' (1982: 124). Families, then, are seen here not only as the supreme guarantor of nation and society, but of freedom as well. In the words of a Haringey Conservative councillor and a Conservative MP, 'children should be brought up to believe in mum and dad, and schools should promote it', and 'it is essential that we support the family'. Conversely, homosexuals threaten nation, society, and freedom. If the ideal family is under attack, then contemporary forms of society, nation, and freedom are under attack – and the pretenders to the family throne must be forced into retreat.

Notes

I would like to thank Annie Whitehead, Eva Mackey, and Jacqueline Brown for critical discussions of this and earlier versions of this paper.

Susan Reinhold is a political anthropologist. Her D.Phil. dissertation at the University of Sussex, 'Local conflict and ideological struggle', details more thoroughly the events related to 'positive images' and Section 28 in late 1980s Britain. Sue and her partner Shannon Dubach live in San Francisco and are planning a family.

1 Count done by counting the number of times the term 'family' used without a definition being specifically defined or contested during parliamentary debate on the sex-education amendments of the Lords Education Bill 1986, questions

tabled on Haringey Council in 1986 and 1987, the Halsbury Bill, and Section 28. Citations from parliamentary debate are drawn from *Hansard*'s copy of the following debates in the Houses of Commons and Lords: Lords 15 April 1986, v. 473, cols. 592–643; Lords 20 May 1986, v. 475, cols. 195–212 and cols. 215–31; Lords 2 June 1986, v. 475, cols. 568–77; Commons 10 June 1986, v. 99, cols. 182–227; Commons 1 July 1986, v. 1, cols. 437–63; Lords 28 July 1986, v. 479, cols. 552–4; Commons 21 October 1986, v. 102, cols. 1055–98; Lords 18 December 1986, v. 483, cols. 310–88; Lords 3 February 1987, v. 484, cols. 179–83; Lords 1 April 1987, v. 486, cols. 570–3; Commons 8 May 1987, v. 115, cols 997–1014; Commons 8 December 1987, v. 123, cols. 1199–231; Commons 15 December 1987, vol. 124, cols. 987–1038; Lords 1 February 1988, v. 492, cols. 864–98 and cols. 928–74; Lords 2 February 1988, v. 492, cols. 993–1020; Lords 16 February 1988, v. 493, cols. 585–643; Lords 29 February 1988, v. 494, cols. 67–84; Commons 9 March 1988, v. 129, cols. 370–432. Full references to parliamentary citations in the text of this article are available upon request.

2 To my knowledge, no one has investigated these aspects of British gay family organization. This is not an assertion that power dynamics in gay relationships are completely devoid of a gendered dynamic.

3 The discourse of family and nation in relation to race is an important one, and one that intersects with the supposed Black threat to nation that I have discussed elsewhere. Implicitly, the ideal family invoked so often in these debates is a *white* family. The statements relating the importance of family to the constitution of the nation takes on an irony in the context of so many Black families being broken up by the British state as a result of stringent immigration law. One might think that the health of the Black family depended on a little more largesse from the state, thus contributing to the health of the nation, but this is not the case.

References

BARRETT, M. and MCINTOSH, M. (1982) *The Anti-Social Family* London: Verso.

CAPLAN, J. (1982) 'Conservatism and the family', *History Workshop Journal* No. 16.

CONNELL, R. W. (1987) *Gender and Power* Oxford: Polity.

DAVIDOFF, L. I. and HALL, C. (1987) *Family Fortunes. Men and Women of the English Middle Class* London: Hutchinson.

FITZGERALD, T. (1983) 'The new right and the family,' in Clarke, J. editor, *Social Policy and Social Welfare* London: Open University Press.

GILROY, P. (1987) *There Ain't No Black in the Union Jack: The Cultural Politics of Race and Nation* London: Hutchinson.

HMSO (1987) 'Sex education at school' Department of Education and Science Circular 11/87.

—— (1990) *Population Trends 60* London: HMSO.

KRAFFT-EBING, R. von (1896) [1965] *Psychopathia Sexualis* London: Staples Press.

METCALFE, A. W. (1990) 'The demonology of class: the iconography of the coalminer and the symbolic construction of political boundaries' *Critique of Anthropology* Vol. 10, No. 1.

MOSSE, G. (1985) *Nationalism and Sexuality: Respectability and Abnormal Sexuality in Modern Europe* New York: Ferti.

PHILLIPS, J. (1988) *Policing the Family: Social Control in Thatcher's Britain* London: Junius.

SEIDEL, G. (1988) editor, *The Nature of the Right: A Feminist Analysis of Order Patterns* Amsterdam: John Benjamins.

WATNEY, S. (1987) *Policing Desire: Pornography, Aids and the Media* London: Methuen.

—— (1989) 'Taking liberties: an introduction' in Watney, S. and Carter, E. editors, *Taking Liberties: AIDS and Cultural Politics* London: Serpent's Tail.

WEEKS, J. (1985) *Sexuality and its Discontents: Meanings, Myths, and Modern Sexualities* Boston: Routledge & Kegan Paul.

WESTON, K. (1991) *Families We Choose: Lesbians, Gays, Kinship* New York: Columbia.

WILLIAMS, R. (1983) *Keywords: A Vocabulary of Culture and Society* London: Fontana Press.

IN SEARCH OF GENDER JUSTICE:
Sexual Assault and the Criminal Justice System

Jeanne Gregory and Sue Lees

Engaging with the law

Within the feminist movement, there is profound scepticism about the value of research into the workings of state institutions, particularly the legal system. When feminists engage with the law, it is argued, they invariably concede too much; the rules of engagement are drawn in a way that contains the feminist challenge while reaffirming the power of law (Smart, 1989). It is not difficult to find examples in the history of feminist campaigns which support this position, documenting the disillusionment of feminist activists who have abandoned attempts to reform the legal system and instead promote their objectives by means of non-legal strategies.

Yet in view of the complex and contradictory ways in which the legal system operates, there is room for a variety of approaches to reform, which are not necessarily mutually exclusive, nor in conflict. The use of legal and non-legal strategies in combination constitutes a safeguard against being 'co-opted' by the law. To abandon legal strategies altogether would be no solution at all; rather, it would be to concede defeat, leaving the law unchallenged, our silence taken to imply that we had no criticisms to make. In developing such a critique, it is important to go beyond an analysis of legal discourse in order to understand the law in action and its impact on women (Dahl, 1987). Only then can we avoid the trap of accepting changes to the legal system which deliver the appearances but not the reality of reform.

In practice, feminist researchers and activists across the world have directed a barrage of criticisms at the failure of the law to deliver justice to women who have been sexually assaulted. They have challenged the dominant discourse that regards rape as an expression of sexual desire, arguing instead that it is an expression of sexual power intended to humiliate. This is confirmed by the way in which rape becomes a weapon of war, used with cruel effect to demoralize an enemy by inflicting permanent physical and psychological wounds on the female members of the 'enemy' community (Brownmiller, 1976). Yet in non-war situations the typical rape trial is conducted on the basis of apportioning blame and it is the character and behaviour of the woman that is placed under the severest scrutiny. Researching the law in action reveals that for many women the trial procedures are almost as traumatic as the initial attack; they describe the experience as a second rape. The outcome of this ordeal is that in over half the cases that reach court the man is acquitted and his behaviour thereby condoned (Lees, 1993).

In attempting to develop a feminist politics from such an analysis, the dilemma is the perennial one so often encountered by feminists: given that' it is not possible to stage a revolution and implement the feminist agenda in toto, what piecemeal reforms will achieve at least marginal improvements for some women and can this be achieved in a way which leaves us free to work for the longer term agenda?

In some situations, feminists have been able to enter into a dialogue with sympathetic governments while lacking a power base from which to ensure that their agenda is fully implemented and not jettisoned. For example, feminists working for Women's Aid in the 1970s were able to play a major role in the drafting of the Domestic Violence Act 1975. They were not able to prevent the restrictive judicial interpretation of its key provisions, combined with an initial unwillingness on the part of the police to play their role fully. Nor have they been able to stop the subsequent cutback in resources for Women's Aid with the steady erosion of any political will to make the law work effectively (see Edwards, 1989).

A more promising scenario occurs when feminists are able to create a power base inside state institutions, developing a 'femocracy' i.e., a bureaucracy with a feminist agenda. The question then becomes how to move forward without selling out and how to retain the links with grass-roots feminist movements. The severing of these links can lead the femocrats to compromise on important matters of principle, believing that they are acting in the best interests of women although they have ceased knowing what these interests are (Watson, 1990). In Canada, the presence of feminists in high places has had a beneficial impact in a number of areas of the law. Yet the failure of the legislators to accept that men and women have very different notions of consent meant that the new sexual assault law passed in 1983 continued to endorse the right of men to define women's sexuality (Los, 1990). In the absence of a successful challenge to this male prerogative, the impact of the legal reforms was limited.

Campaigning from the margins in the hostile political climate of the 1990s, there are obstacles to having any voice at all. The first task is to break through the official rhetoric, which unreservedly condemns acts of sexual violence, by demonstrating the extent to which the current legislation is failing to bring the perpetrators of such acts to justice. The maximum penalty for rape or attempted rape is life imprisonment and for serious sexual assault ten years (Sexual Offences (Amendment) Act 1985).

The availability of such harsh penalties provides the illusion that the state has taken appropriate action to control rapists, although in practice the maximum penalties are almost never used. This illusion is compounded by a deeply rooted complacency emanating from the judiciary, conveying the belief that the system delivers justice to the small number of women deemed worthy of protection at the same time as protecting men from the hoards of women who make false allegations. The occasional expression of public outrage when the media report a particularly lenient sentence or an offensive and insensitive judicial comment is greeted with expressions of pained surprise and has no lasting impact on subsequent cases.

If the judges seem impervious to criticism, a chink has appeared in the armour of the criminal justice system, at a point more responsive to public pressure than the judiciary. The police service, in adopting new policies and practices in its treatment of women reporting domestic violence, rape and sexual assault, broke ranks with the dominant discourse, producing tensions within the institutions of the state and opening up the possibility of change. It was the appearance of this ideological fracture and the potential it provided for creating new alliances that provided the inspiration for our research. The timing of the project also enabled us to assess the impact of the formation of the Crown Prosecution Service (CPS), a major new state institution, established in 1985 to take over from the police the task of prosecuting offenders.

Devising the research plan

Our interest in researching rape and sexual assault arose from the disturbing finding of previous research, including our own earlier involvement in this area.[1]

Our concern was triggered by evidence of extremely high rates of attrition in cases of rape and sexual assault; at each stage of the criminal justice process, cases were falling away in large numbers, which meant that only a tiny proportion of cases reported to the police were resulting in a conviction. As the vast majority of women who have been sexually assaulted do not even take the initial step of reporting to the police, those who do report are merely the tip of the iceberg and yet this tip is further decimated as the criminal justice system runs its course. It appeared to us that this evidence stood in sharp contrast to the rhetoric of the politicians and of the media, who gave the impression that more women were coming forward to report sexual attacks and that more men were being convicted and receiving their 'just deserts' in the shape of longer sentences. Under these influences, the tide of public opinion was beginning to turn, caught up in the quite legitimate concerns precipitated by a number of well-publicized cases of miscarriages of justice, mostly occurring in another area of the criminal law altogether. The old myth that allegations of rape 'may be very easy to make and very difficult to refute' (Lees, 1993) reasserted itself in the popularity stakes.

There was indeed some statistical evidence that more women were reporting rape and sexual assault, either because of an actual increase in the incidence of this crime, or because they had been encouraged to expect a more sympathetic reception at the hands of the police. A documentary television programme about the Thames Valley police transmitted in 1982 had drawn attention to the harsh treatment meeted out to women complaining of sexual assault and this, together with a report on violence against women published by the Women's National Commission (WNC, 1985) had provided the impetus for a fundamental shift in the way that complaints were handled.

Our research plan was developed on the basis of three major objectives: firstly, to investigate the impact of the innovations in police practices on women reporting sexual offences, to see whether they were satisfied with the way their complaints had been handled; secondly, to take a new look at the rates of attrition (the process by which cases are dropped) to see whether these had declined as a result of the new policies; thirdly, to assess the role of the CPS in terms of its impact on service delivery and attrition rates. In order to accomplish these objectives, we required access to police records and we also needed to interview complainants, police officers and other professional people working in this area.

Gaining access to state institutions

There is very little research on the workings of the legal system in the area of violence against women. There are two main obstacles: gaining access to records, court officials and courts and obtaining funding for the research. Gaining access requires time, patience and energy. Officials employ a variety of delaying tactics, in the hope that researchers will give up and go away.

When we first approached local police stations with a view to gaining access to police records, we were fortunate enough to be put in contact with a woman deputy chief superintendent who was extremely supportive. We also had to clear the research with Scotland Yard and this proved to be more difficult. The initial response was that we would have to delay the research for at least a year, until another project (which we have been unable to trace) had been completed. By the time this period had elapsed, the deputy chief superintendent was on sick leave and a new chief superintendent had been appointed; he felt unable to grant us the access to police records which we believed we had already negotiated.

After several months of further negotiation and a number of intimidating interviews, a compromise was agreed. The police were anxious that they should not be required to shoulder alone the blame for any shortcomings in the system and we were able to assure them that we were interested in examining multi-agency responses to the problem of sexual assault. An agreement to that effect was signed by all parties. It was also agreed that two women police officers would be seconded to obtain information from the police records according to our instructions. We had certain reservations about this arrangement, as we would have no way of telling whether data was being withheld for some reason, perhaps in order to present the police in a more favourable light. In the event, however, because of the commitment and enthusiasm of the policewomen who were seconded to this task, we were able to obtain better quality information than if we had been given permission to undertake it ourselves. Many record forms, particularly when cases are still ongoing, are not filed but have to be tracked down and may even be held at a different police station. A combination of determination, inside knowledge and personal contacts enabled the women officers to achieve a much higher success rate in the data collection than we could ever have hoped to achieve. In response to our requests, they collated crime report forms held at two police stations relating to a two-year period (September 1988 to September 1990) and presented us with detailed information on 301 reported cases of rape and sexual assault.

Criminal justice professionals have their own concerns and agenda for change. In deciding whether or not to grant access to outside researchers, they have to weigh the possibility that the findings will be critical rather than supportive against the possible adverse consequences of non-co-operation. It may be more desirable from their point of view to grant at least partial access, in the hope of retaining some control over the shape and direction of the research. Not all the gatekeepers of different parts of the criminal justice process necessarily resolve this dilemma in the same way. In our research, there was a marked difference between the reaction of the police who, after some initial hesitation, co-operated fully with the project, and the Crown Prosecution Service, who retained a defensive stance throughout, blocking our access to the 'front line' lawyers with the most experience of handling rape and sexual assault cases.

Instead, after a considerable delay, we were offered an interview with the branch crown prosecutor. He cancelled the first appointment and attempted to cancel the second, but the notification did not reach us and we presented ourselves at the offices of the CPS. The interview did go ahead but the prosecutor chose his words with extreme care, constantly referring to the Code for Crown Prosecutors and adding very little of significance. He did suggest that if there was any specific information we needed, we should write to him yet again, but by that time our research was in its final stages and the delaying tactics had proved effective, in so far as we did not pursue this line of inquiry any further.

The search for funding

Obtaining funding for the research, without relinquishing control of the research design or the research output, presented a second major obstacle. The funding councils, such as the Economic and Social Research Council, while fully respecting the need for academic autonomy, are exercising an increasing influence over the type of projects that receive funding. They do this by allocating a substantial proportion of the available money to specific research initiatives for which researchers are invited to bid. The problem then is to persuade them that, at a time of shrinking budgets and tighter controls, research into violence against women should be regarded as a priority area.

If funding is sought directly from the state, rather than via the research councils, the issues of priority and autonomy both have to be addressed. The controllers of the purse strings have to be persuaded that the project is worthwhile and also that it is not in their interests to censor or suppress the findings, however controversial. We made several approaches to the Home Office, which was about to publish the findings of its own 'in-house' research into attrition rates in rape cases. This was a study conducted in 1985, prior to the setting up of the Crown Prosecution Service (Grace *et al.*, 1992). It is possible that this study will be repeated for the period since 1985, but it seems unlikely that it will be 'contracted out' to independent researchers. Certainly, our negotiations have so far proved fruitless. Most Home Office research in this area is conducted 'in-house'; the only commissioned project of which we are aware is a psychological study of convicted rapists (Grubin and Gunn, 1990). Presumably, psychological profiling, in which the focus of attention is on individuals who rape, is seen as less threatening to the state than a more statistical and sociological study which places state practices under the spotlight.

It was the local state, in the shape of Islington Council's Police and Crime Prevention Unit, that provided us with funding, after more than a year of negotiation through the Department of the Environment's Inner Cities programme. The Islington Police Committee has been at the forefront of a number of crime prevention research initiatives, beginning with the Islington Crime Survey, the first local crime survey to investigate the extent of violence against women (Jones *et al.*, 1986), and most recently, the Domestic Violence Project (Mooney, 1993). The Police and Crime Prevention Unit reacted positively to our initial proposal. Islington has a high proportion of women counsellors, many of whom take an active part in promoting safety for women and their support through the Women's Committee was useful. It was a unique combination of an imaginative Police and Crime Prevention Sub-Committee and some central government funding for inner city projects that enabled this research to go ahead, not to mention our persistence!

Ethical considerations

For feminist researchers, ethical considerations are paramount, particularly when working in such a sensitive area as sexual assault.
Confidentiality is particularly important where issues of violence
against women are involved. Since we did not have access to the
women's addresses, our letter asking whether they would be willing to
be interviewed about their experiences was sent out by the police. This
might have led to some confusion as to the identity of the researchers.
Two women contacted assumed it was the police, although our letter
specifically stated that we were independent researchers. Their confusion is understandable, since the letter was written on police headed
notepaper and this may have deterred some women from replying. Only
thirty-eight women responded, some 12 per cent of those to whom the
letter was sent. Twenty-eight wrote to say they were willing to be
interviewed; two of those contacted cancelled the appointment on three
occasions and failed to answer a letter inviting them for another
interview. Therefore twenty-six women were interviewed, two on the
telephone, as they indicated that they would have found a face-to-face
interview too distressing. Despite the small size of the sample, it did
include women from different racial and ethnic groups. Two of those
interviewed were African-Caribbean, one was Asian and the rest were
white, two from Ireland and one from France.

Ten women who were not prepared to be interviewed wrote to tell us
that they would have found it too painful. Most of them had gone to court
and the suspect found not guilty. The reasons they gave for not speaking
to us are a moving testimony to the pain they had experienced and
wanted so desperately to forget. It is significant that none of the
defendants in these cases had been convicted and several cases had been
'no-crimed', in other words, not recorded as offences. The following are
typical of the replies:

> I just try to forget what happened. (From a woman who had gone to court
> and the defendant, an acquaintance, had been found not guilty of rape
> and Actual Bodily Harm)
> I am just getting over the assault and do not wish to discuss the matter,
> because it is still painful to do so. (From a woman allegedly raped by her
> ex-boyfriend who was found not guilty at the Crown Court)

We can only guess at the pain and anguish and destroyed lives that lie
behind the silence of the women who chose not to respond.

The findings:

Service delivery to complainants
Three-quarters of the women interviewed were satisfied with the way
they were treated by the police; they appreciated the increase in the

number of female officers dealing with cases of sexual assault and some were surprised that the police treated their complaint so seriously and sympathetically. On the other hand, several women commented on the poor flow of information on the progress of their case; many received no information whatsoever. There appears to be a serious communication gap occurring across the spectrum of case outcomes, although we have no way of knowing whether there was a similar pattern of experiences among the women who declined to be interviewed. It is possible that the most dissatisfied group were the least willing to come forward, especially as our letter was sent to them by the police.

The medical examination was described by almost all the women as a horrific endurance test and several described it as utterly degrading. One woman even said it was as bad as the rape itself. Only one woman interviewed described her medical examination positively. Some doctors appear to have been callously unsympathetic. Others may not have been deliberately heartless but do not appear to have appreciated the acute sensitivity of women whose bodies have been bruised and denigrated. Doctors need specialized training in how to examine sexual assault survivors, so that they are taught to avoid humiliating women who have already faced appalling degradation. One woman described how she was made to feel like an object, rather than a human being:

> I looked down at myself with this sheet wrapped around me and he (the doctor) turned to the woman police officer and said: 'Cover her up will you?' I felt like a piece of something on a slab – cover that up, we should not be looking at that.

These findings suggest that forensic requirements are put into effect with little flexibility. It is questionable whether a full medical was really necessary in the case of one woman, whose bedroom was broken into by a man with a knife and who had not in fact been raped.

> They did the whole bit – spit in the tube and swabs for this and swabs for that. It was all very degrading. They didn't explain what they were doing it for.

Women experienced going to court as an ordeal in itself. The prospect of coming face to face with the man or men who attacked them was universally dreaded. They described the appalling inadequacies of court facilities where there was often no heating, sparse furnishing and poor canteen arrangements. Having to share this space with the suspect understandably unnerved a number of complainants. As one woman put it:

> I would have liked not to have to sit where he had to sit. I don't see why I had to sit in the same room. It's the same kind of personal space invasion, so the perpetrator should have to sit in a separate room. I've never seen

him again, thank goodness. I'm not sure what I would do if I saw him again.

Research has shown that women who have been raped and sexually assaulted suffer from what has been called 'rape crisis syndrome' (Holmstrom and Burgess, 1978), which involves symptoms such as sleeplessness, panic attacks, unreasonable fears, horror of smells associated with the rape, disinterest in sex and depression. All the women we interviewed who had been subjected to attacks, even of a relatively minor kind (such as being touched over clothing) experienced some anxiety. Those who had experienced serious sexual assaults suffered from sleeplessness, nightmares, fear of going out alone or of being alone. Our findings were also in line with earlier research in that such symptoms often did not appear immediately, which indicates the importance of long-term counselling for the survivors of sexual attacks.

There are two main organizations in London that aim to provide some form of counselling for the survivors of sexual assault. Rape Crisis is predominantly a telephone helpline set up by rape survivors and providing some counselling, mainly over the telephone. In London, the training of volunteers has been regarded as a priority but limited funding means that the Centre is currently unable to provide face-to-face counselling and operates one telephone line for only a few hours a day. Victim Support is a nation-wide service partly funded by the Home Office and providing help to victims of all types of crime. Unlike Rape Crisis, it does not specialize in sexual assault cases. It does provide some face-to-face counselling, but the service varies from one local authority to another. In Islington a special attempt has been made to provide counselling for the survivors of sexual assault and the feedback from these women was more positive than from those living outside the borough, although some said they would have liked more intensive counselling.

Researching the role of the police
Once the research was underway, regular contact was maintained with the two women officers assigned to collate the records on our behalf. Meetings were held with the two chief superintendents at crucial points in the study; both of them were fully supportive of the research and allowed free access to their officers as required. All the officers seemed willing to talk to us and were very keen to describe the transformation that had taken place in recent years in the treatment of women reporting rape and sexual assault. Many made reference to the 'bad old days' depicted so vividly in a 1982 television documentary programme on the Thames Valley police, which showed a woman complainant undergoing a harsh interrogation. Since the furore generated by that episode, the police have operated under a clear instruction that no one reporting a serious sexual assault is to be disbelieved. As an example of this new policy in action, one of the detective inspectors related a case in which a woman reported that she had been raped by a taxi driver but at

the same time admitted that she may have dreamt it. The inspector acknowledged that in the past 'she would have been laughed out of the station', but in accordance with the new policies, the complaint was treated seriously. Semen found on her sheets matched with samples obtained from the taxi driver and he was convicted.

Current police practice in this area is to assign a female officer who has completed the training programme on Sexual Offences Investigation Techniques to a case from the outset and she assumes responsibility, as far as possible, for all communication with the complainant. Although a detective inspector (most of whom are male) takes overall charge of the investigation, it is the female officer who takes the complainant's statement, stays with her during the medical examination, provides her with information and support and, should the case reach court, accompanies her. If it seems unlikely that the case will go to court, the officers are required to emphasize that what happened was not the woman's fault and that it was just a problem of evidence.

At one level, the police officers seemed committed to making the new policies work. The female officers interviewed were particularly impressive; they were attempting to provide some support for complainants, despite the tendency for the rest of their work to 'pile up' while they did so and they were genuinely concerned that so few cases went to court. At another level, it is important to realize that old attitudes die hard and also that the police are subjected to conflicting pressures. On the crucial question of false allegations, for example, it was apparent from the interviews that many officers believed these to be a frequent occurrence. They gave hypothetical examples of mischievous reports of rape, such as the woman who has had a row with her boyfriend, the prostitute who has not been paid, the young woman who becomes pregnant or stays out all night and wishes to escape parental wrath. One inspector commented that the last three rapes he had dealt with were not rapes at all and a female inspector believed that 50 per cent of the rapes reported were probably false allegations.

Apart from that particular inspector, women officers were less likely to express such scepticism. In view of the roles they as policewomen are expected to perform and their concentration in the junior ranks, women officers find themselves on the front line in rape and sexual assault cases. It is this 'hands-on' experience which dispels the myth of false allegations; the female inspector quoted above was part of the dominant culture, operating at one remove from complainants and having served her time in the lower ranks before the new 'sympathetic' policies were adopted.

It is indicative of the fragile nature of the changes in police policies that by the end of the 1990s they had had no noticeable impact on the practice of 'no-criming' cases, i.e., not recording them as crimes. This is a long-standing police practice, justified as a way of avoiding wasting time on 'hopeless' cases and previously encouraged because it produced a higher 'clear-up' rate in the official statistics. Home Office circulars produced during the 1980s, directing the police to handle sexual-assault complaints more sympathetically, also established new guidelines for the practice of 'no-criming'. Cases of serious sexual assault were only to be placed in this category if the complainant withdrew the allegation and admitted that it was false. Yet our findings indicated that during the two-year period covered by our study 38 per cent of the reported cases (116 out of 301) were treated as 'no-crimes' and that the reasons given for classifying them in this way fell outside the official guidelines.

Cases in which there was some kind of a relationship between the complainant and the suspect were much more likely to be 'no-crimed' than stereotypical 'stranger' attacks. These were also the cases least likely to be taken up by the Crown Prosecution Service or to result in a conviction. In 'no-criming' such a high proportion of cases in which there was some kind of prior acquaintance or even intimacy between the complainant and the suspect, the police are anticipating outcomes at later stages in the criminal justice process. They are 'screening out' those cases in which the complainant will not be seen as a credible witness by the CPS or by a jury.

As the police attempt to resolve this dilemma, the tensions are likely to be accentuated rather than reduced. On the one hand, they informed us that there had been a further tightening of the 'no-criming' procedures since the two-year period covered by our research; on the other hand, they are being encouraged to pass to the CPS only those cases with a reasonable prospect of resulting in a conviction. This leaves them with an ever increasing number of cases on file that cannot be resolved, particularly as more women are coming forward to report sexual attacks now that they can expect a sympathetic hearing. The police are themselves being subjected to stringent performance criteria, so that the tension between the conflicting demands of service delivery to complainants and demonstrated success at solving crimes is likely to increase.

The role of the CPS and the courts

Less than a third of the cases originally reported to the police went forward to the Crown Prosecution Service, i.e., 88 out of 301 cases. Despite this draconian sweep of 'weak' cases, the CPS took no further action in 17 of those referred, so that 71 cases proceeded to a prosecution. In 41 of these a conviction was secured, although one of these was quashed on appeal. Three offenders were detained under the Mental Health Act and in the remaining 27 either the proceedings were discontinued at some point or the suspects were found not guilty.

In only 29 cases were custodial sentences given, ranging from one month to life imprisonment and in only 5 of these cases had there been a prior acquaintance between the offender and the complainant; the rest were all stereotypical stranger attacks. All 5 of the 'acquaintance' cases involved a considerable degree of violence; in two cases, this included buggery as well as rape and in three cases there was an age gap of some twenty-five years between the woman and her attacker. In other words, although more women are being encouraged to report assaults by men they know, these assaults are not being recognized as such by the criminal justice system. The fact that the police deal sympathetically with these women and accept their account as true is important in helping their recovery, but in failing to convict all but a handful of the men responsible for the assaults, the criminal justice system is condoning their actions and encouraging them to attack again.

The way forward

As our research focused mainly on the work of the police and was conducted on behalf of a local authority, it was easier for us to make recommendations for further improvements in service delivery than to tackle the underlying problem of the attrition rate. The recommendations included strategies for improving the flow of information between the police and complainants and for reducing the trauma of the court appearance; also for the development of a much more comprehensive and sensitive medical service, including advice and support in relation to pregnancy, venereal disease and HIV testing and for ensuring the availability of long-term counselling. We also recommended a fundamental review of police recording procedures, in order to yield a more objective picture of precisely why cases fail to proceed and the abolition of the 'no-criming' category altogether. The local police seemed receptive to our suggestions for further reform and recognized the need to monitor how the changes were working in practice. We were subsequently invited to speak to the Sexual Offences Steering Committee at New Scotland Yard, who were equally receptive, while rightly pointing out that the key to solving many of the problems we had identified lay elsewhere, in the courts and in the wider society. Detective inspectors, police superintendents and senior medical officers expressed frustration with the practices of the judicial system and agreed that changes were overdue.

One of the dominant themes of official discourse concerns the rights of individuals, encouraged to demand high standards of service delivery in various walks of life, whether as patients, passengers or victims of crime. Yet as these 'charters' proliferate, each in turn meets the stumbling block of scarce economic resources and the criminal justice system is no exception. On the one hand, there is a new official concern with 'witness care' and users groups are being established in a number of crown courts. On the other hand, the CPS is under pressure to reduce the number of jury trials by extending the practice of 'plea-bargaining'. In relation to rape and sexual assault cases, this could mean even more men accused of serious sexual crimes pleading guilty to indecent assault, a crime which can be disposed of in the magistrates' court with the imposition of a light sentence, such as a fine or community service order. Unlike police officers, CPS lawyers have no direct contact with complainants; their main concern is to reduce time delays, improve conviction rates and keep costs under control. Their current strategy for achieving these goals is to anticipate judicial decisions rather than challenge them.

Conclusion

Within the police service, the dominant discourse which holds that women complaining of rape or sexual assault frequently make false allegations is under attack. It is caught in a pincer movement between senior policy-makers, who instruct officers to deal with complainants as though they believed them, and the junior officers most closely involved with the cases, who really do believe them. Despite these powerful pressures, there is a real danger that the police, believing themselves to be isolated, may take the line of least resistance and retreat from the advances they have made. In order to prevent this occurring, it is essential to sustain the attack on the dominant discourse as enshrined in judicial pronouncements and in the trial itself. Support for such a campaign can be found within the media. Recent television programmes have highlighted lenient sentences in rape cases (BBC, *Panorama*, July 1993) and the scandal of serial rapists who escape justice only to rape many times again (Channel Four, *Dispatches*, February 1994). The CPS has been criticized for dropping too many cases, particularly when complainants then go on to pursue a successful civil action (Channel 3, *The London Programme*, August 1993). Such anecdotal evidence is confirmed by Home Office statistics, which show that between 1985 and 1991 the conviction rate for crimes of rape and sexual assault fell from 24 per cent to 14 per cent (Home Office, 1993).

Whether legislative reforms are introduced from within, by femocrats or sympathetic politicians, or by a less sympathetic government implementing its own agenda, their impact in the courtroom will be minimal until sexual offence cases are heard by judges, including Appeal Court judges, who have been carefully screened and received intensive training from counsellors experienced in dealing with the survivors of sexual assault. It is time to challenge the simplistic notion that the only 'politically correct' stance for anyone on the left is to side with the defendant against the state. As James Garvie perceptively argues, it is possible to develop a radical position with regard to the role of the prosecution and the needs of the victim, without attacking the civil liberties of the defendant (Garvie, 1993).

At present, the balance in rape trials is very much in favour of the defendant. His sexual history and past criminal record is protected even if he has attacked the character of the complainant. He also has his own highly paid legal representative, whose main task is to destroy the credibility of the complainant. She, by contrast, has no lawyer specifically to represent her interests, nor to protect her when her version of events is challenged and her good character and past sexual behaviour are called into question. Until this imbalance is corrected, the attrition rate in cases of rape and sexual assault will remain high, leaving the perpetrators of these crimes free to attack again.

Notes

Jeanne Gregory is Professor of Gender Studies and Head of the Gender Research Centre at Middlesex University.

Sue Lees is Professor of Women's Studies and Director of the Centre for Research in Gender and Ethnicity at the University of North London.

1 Sue Lees had observed a number of rape trials at the Central Criminal Court (see Lees, 1993) and Jeanne Gregory had assisted in the design of the questionnaire used on the Channel 3, *World in Action* programme on marital rape ('The Right to Rape', shown on 25 September 1989).

References

BROWNMILLER, Susan (1976) *Against Our Will* Harmondsworth: Penguin.

DAHL, Tove Stang (1987) *Women's Law, an Introduction to Feminist Jurisprudence* Oxford: Oxford University Press.

EDWARDS, Susan (1989) *Policing 'Domestic' Violence* London: Sage.

GARVIE, James (1993) 'In defense of the prosecution' *Guardian* 31 August.

GELSTHORPE, Lorraine and MORRIS, Allison (1990) editors, *Feminist Perspectives in Criminology* Milton Keynes: Open University Press.

GRACE, et al. (1992) *Rape: From Recording to Conviction* London: Home Office, Research and Planning Unit Paper 71.

GRUBIN, Donald and GUNN, John (1990) *Imprisoned Rapists and Rape* London: Home Office Research Unit.

HOLMSTROM, Linda and BURGESS, Ann (1978) *The Victim of Rape: Institutional Reactions* New York: Wiley.

HOME OFFICE (1993) Unpublished statistics, obtained by Channel Four *Dispatches* programme, Home Office Research Unit.

JONES, Trevor, MACLEAN, Brian and YOUNG, Jock (1986) *The Islington Crime Survey* London, Gower.

LEES, Sue (1993) 'Judicial Rape' *Women's Studies International Forum* 16(1).

LEES, Sue and GREGORY, Jeanne (1993) *Rape and Sexual Assault: A Study of Attrition* London: Islington Council.

LOS, Maria (1990) 'Feminism and rape law reform', in GELSTHORPE and MORRIS (1990).

MOONEY, Jayne (1993) *The Hidden Figure: Domestic Violence in North London* London: Islington Council.

SMART, Carol (1989) *Feminism and the Power of Law* London: Routledge.

SMITH, Lorna (1989) *Concerns About Rape* Home Office Research Study No. 106, London: HMSO.

WATSON, Sophie (1990) *Playing the State: Australian Feminist Interventions* London: Verso.

WOMEN'S NATIONAL COMMISSION (1985) *Violence Against Women* London: WNC.

GOD'S BULLIES: Attacks on Abortion

Janet Hadley

In recent years in the United States, in Poland, and in Ireland too, national politics has at times been convulsed by the issue of abortion. In Germany the historic reunification of East and West almost foundered amid wrangling about conflicting abortion laws. How can abortion, hardly an issue comparable to the great affairs of state, such as the economy or national security, have an impact such as this?

This is an account, first, of how post-Communist Poland found itself in the grip of the abortion debate and secondly how the issue came to be such a seemingly permanent shadow on the political landscape in the United States, in the wake of the Supreme Court's 1973 landmark decision on abortion in the case of *Roe v. Wade*. It offers some ideas about why.

The account focuses on abortion, primarily as a method of birth control, which women have always sought out, legally when they can, illegally when they must. The controversies and campaigns recorded and the ideas offered here concentrate on women's access to affordable, safe and legal abortion – an essential part of women's reproductive freedom in a world where five hundred women die every day from the complications of unsafe abortion (World Health Organization, 1993).

The way abortion has at times dominated public debate in both Poland and the United States can hardly be exaggerated, but the contexts are very different. At times, during the 1992 American presidential election campaign, it seemed as if the fate of the United States for the next four years hung solely on the thread of the abortion issue. Economic issues, national security, even political scandals were all pushed into the background. But no one was too surprised to encounter this wild card in the United States' electoral politics. It had been thus, on and off, for around twenty years, since the 1973 Supreme Court judgement which had sanctioned abortion as a woman's constitutional right.

It was, however, probably a lot harder for anyone to have predicted events in Poland where, for more than four years, well before the forty-year-old Communist regime was finally sloughed off, abortion took centre stage. The renascent right in Poland selected abortion as the first block of the social welfare system for demolition. The battle over it highlights the new relationship between the Roman Catholic Church – once the main element of opposition alongside Solidarity – and the state. As the democratization of Eastern Europe got under way, abortion was one of the first laws to come under fire (Einhorn, 1993).

In some ways the abortion debate in Poland, which of all the former Soviet bloc countries has undergone far the most draconian reversal of its abortion law, is quite straightforward: the opponents of abortion are solidly Roman Catholic and perceive their efforts as part of the task of rescuing Poland from its years of godlessness. The debate in Poland harks back to the relatively straightforward arguments which took place in Britain at the time of the passing of the Abortion Act in 1967.

In the United States on the other hand, the issue has been linked to a much more extensive catalogue of perceived 'social degeneracy'. Opposition to abortion in the United States involves a curious alliance of religious and secular New Right groupings and much of the driving force has been provided, not by the Roman Catholic Church, but by evangelical Christians.

I have chosen to look closely at Poland and the United States for no particularly lofty reasons. They are very different, that's the main thing, and what's more, when *Feminist Review* published a special issue on abortion in 1988, there was no article on the United States (*Feminist Review* 29, 1988). Also, I believe that the Polish case serves powerfully to remind feminists in the West that access to safe, affordable, legal abortion remains a fundamental and precious element of reproductive freedom, and is something which the majority of women in the world either lack completely or, as in Poland, cannot ever take for granted (McLean, 1989). This needs to be underlined at a time when much of the feminist and public debate around reproductive freedom has switched, in response to the advancing juggernaut of medical biotechnology, to more esoteric matters such as infertility treatment and its spin-offs, as well as to fetal 'rights'. Such issues are indeed important, now and for the future, but for many women they are a luxury way beyond reach.

Poland: no place to be a woman

> Polish Church may sink government over abortion. (*National Catholic Reporter* 15.1.93)

> Fierce political battle to amend 'God's law'. (*Catholic Herald* 1.1.93)

What we have been witnessing in Poland since 1989, according to one observer, is the 'Church's colossal efforts to replace a totalitarian state with a theocracy' (Kissling, 1992). Weekly Masses from Rome are broadcast on Polish TV these days. Scientific conferences open with High Mass, blessings and so on, and military personnel are sent on pilgrimages. Classes in religion (i.e., Roman Catholicism) are mandatory for children in state schools. There is little doubt that the bishops of Poland, who behave more like leaders of a political party than as simple guardians of moral values, have their sights set not only on banning abortion but also divorce, provision of contraception, and other hallmarks of a secular society. One commentator wrote in 1991:

> From the very beginning until its unexpected culmination in June [1991 –
> when a draft anti-abortion bill was rejected by parliament in the face of
> huge pro-choice demonstrations] the Polish controversy on abortion was a
> classic example of political conflict. Nobody cared any more about subtle
> moral or political arguments. It was clear that who wins the abortion
> debate will control the political situation in Poland. (Szarwarski, 1991)

The irony is that not only was June 1991 far from being the 'culmination', but also that nobody today could be said to have won. (Women, of course, lost.)

The final law, signed by President Lech Walesa in February 1993, was seen by opponents of abortion as a compromise. It is much weaker than they would have liked. The original anti-abortion bill, first published in 1989, promised three years' imprisonment for a woman who induced her own abortion, as well for any doctor caught performing an illegal operation. Under the new law, two years' imprisonment awaits an abortionist, but a woman inducing her own abortion will not face gaol.

The new law allows abortion when a woman's life or health is in danger, after rape or incest, or if there is suspected fetal abnormality. But prenatal testing is only permissible if there is a family history of genetic disorder. There are token provisions urging local authorities to provide contraceptive services.

The Church's power and influence
The religious context of the abortion row in Poland goes a long way to explaining how it came to be such a passionate, extreme and dominating issue. Around 95 per cent of its 39 million people consider themselves Catholic and there is a very strong family tradition of Catholicism, which during the Communist era greatly strengthened the Church as a focus of national identity and a shelter for opposition. Having a Polish Pope helps too; when John Paul II visited in 1991, he urged his fellow Poles to free themselves from a law permitting abortion, which he called a tragic inheritance of Communism.

Even when the Communist grip seemed at its most unyielding, the Church consistently harried the authorities on issues of sexual control. In a recent survey, conducted since the fall of the Communists, and reported in the *Guardian* (14.9.93), 95 per cent of Polish women said they rely on personal experience for their sex education and 73 per cent said they had had an unplanned pregnancy.

The only sex-education manual ever produced in Poland had to be withdrawn because of Church protest. Roman Catholic opposition to contraception has been effective – 76 per cent of the urban population and 87 per cent of the rural population use only Church-approved 'natural' methods of fertility control (Mrugala, 1991). (Priests often determine what is sold in local pharmacies.) Poland's 1956 abortion law contained no conscience clause, but the Church's success in pressuring doctors can be judged from the fact that in some state hospitals, staff refusal made it impossible to get an abortion. As early as 1973, Church protests over the rising abortion rate and the behaviour of 'callous young women' forced the government to set up a commission to consider whether the law needed amending (Okolski, 1988).

But the pressures on women to have abortions were very strong. Even for those who wanted it, contraception has never been easily available, and was of notoriously poor quality. Abortion – which was free in state hospitals after 1959, and easy to obtain – was therefore the main method of birth control. Women only had to report that they were 'in a difficult life situation'. 'Poland's hard life finds more and more women choosing abortions', reported the *New York Times* in 1983, citing families in some cities waiting eighteen years to obtain a small apartment. Despite the Church's denunciations, there were an estimated 600,000 abortions a year, compared to just 700,000 live births.

Times may have been hard in 1983, but the economic 'shock therapy' of post-Communist Poland has brought unimaginable hardship in its wake. Unemployment is now 2.8 million and will be one-fifth of the workforce in three years' time. The bishops have deplored this, by urging *women* to leave the labour market, to ease unemployment and ensure that men's wages increase. They have made no adverse comment on the virtual shutdown of state-financed child care.

The bishops, the state, and the medical profession

The episcopate first floated the idea of outlawing abortion in 1988, deeming it to be a mortal threat to the 'biological substance of the nation'. In the spring of 1989 an Unborn Child Protection Bill was published and the Pope hurried to send his congratulations.

In 1990, however, long before the legislative battle had got into its stride, the Ministry of Health took its own initiative, saying that women wanting abortion would now need the permission of three physicians and of a psychologist, whose appointment had been approved by the local bishop, and that an abortion for social reasons must be requested in writing (*New York Times*, 21.4.92). The psychologist's job is to dissuade women, mainly by putting the frighteners on them. Sterilization and the in-vitro fertilization programme were suspended.

As Poland created its first parliament, abortion became the bellwether for fitness to serve. Anyone supporting abortion rights was traduced as a surreptitious advocate for Communism. Throughout 1990 and 1991 the battle raged, overshadowing the upheavals of the new market economy. Huge demonstrations in favour of abortion took place in Warsaw and women's groups began to get organized to defend abortion rights. Solidarity was split on the issue. Bills were proposed and defeated in dizzying succession. Parish priests threatened to withhold sacraments from anyone who did not sign the petitions against 'killing innocent children'.

The anti-abortion movement targeted not only abortion but family planning provision too, blocking the launch of an information campaign in the textile city of Lodz, where there has been an unusually high rate of congenital abnormalities among babies born to women working in the textile factories (Rich, 1991). Their activity was partly financed by pro-life organizations from the United States, such as Human Life International. This evangelical group, fired by a vision of a 're-Chris-tianized united Europe stretching from the Atlantic to the Urals', vowed to 'flood Eastern Europe' with films, videos (such as *The Silent Scream*, which has been shown in Polish schools), fetal models and other propaganda. In 1992, Operation Rescue blockaded a clinic in the Baltic port of Gdynia, with protesters from USA, Canada and the UK.

Although one smear in circulation was that 'only communists and Jews favour abortion', there is little direct evidence that the anti-abortion campaign was fuelled by a nationalist pro-natalism – a desire to demographically overwhelm Poland's minorities. There was, however, a definite bid to appeal to a repressive notion of proper and traditional Polish 'womanhood'. The term 'emancipation for women' is laden with Communist overtones and has often in reality meant the notorious 'double burden' or overloading of women, in Poland and Eastern Europe in general, in which they have been expected to shoulder full-time jobs as well as forty hours a week shopping, cooking, cleaning, laundry, with only the aid of very poor-quality pre-school child care and medical care (Jankowska, 1993). Against such a reality, a misty vision of womanhood may have a definite allure.

May 1992 brought another turn of the screw. A new code of medical ethics made it professionally unethical for doctors to perform abortions except in cases of rape or incest or when the woman's life was in danger. Violations would lead to suspension of the doctor's licence. The code effectively ended hospital abortions and prenatal testing: some insti-tutions put up signs, 'No Abortions'.

The issue continued to rock the government, which twice postponed a final vote on abortion. By the end of 1992, the conflict was extreme enough to threaten the fragile coalition government, an improbable seven-party affair. A million people signed a petition for a referendum. Meanwhile, 61 per cent of Poles said they favoured the provisions of the 1956 law.

Turning the clock back
Nevertheless, when the government could postpone a vote no longer, a law was finally passed early in 1993. Under the new law, only 3 per cent

of the abortions previously performed in Poland are now deemed legal. Two years in gaol awaits an illegal abortionist, but there is no punishment for a woman who obtains an illegal operation. Although it is the most restrictive abortion law in Europe, apart from Ireland's, pro-choice campaigners comforted themselves with the rueful thought that things could easily have been much worse.

The legislation satisfies no one. Both sides have vowed to fight on. Even before President Lech Walesa signed the new law, the 1992 doctors' code – a *de facto* ban on abortions in Poland – was having its effect. The Warsaw police morgue has begun receiving bodies of women bearing witness to botched abortions. For the last three years, cases of infanticide have steadily increased.

Deaths will be outnumbered by injuries. Romania, where abortion was illegal until the fall of Ceauşescu in 1989, shows the way. Staff at a clinic for women in Bucharest, set up by Marie Stopes International, found that 80 per cent of patients were suffering from past incompetent abortions.

A helpline set up in Warsaw by pro-abortion campaigners is receiving calls from men seeking advice because their wives are refusing to have sex any more. Women are phoning for help, reporting that even in circumstances which comply with the new law, they are being refused operations. In Poland's deep Catholic south, a pregnant Cracow woman, furnished with a police report confirming that she had been raped, was refused help at the hospital (Hoell, 1993).

All the desolately familiar symptoms of outlawed abortion are there: police raids on clinics, small ads appearing in the newspapers: 'Gynaecologist: Interventions'. The price is $350–1,000: the average monthly wage is $200. For professional women, 'medical tours' can be arranged – to the Ukraine, to Kaliningrad, even to Holland. (But not to the Czech Republic, which in the wake of Poland's new law, moved swiftly to outlaw abortions for foreign visitors.)

Paradoxically, the last few years have seen a burgeoning of women's organizations, formed to defend abortion and women's rights. It is an irony, comments Hanna Jankowska, when 'the word "feminist" sounds in this country like an insult' (1993). But sustaining the momentum of such organizations is uphill work. People are consumed by the effort to cope with the effects of 38 per cent inflation.

There are signs that the Church may have overplayed its hand in its attempt to introduce a legislative version of 'absolute morality' as part of a plan to create a theocratic Poland. There was strong public support for a referendum on abortion, which the Church opposed, and its popularity has dropped by half since Communism collapsed, according to opinion polls (*Catholic Herald* 9.9.93). The Irish Church found itself in similar trouble after the referendum on abortion in Ireland in 1992, an event which was much reported in the Polish media.

But it is hard to draw sound parallels with Ireland: the Republic is certainly behind the times, but there are signs that slowly things are creeping forward for women in Ireland. Nothing compares with the crudeness with which the clock hands have been wrenched *back* in Poland.

In September 1993 the political coalition which fostered the anti-abortion legislation suffered a crushing defeat in national elections. The pace of reform was thought to be the main culprit, but the unpopularity of the anti-abortion law was also held to blame. Pro-abortion campaigners are preparing a new bill to reverse the law, scarcely before the ink is dry. In January 1994, Polish doctors amended their medical code, somewhat relaxing the abortion guidelines and increasing scope for prenatal diagnosis of fetal abnormalities.

The bishops and their allies intend to press on towards a theocratic state. They have stated: 'We must reject the false and harmful belief – which unfortunately is grounded in social consciousness – that a secular state is perceived as the only and fundamental guarantee of freedom and equality of citizens' (Szawarski, 1991). If they succeed in creating a model Roman Catholic state, it will be women who suffer most directly. That is why no one in Poland, on whichever side of the abortion divide, underestimates the importance of the struggle around abortion as a stalking horse for what may yet come.

It is not possible to yoke together the national experience of abortion politics in Poland with that of the United States, only to offer them as two distinct examples of how abortion seemed at times to be the tail that wagged the dog of national politics. It has been quite remarkable to find abortion ricocheting around the political arena in Poland and other Eastern European countries. But the issue has played a crucial part in the politics of the United States for almost twenty years: in itself an astonishing phenomenon.

USA, 1973 – the Supreme Court lights the fuse

Until the historic US Supreme Court judgment of 1973, in the case of *Roe v. Wade* (which I shall call plain *Roe*), abortion was not a major issue in the United States. In the late 1960s, when campaigners for abortion reform in California asked people to sign petitions, it took so long for people to think and talk before deciding where they stood that no more than four or five signatures could be gathered in an afternoon's work (Luker, 1984).

But the spark of *Roe* caught dry tinder at once and is still burning. Today, everyone has an opinion on abortion: after thousands of opinion polls, hours of TV debating, radio phone-ins and miles of newsprint, people know with certainty whether they are 'pro-choice' or 'pro-life'.

In the late nineteenth century it was doctors who pressed for anti-abortion legislation in the United States, partly to strengthen the delineation of medicine as a regulated, élite profession. Making abortion illegal, unless performed by a doctor, was an effective way of cutting the ground from under the 'quacks'. The laws granted doctors alone the discretion to decide when a woman's life was sufficiently endangered to justify the loss of fetal life.

For almost seventy years legal abortion was a matter for medical judgement. Its prevalence and the criteria used varied enormously. Women who could not get legal abortions resorted to illegal practitioners and practices. But in the 1950s and 1960s exclusive medical control over abortion began to crumble.

Briefly, women's lives were changing as they entered the labour market in increasing numbers – for a married woman an unintended pregnancy became much more of a disaster than in the past; secondly, the improvements of medicine and obstetrics made pregnancy and childbirth much safer and made it harder for doctors to cloak a decision to perform an abortion for a wealthy patient behind the excuse that continuing the pregnancy would gravely endanger her health. Doctors' work became much more hospital-based and could be more easily scrutinized and regulated than when they worked in private consulting rooms.

Thirdly, women began to question the right of doctors and lawyers, or anyone, to decide whether or not they should have to continue an unintended pregnancy. Finally, the effects of the Thalidomide cases and the advent of effective contraception all played a part in dragging decisions and policies on abortion into the harsh public light of politics.

Some states began to permit abortion. Between 1967 and 1973, seventeen states rescinded their restrictions on abortion. Thousands of women crossed state boundaries to obtain abortions (Gold, 1990). Abortion was happening, despite its continuing prohibition under federal law.

Several decades of Supreme Court decisions – for instance, acknowledging it was no business of the state (or states) to seek to outlaw the use and purchase of contraceptives – had smoothed the path towards the *Roe* judgment, but none the less, when it eventually came, it was quite dramatic. The court said that a woman's right to obtain an abortion, like her right to use contraception without government interference is constitutionally protected, as part of her fundamental right to privacy. And that because the right to privacy is fundamental (rights under the American constitution are ranked, and *fundamental* trumps every other kind of right) states must show a 'compelling interest' before they can intervene.

The court stressed that, of course, the decision to abort must be made together with a doctor. But it devised a sliding scale of maternal/ fetal rights, practically sanctioning 'abortion on demand' in the first trimester and gradually increasing the amount of protection afforded to the fetus as the weeks of pregnancy progressed.

No room for compromise

The significance of the Supreme Court ruling in 1973 was that it turned abortion into a constitutional issue, declaring it a fundamental right of the female citizen, and sweeping away all the various state restrictions.

In doing so it called into question the deeply held beliefs of people accustomed to thinking that *theirs* was the majority opinion and set the state on a collision course with an indefatigable group of its citizens. As long as abortion had been purely a medical issue, as it is in Britain (see below) it had been much more difficult to challenge, and far less in the public domain.

The absolute divide between right-to-life/pro-life/anti-choice/anti-abortion people, and the rest is the embryo or fetus. If you believe that the embryo or later the fetus is a person, a human being in the fullest sense, the moral equivalent of a woman, everything else falls into place. The Supreme Court questioned this notion and opened the door to the years of court challenge, endless legislative pressure and single-issue pressure-group politics. For those who believe that abortion is the equivalent of homicide there can hardly be a compromise.

The impact of the *Roe* judgement was enormous. Overnight, literally, the opposition mobilized.[1] Its attack has had two aims: to upset and overturn the judicial applecart and at the same time to erect as many obstacles as possible between a woman and a legal abortion. It's been a busy twenty years: *Roe* has been harried almost to extinction by state regulations, such as imposed waiting periods, demands for 'informed consent', such as making the woman look at images of fetal development – at all stages, no matter how early her own pregnancy. As pro-choice campaigner Lawrence Lader said, after *Roe*, 'We thought we had won. We were wrong' (*Family Planning World* Jan/Feb 1992).

At first, state attempts to regulate abortion after *Roe* received a cool response in the Supreme Court, but as the new right has gained power and judges appointed to the court became more conservative, so the judgements have hardened against abortion rights.

Wide-ranging success for abortion's opponents
The cultural and political climate today is of course very different from that surrounding *Roe* in 1973. On the day of the Supreme Court's ruling on *Roe*, newspapers reported an agreement which might bring an end to the war in Vietnam and carried obituaries of former President Lyndon B. Johnson, whose presidency was marked domestically by the civil rights movement, Black Power and the movement against the war in Vietnam. This is not the place to rehearse the cultural 'backlash' of the years since then except to highlight how wide-ranging it has been.

Susan Faludi, for instance, recounts the fate of a script for the TV show *Cagney and Lacey*. In 'Choices', as the early 1980s' episode was to be called, Cagney – the single woman in the feisty female cop duo – became pregnant. CBS programming executives went beserk at the mere idea of abortion (even as an option to be rejected). They demanded numerous rewrites until in the final version, Cagney only mistakenly thinks she is pregnant. 'Lacey . . . tells her that if she had been pregnant she should have got married. Abortion is never offered as a choice' (Faludi, 1992: 186).

The anti-abortion lobby drew comfort not only from *Cagney and*

Lacey but also from the White House. As the violence against clinics increased in 1984 after Ronald Reagan's election to a second term as president, he refused to condemn the actions and their perpetrators (Blanchard and Prewitt, 1993).[2]

Opinion polls show that Americans' attitude to abortion was and generally remains 'permit but discourage'. It was not very hard to convert such ambivalence into support for restrictions on government funding and so on. The most significant curtailment of rights for low-income women was the Hyde Amendment of 1979 which denied Medicaid funding for abortion, except where a woman's life is in danger. There have also been severe and wide-ranging restrictions on the use of public facilities for abortion: it is illegal, for instance, to perform a private abortion in a private building standing on publicly owned land. By 1979 no federal funds could be used to provide abortion or abortion-related services (Petchesky, 1984).

Today, only half the United States' medical schools even offer the option of training in abortion procedures, and fewer and fewer young doctors are willing to perform abortions. Many gynaecologists still performing abortions are reaching retirement, and in a 1985 study, two-thirds of the gynaecologists in the United States stated that they would not terminate pregnancy. Who would choose to conduct their professional working life in a bullet-proof vest, with an armed guard at the clinic door? In 1988, 83 per cent of all United States counties lacked any facilities for abortion, and those counties contain 31 per cent of US women aged between 15 and 44 (Alan Guttmacher Institute, 1993).

A shadowy world of unlicensed, unregulated abortion facilities in private doctors' offices is beginning to emerge. There are estimated to be several dozen in New York City alone and a doctor there was recently prosecuted for a botched abortion on a 21-year-old immigrant woman, who subsequently gave birth to a severely mutilated infant (*Family Planning World* May/June 1993).

And yet, despite all the legislative obstacles and the physical harassment, the anti-abortion movement has made no dent in the number of abortions taking place in the United States. The overall figure has hovered steadily around 1.6 million a year.

Who opposes abortion rights?
The intimidation of anti-abortion activists, such as Operation Rescue, or the Lambs of Christ, and the violence and terrorism against abortion clinics is what immediately comes to mind when thinking about abortion's opponents, but it is not the only face of the opposition.

After the *Roe* judgment, the Catholic Church was the first into action, with plangent denunciation and millions of dollars poured into new anti-abortion organizations. But as the New Right in the Republican party set out deliberately to woo the anti-abortion voters, as part of its efforts to shift the party itself to the right, the anti-abortion alliance became a curious blend – from Catholics to born-again Christian evangelicals, to more secular 'New Right' types. It was ultimately to prove a volatile coalition.

Abortion has been and still is the kernel of a protracted campaign against the social trends of the second half of the twentieth century, and for a reinstatement of 'traditional family values'. The Reagan presidency boosted the legitimacy, power and influence of 'God's bullies' as they have been aptly called. Although the specific goal of the anti-abortionists is to outlaw abortions, it is important to see this in a wider context of conservatism, attacks on welfare and so on.

The movement has two faces – first, the lobbyists and court challengers, as well as the image-makers, whose ideological offensive has sought to control the public perception of abortion and the women who seek it (Petchesky, 1984). In 1990 alone there were 465 abortion-related bills presented to state legislatures (McKeegan, 1992). The anti-abortion lobby has used its muscle in the ballot box with considerable effect. Single-issue voting can tip the scales when results are close and election turnouts are low. Packing state legislatures and other elected bodies has been a systematic strategy and for twenty years abortion has wracked the United States, from school boards to Congress.

Secondly, there is the face of direct action, some of it peaceful, but nevertheless extremely intimidating, some of it violent and explicitly women-hating. In 1991 in Wichita, south Kansas, there were more than 2,600 arrests as 30,000 anti-abortion protesters blockaded an abortion clinic. In the last 15 years around a hundred clinics have been bombed or set on fire. Others have had medical equipment wrecked. Clinic staff and their families have been harassed; doctors have been shot at; in March 1993, one was even killed. Pregnant women arriving at abortion clinics have had to run a gauntlet of screaming demonstrators, some hurling plastic fetal models, some videotaping their faces and noting the numbers on their car licence plates for subsequent tracing and personal harassment.

A study of men convicted of anti-abortion violence concluded that they are 'clearly acting out of a desire to maintain the dependent status of women'. Many also favour policies such as capital and corporal punishment (Blanchard and Prewitt, 1993). Somewhat in a grey area of legality lie the fake abortion clinics which have been set up and are listed in the Yellow Pages, which harangue women who turn up hoping to arrange an abortion, and force them to look at often gruesome pictures of fetuses.

The 1992 presidential election
For presidential candidates in 1992, as in all the presidential elections since 1980, abortion was an impossible issue to duck. In March 1992 a *Newsweek* review of six candidates – 'What They Think' – about economic growth, national security, environment and so on, put the candidates' abortion views at the top of the list of social policy issues, before even mentioning welfare or education. When, in August 1992, the

Operation Rescue anti-abortion protesters outside a New Jersey women's clinic in 1990. Violent attacks and clinic blockades heighten the difficulties and distress for women seeking abortions where service provision is limited and numerous legal restrictions exist

Republican Party voted 84 to 16 at its convention to outlaw abortion policy even for victims of rape or incest, and in the same week the President's wife, Barbara Bush, told *Newsweek* she considered abortion to be a 'personal choice', the horns of President George Bush's dilemma could not have been more pointed.

The immediate cause of the dilemma for Bush and the Republican Party was that there had been a shift, once again in response to a Supreme Court case – this one in 1989 – the case of *Webster v. Reproductive Health Services*. In its adjudication of *Webster*, the court said that many of the state restrictions on abortion which had in the past been thrown out by the Supreme Court as unconstitutional, might after all be legitimate. This had wobbled the *Roe* judgment to the extent that its very existence seemed in jeopardy. People were beginning to see a distinct possibility that abortion would once again become virtually illegal, a step beyond merely putting it out of women's reach – already a reality in many states.

Abortion was becoming a liability for the Republican Party, as women supporters were being put off by the success of the extremists on party policy and, just as damagingly, persuading their wealthy husbands not to donate to party coffers. Republican strategists feared that if they were seen to go 'soft' on social issues such as abortion, many of their single-minded anti-abortion supporters would 'go back to voting their economic interests, which are decidedly not Republican' (McKeegan, 1992). With this change in the current of popular opinion, Clinton took a calculated gamble in appearing at a huge pro-abortion march in Washington in May 1992.

A month later, the Supreme Court intervened again. It came as a great surprise to campaigners on both sides when the court's judgment on *Planned Parenthood of southeastern Pennsylvania v. Casey* in June 1992 stood by the principles of *Roe*. Nevertheless, the ruling allowed states to create a raft of restrictions, so long as they did not impose an 'undue burden' on the pregnant woman. Compelling women to view pictures of fetal development at all stages of gestation, no matter how early on in pregnancy they might be, in order to ensure that her consent was 'informed', was judged not to be an undue burden.

It was most confusing. While most activists, on whichever side, saw the ruling as a victory for their *opponents*, popular opinion reflected an impression that the right to abortion was home and dry. The ruling hardly helped George Bush out of his difficulties.

While Governor of Arkansas, Bill Clinton had signed a state law restricting access to abortion for minors and opposed Medicaid-funded abortion. But he campaigned as a pro-choice presidential candidate and once elected quickly repealed some of the more bizarre restrictions, such as the 'gag-rule', which prohibited anyone working in a family planning clinic in receipt of federal money from even mentioning abortion to clients seeking advice about unwanted pregnancy.

Clinton's presidency

Some pro-choice groups wanted Clinton to put his weight behind a Freedom of Choice Act to enshrine the *Roe* principle safely in legislation. But he is clearly terrified of getting embroiled in a furore such as that would entail, and the bill's chances look remote. Others are concentrating on trying to ensure that Congress includes pregnancy-related services in the much-heralded new health package.

Opinion polls show that most people in the United States favour access to safe, legal abortion. But the power of the anti-abortion campaign is totally disproportionate to their numbers, or anything that is reflected in general opinion polls. It is similar to that of another vocal minority, the National Rifle Association, the lobby for gun-owning Americans. As the Republican Party picked itself up in the aftermath of the Bush defeat, a senior Republican remarked, 'I will not allow abortion to be a litmus test for membership', a tribute indeed to the way the anti-abortion lobby has twisted the tail of the Republican Party in the last fifteen years (*Guardian* 1.2.93). Some Republicans are attributing their 1992 defeat to the hard line on abortion and there are signs that the tide of popular opinion may be turning against the aggressive 'pro-lifers'.

It is not easy to assess the current strength of the protagonists. The flow of dollars into Operation Rescue has dramatically dwindled and it's getting harder to mobilize large numbers for the mass blockades. Federal legislation, passed in autumn 1993, has forbidden protesters from obstructing or threatening to use force against clinics.

Beneath the froth of politicking, the current scarcity of abortion services and the web of state restrictions contrive to put access to abortion beyond the reach of all but the wealthiest, the luckiest or the most persistent. A 24-hour waiting period imposed by the largely rural state of Mississippi, for instance, increases the cost of an abortion by the price of an overnight stay or a tankful of petrol. Clinton's election has done nothing so far to remove the major obstacles for poor women, such as public funding for abortion.

While it's certainly been the activities of the anti-abortion campaigners which have kept abortion in the public eye and on the political agenda, and the violence and mass blockades do seem on the wane, it is unlikely that the issue will fade from the scene. There are several abortion-related issues in the sights of the anti-abortion lobby. The new abortion drug RU-486, the use of fetal material in embryo research, prenatal diagnosis and extending fetal rights in a way that is punitive to pregnant women are all matters on which the opponents of abortion are eager to express their distinctive opinions. Fading into demure silence is the last thing on their minds.

Why has Britain's abortion debate been different?

It seems worth briefly comparing the struggle in the United States with that in Britain, whose political process has never been gripped by the throat as it has in the United States. Pro-choice Republican Senator Robert Packwood explained what the attentions of a single-minded group such as the US anti-abortion lobby mean to his daily political life:

> [The pro-lifers] are a frightening force. They are people who are with you 99 per cent of the time, but if you vote against them on this issue it doesn't matter what else you stand for. (Tribe, 1992)

That's hard to imagine in Britain. Of course, there have been times when abortion has been a hot issue in the UK, swelling MPs' mailbags and prompting heated exchanges on *Question Time*, but it has at no time been such dynamite, compelling British MPs to refer their every political step to its impact on those of their supporters' who oppose abortion. Part of the reason is that Britain is relatively indifferent to religion and has no comparably powerful, organized fundamentalist or Roman Catholic population. Also, laws made in the United States' Supreme Court positively invite legal challenge and counter-challenge. Laws made by Parliament are more resilient in general.

What's more, part of the reason is in the abortion law itself. It is for doctors, says Britain's 1967 Abortion Act – two doctors – to decide whether a woman needs an abortion, under the terms specified by the law. The rights of women do not remotely enter into it. Many campaigners who have defended the provisions of the 1967 Act, from no less than sixteen parliamentary attempts to curtail its scope, believe that it is the Act's reliance on doctors, that has allowed it to escape relatively unscathed after twenty-five years.

When opponents of abortion in Britain have attacked the Act, its defenders have quite legitimately and cogently been able to point out that it is not *women* who make the final decision, but (respectable) professionals. (Funding cuts in the National Health Service and excessive Department of Health regulations have more stealthily debilitated abortion provision in Britain – that is another story.) Although the inherent paternalism in the framing of the Act is not only demeaning but has also lead to unfair geographical differences in women's access to a sympathetic, prompt abortion service, the pragmatic, defensive value of investing the responsibility in the medical profession is worth noting.

New issues in the abortion arena
When Britain's Abortion Act was framed in 1967, it was almost entirely in the context of fertility control and health. Most women then wanted abortions because they did not want a baby, or another baby, not because, having undergone specific tests, they did not want this particular baby. While suspected fetal deformity was included as a criterion for abortion, twenty-five years ago the scope of prenatal diagnosis was comparatively limited.

Today dozens of genetic conditions can be and are prenatally diagnosed. Does this mean that we can look forward to a time when some hereditary conditions are wiped out entirely? It's happening already. In Sardinia, for example, where thalassaemia – an hereditary wasting disease – is prevalent, all pregnant women on the island are offered screening and terminations. Take-up of the service has been enormous. Thalassaemia could be on its way out.

There are genetic links with breast cancer, depression, Huntingdon's chorea, Alzheimer's disease. Should we start prenatal screening for them as soon as it becomes practicable? Where do we stop? And who decides? Many doctors, and others too, argue that there is no point in prenatal diagnosis unless a 'bad result' is terminated. Where does genetic screening and 'therapeutic abortion' shade off into eugenics and totalitarianism? Some provinces in China have forbidden marriage between individuals judged to be mentally retarded or carrying hereditary disease and require *compulsory* abortion of any pregnancies resulting from marriages deemed illegal. There are plans afoot to make this a national law.

The abortion pill RU-486 has to some extent challenged the historic medicalization of abortion – it offers the prospect, in theory, of abortion being available without the involvement of doctors. HIV/AIDS may also play a part in altering the landscape of abortion ethics and public policy in countries where the law has hitherto been hostile to abortion. There may also be pressure placed on women who are HIV positive to terminate pregnancies unwillingly.

All three issues, as well as the wider issue of reproductive technology may influence national abortion debates as the political, social and ethical issues are fought over. And much depends on how the debate is defined and who controls that definition.

Starting line values

Is abortion a moral issue or a public health issue? Is it a feminist issue? Is it a personal issue of individual rights or a matter for legitimate state involvement? The answer is hardly ever clear cut, but the emphasis exercises a powerful influence on the type of policy which ensues. The more the anti-abortion movement fulminates, the more important it is for defenders of abortion rights to be clear about the underlying principles of their campaigning. Playing for respectability can be a dangerous game: abortion gets isolated from the mainstream issues of reproductive rights – exactly what the anti-abortion lobby wants.

The bottom line for much of the anti-abortion lobby is the moral question: abortion is murder. But abortion is often also portrayed, by anti-abortionists in the Third World as well as by opponents of abortion in Europe and the United States, both secular and religious, as a contributory factor in a general breakdown of 'social values' and the 'traditional family'. It is lumped in with street crime, drug abuse, sex education and contraceptives for adolescents, pornography, 'excessive' welfare and suchlike.

The terms in which access to abortion is argued *for* also frame the policies. Feminists must choose their allies clear-sightedly. Right-wing MP Teresa Gorman has no difficulty supporting abortion rights on straightforward libertarian grounds. It is not a matter for the state, she argues, it is an individual choice, a 'woman's right to choose'. But choice is no abstract affair: giving women choice under the United States' constitution has done nothing whatsoever to enable women to exercise choice. And what choice is it anyway, when women, not just in the United States, seek abortion because the alternative is being thrown out of school, or out of a job, or into the poverty of single motherhood? The availability of prenatal diagnosis, for fetal abnormality or even for sex selection throw up further paradoxes which underline the limits of the concept of a woman's 'choice' (Himmelweit, 1988).

Far more numerous than right-wing libertarians such as Teresa Gorman are those who argue for the provision of abortion services out of concern for public health or even for social control. Their case is that it is in society's interests to prevent both unwanted births and the deaths and injuries of illegal abortions.

Britain's 1967 Abortion Act sits firmly within this framework, and also implicitly accepts the notion that abortion is for any woman a last resort, not a contraceptive method of 'choice'. The wording of a great many countries' abortion laws encompasses the notion that ideally there should be no abortions, 'unless A or B or C'. It is left for doctors, or committees of some kind to judge whether the woman's circumstances meet the particular criteria.

For reasons which may be patriarchal, religious, social, imperial (e.g., population control or prevention of 'social problems') nationalist or medical, the woman is never the shaper of her destiny. She can never simply say: 'I just can't have this baby at this time.' So women tell lies, which are sanctioned by their doctors. In Britain the state permits abortion mainly on health grounds (in the broad sense of 'health'), in West Germany on social grounds, and in Switzerland on psychological grounds. The result? Most abortions in Britain are performed for health reasons, most abortions in Germany for social reasons and most abortions in Switzerland . . . (Ketting and Praag, 1986). Women plead whatever hardship it is necessary to plead to get an abortion and, as Marge Berer has pointed out, the state condones 'seemingly transparent hypocrisy . . . enshrined in law and practised daily with a straight face', by all concerned (Berer, 1993).

A distinctive message

Defending women's rights against the criminalization of abortion and extending access to safe, affordable services cannot be campaigned for in the same terms as it was in 1967. A feminist advocacy of abortion must not only take account of the arrival of genetic testing, RU-486 and HIV/AIDS, but must also stand distinctively apart from its *laissez-faire* political allies or the lobby for population control. The white-dominated feminist movement blundered twenty-five years ago when it failed to comprehend the significance of population control, and had to be woken up to the racist aspects of state-delivered birth-control programmes. Today there is a much better understanding that the meaning of abortion services can have a very different resonance among black communities, against a background of aggressive state-funded steriliz-ation programmes and promotion of long-term contraception such as injections and implants (Petchesky, 1984).

Abortion remains a dirty word and that continues to influence profoundly the terms in which it is defended or fought for. On the other hand using contraception, in the sense of 'family planning' is seen by and large as a prudent and responsible form of behaviour, not a subversive attack on 'family values'. (This argument tends not to apply to teenagers, where providing contraception is still perceived as a sure road to sexual depravity.)

It is a mark of the success of the anti-abortion image-makers that the 'pro-choice' lobby, as it likes to call itself, sometimes eschews even the word abortion, aiming for respectability and preferring to talk about choice, and human rights, and 'terminating a pregnancy' – though that could mean all sorts of things: birth terminates a pregnancy, so does shooting a woman dead. But if personal fertility control is an acceptable goal, and contraception is deemed responsible, then 'acceptance and validation of the practice of abortion should be seen as a logical extension of the same principle', not a procedure laden with stigma and shame (Berer, 1993).

Given the health hazards and unpleasant side-effects of so many contraceptives, such an unswerving approach to abortion becomes even more important. Most women, given the option, would probably prefer a contraceptive that worked *and* did not damage their health rather than the prospect of abortion. Most settle for far less than that (Doyal, 1994). It has been calculated that the safest contraceptives, from a woman's point of view, are condoms *plus* easy access to safe, early abortion. Yet women seeking abortions continued to be stigmatized as 'bad girls', with no excuse for not using 'effective' methods of fertility control, such as the Pill or the IUD, at whatever cost to their health.

Defensive campaigning for abortion does women no favours and does not lead to good abortion law. This is not to deny the powerful case for abortion on grounds of public health. But abortion should not be advocated solely as a last resort method – for women who have been 'unlucky' or 'foolish'.

> The current status of contraceptive techniques underlines more than ever that as long as it remains possible for a woman to be pregnant without wanting to be, abortion will be a necessity and its denial a punishment of women – for having sex. (Petchesky, 1984: 190)

If abortion is a quintessential element of women's reproductive freedom, and it is, that means that the abortion debate has to be unflinchingly and unapologetically reclaimed.

Stop press (July 1994)

In the summer of 1994, an amendment to the 1993 abortion law, primarily permitting abortion on 'social grounds', was passed by both houses of the Polish parliament. But Lech Walesa, President of Poland, refused to sign the amendment, on the grounds of his Roman Catholic beliefs, and returned it to the parliament. It now requires a two-thirds majority in both houses. The only certainty is that abortion has returned to centre-stage of the Polish political process and a constitutional quagmire lies ahead.

Notes

Janet Hadley is a journalist and writer on health issues, particularly those which affect women. She writes the health column for *Everywoman* magazine and is currently writing a book about the international politics of abortion, to be published by *Virago* in 1996.

1 Kristin Luker (Luker, 1984) describes how would-be activists phoned round frantically in the days after the court decision, trying to find an organization to join. Many of them – women, married, housewives with small children, had never joined anything before – not even the school parent-teacher association.
2 Ronald Reagan not only refused to condemn the violence, in 1984 he wrote a bizarre call-to-arms against abortion, with help from Malcolm Muggeridge. (*Abortion and the Conscience of the Nation* Thomas Nelson, Nashville, 1984).

References

ALAN GUTTMACHER INSTITUTE (1993) *Abortion in the United States: Facts in Brief* New York.

BERER, Marge (1993) 'Abortion in Europe from a woman's perspective', in *Progress Postponed: Abortion in Europe in the 1990s* International Planned Parenthood Europe Region.

BLANCHARD, D. and PREWITT, T.J. (1993) *Religious Violence and Abortion* University Press of Florida.

DOYAL, Lesley (1994) *What Makes Women Sick: Gender and the Politics of Health* London: Macmillan.

EINHORN, Barbara (1993) 'Polish backlash' *Everywoman* April 1993.

FALUDI, Susan (1992) *Backlash* London: Vintage.

FEMINIST REVIEW (1988) *Abortion: The International Agenda* No. 29, Spring.

GOLD, Rachel Benson (1990) *Abortion and Women's Health: the Turning Point for America* New York: Alan Guttmacher Institute.

HIMMELWEIT, Susan (1988) 'More than "a woman's right to choose?"' *Feminist Review* No. 29, Spring.

HOELL, S. (1993) 'Strict new law drives abortion underground in Poland' *Reuters* 14 December.

JANKOWSKA, Hanna (1993) 'The reproductive rights campaign in Poland' *Women's Studies International Forum* Vol. 16, No. 3: 291–6.

KETTING, E. and PRAAG P. (1986) 'The marginal relevance of legislation relating to abortion' in LOVENDUSKI, Joni and OUTSHOORN Joyce (1986) editors, *The New Politics of Abortion* London: Sage.

KISSLING, Frances (1992) 'The Church's heavy hand in Poland' *Planned Parenthood in Europe* 21(2), May: 18–19.

LUKER, Kristin (1984) *Abortion and the Politics of Motherhood* Berkeley: University of California Press.

McKEEGAN, Michelle (1992) *Mutiny in the Ranks of the Right* New York: The Free Press, Maxwell Macmillan International.

McLEAN, Sheila (1989) 'Women, rights and reproduction' in McLEAN, Sheila (1989) editor, *Legal Issues in Human Reproduction* Aldershot: Gower.

MRUGALA, G. (1991) 'Polish family planning in crisis: the Roman Catholic influence' *Planned Parenthood in Europe* 20(2), September: 4–5.

OKOLSKI, M. (1988) 'Poland' in SACHDEV, P. (1988) *International Handbook on Abortion* New York: Greenwood Press.

PETCHESKY, Rosalind (1984) *Abortion and Woman's Choice* New York: Longman.

RICH, Vera (1991) 'Poland: abortion and contraception' *Lancet* Vol. 338, No. 875, 13 July: 108–9.

SZAWARSKI, Zbigniew (1991) 'Abortion in Poland' *British Journal of Obstetrics and Gynaecology* Vol. 98, December: 1202–4.

TRIBE, L. (1992) *Abortion: The Clash of Absolutes* New York: Norton.

WORLD HEALTH ORGANIZATION (1993) *Progress in Human Reproductive Research* No. 25, Geneva.

SEX WORK, HIV AND THE STATE:
An Interview with Nel Druce

Cheryl Overs

Nel Druce: We are now over a decade into the HIV epidemic. What's your view about the changes that have occurred in state responses to prostitution since HIV was first perceived as a threat?

Cheryl Overs: There's always been a close relationship between government and prostitution. Of course prostitution is illegal – and sex workers penalized – in some form or other in most countries, but it's often tolerated and permitted to continue in a controlled fashion. Agencies of the state benefit from the sex industry in many ways. For example, police and court officials extract protection money, and income is generated through state-run brothels, or taxing sex-worker earnings.

Since HIV was first perceived as a threat to heterosexuals (the so-called general public) in the mid 1980s, we've started to see some major changes in this relationship. Politicians and public health experts assumed from the start that prostitutes are 'vectors of transmission', acting as a core group from which infection spreads to endanger the lives of good, clean-living men. This is in spite of evidence showing that sex-workers – especially in countries where health care and condoms are easily available, and where the law defends prostitute rights – have practised safer sex to avoid sexually transmitted diseases (STDs) for decades, and are often more likely than other citizens to perceive the risks and adopt safer behaviours.

The stereotype of the free-living amoral prostitute has been strengthened by fears of AIDS. Not only does she have sex for money rather than love, but she has become deadly as well. It is the sex worker who is blamed, and who is therefore the target for education and further restriction. Predictably, a number of repressive policies have been adopted in an attempt to control prostitution.

HIV-positive sex workers are particularly vulnerable to horrific human rights abuses, even execution. In April 1992, human rights groups reported that in Myanmar at least twenty-five women had been killed by officials acting on behalf of the ruling party. They had been tested for HIV while working in brothels over the border in Thailand, and repatriated if HIV-positive. This is not seen as an isolated incident, but part of wider oppression by the ruling party against ethnic and religious minorities and those deemed socially undesirable, including people who are HIV-positive and drug users. Prostitutes are regularly rounded up in many countries and tested for HIV and other infections. HIV-positive women have been quarantined in countries including India, the USA and Australia.

Registration systems, where sex workers can work legally if they are known to the local authorities, are also being widely introduced. Greece and Thailand have explicit policies legislating for registered sex workers to be regularly tested for HIV to ensure that 'the product for sale is clean'. Women who are not registered are working illegally and vulnerable to arrest. These policies are adopted in spite of the fact that the familiar public health model, whereby diseases like TB are controlled through treatment and quarantine procedures, just can't work for HIV. A negative test for HIV is not always conclusive. It takes up to three months after initial infection for HIV antibodies that are detected by the test to develop, so a person who is infectious can test HIV-negative.

Not only is this model ineffective, but it increases risk. Coercive policies fly in the face of sound public health practice, making people fearful and reluctant to seek health care, information and condoms. Such policies also reduce the motivation of clients to use condoms, and endanger sex worker's health – if he thinks she's clean, he may be more likely to want unprotected sex. The blame for infection can be placed firmly in the lap of the sex worker. The idea of 'clean women' also undermines efforts at public education which promote the idea that you can never know for certain if someone is HIV-negative and that safer sex is the safest option.

A 1992 case in Victoria, Australia, has particular notoriety. There, the law was changed to permit a person to be prosecuted for 'recklessly endangering life'. The health department and police came to an agreement about control of an HIV-positive sex worker. She was put under house arrest, and a social worker was assigned the full-time job of social control – to prevent her from working.

Some changes have occurred in legislature which may benefit sex workers. Violence against prostitutes is endemic. But in a few countries men have been prosecuted, including for rape. And for what I think is the first time anywhere in the world, in the Australian state of Victoria both sex worker and client can be fined if they have penetrative sex without using a condom . . . This could backfire into prostitute blaming. However skilful, it's of course often impossible for women to insist on safer sex and use a condom. Ultimately the power lies with the client.

As with the anti-syphilis campaigns and Infectious Diseases Acts in Britain during the last century, prostitution is being medicalized once again, with changes in the nature of the intervening state agencies.

Whereas the most common figure was from the criminal justice system, now it's more likely to be the doctor, the outreach or education worker, and the social worker who receive funding in order to generate change on behalf of the state.

Nel: So, soft approaches to HIV prevention are being adopted as well as, or instead of, the more repressive tactics. Could you expand on how this operates in terms of state approaches to prostitution?

Cheryl: It's true – more people are realizing that the heavy-handed control model is counter-productive. There is seemingly a new benevolence in state policy at local and national levels. But this must not be taken as evidence of any fundamental rethink by the state. It's a continuum – at the soft end is distribution of free and flavoured condoms and education about how to use them, often by funded prostitute organizations. Great. Further along the line, though, are registration, compulsory testing and rehabilitation, and quarantine.

We're seeing health and social workers with effective policing powers, but perhaps without proper controls and certainly without properly articulated aims in terms of social policy. And who is meant to benefit from the benevolence? Sex workers themselves or those who seek unprotected sex from them? This makes the overture of the state to the sex worker, via the social worker, dangerous indeed for prostitutes themselves. As for the efforts to improve sex workers' health, during the HIV decade, more public money has been directed by local and national state structures towards people considered to be members of 'core groups' – men and women with multiple partners who are assumed to be having lots of unprotected sex and frequent sexually transmitted infections, and are therefore at risk of HIV. Sex workers are seen as one such group – and are being intensively targeted. Their clients (also at risk) are much harder to reach, and have a lot less to lose if they don't comply with instructions. The number of client-focused initiatives is minimal, given the billions of men who have paid sex regularly. Yet it's they who control condom use.

Mass education campaigns in the North have meant that the excuse of ignorance is running out as we live longer with the epidemic. A client's claim of 'poor innocent me' has less validity. However, often education is targeted only at people deemed to be members of core groups – especially in high-prevalence areas. This is problematic because it can lead to a belief that those people are the only vulnerable ones, and that no one else need worry. More and more, in higher prevalence countries, it is women in 'stable relationships' who are getting sick, partly because neither they nor their stable partners have been targeted, and the ones who have – women paid for sex – have limited power with which to control what happens in sex.

An enormous amount of money is being spent on research. The scientific community is fascinated by sex workers' behaviour and their lifestyles, their feelings and why they do it. A research organization studying prostitutes in Nairobi is gaining particular notoriety. They have tracked several women known to have had multiple exposure to

WE ARE
PROFESSIONAL
ABOUT
PREVENTING
AIDS
ARE YOU?

NEW ZEALAND PROSTITUTES COLLECTIVE

the virus over several years. They watched and measured as women were diagnosed and then resumed work providing unsafe sex. No group but prostitutes – always on the edge of legality, always just tolerated – would be subjected to this.

Globally, there are now hundreds of projects funded by state health departments to 'educate prostitutes'. There's no doubt that funding is enabling development of some initiatives. In the South, the prostitutes' rights movement is becoming stronger in the context of HIV. But the main aim of these efforts is to ensure that clients are safe. The funds are not directed at sex workers for their own sake, but because they are viewed as people particularly liable to infect others. Helping sex workers to protect themselves is not the priority.

It is important not to misunderstand the nature of this benevolence – it has nothing to do with women's health, or the rights of prostitutes. There has been no change in policies or motivation, but rather these are pragmatic moves to protect the client. If prostitute rights were the priority, the focus of prevention efforts would be to improve working conditions, to enable women to insist on condom use and to work in safety without fear of male violence, or to prevent them from being unwillingly dependent on the protection of other people or the police. Human rights would be the central issue, as this would lead to greater control over working conditions and greater self-esteem.

Almost always, funding is for sexual health work – with the emphasis on fairly traditional health education and clinical services for STD treatment, along with HIV and hepatitis testing. Initiatives in Britain – through local health authorities for example – have been very constrained, using a narrow definition of health promotion. Distribution of condoms, lubricants and information about STDs is about the limit. In some places, service delivery has been improved by working to make STD clinics more open to sex workers.

There has been more scope elsewhere. In The Netherlands, Australia, Germany, New Zealand, Canada and the USA, for example, existing prostitute rights groups have been funded to do outreach work on HIV. But these funding possibilities have placed sex-worker activists and rights groups in invidious positions. As always the relationship between the state and action groups is tense. They are perceived to be in a position to provide services to people who are seen as unreachable in other ways by conventional services. But many have become dependent on government funding, and are vulnerable to losing support and their infrastructure, ending up not surviving, losing the ability to carry on without funding.

The Red Thread, a large prostitutes' rights organization in The Netherlands, already receives substantial state funding. It has decided not to take any money for specific HIV education activities, because it believes that it may be forced to compromise. Elsewhere, other prostitutes' organizations have become much more limited in what they do. After a few years of government funding for health promotion, one organization was faced with the choice of closing its services or changing to fit the priorities of a new (conservative) government. Its activities now include an 'exiting and retraining house' for repentant prostitutes . . .

Many organizations are funded to run clinical services to test and treat a wide range of infections. With HIV, sex workers are perceived as a repository for infections of every sort – and it becomes legitimate to test for everything. At first, sex-worker groups decided not to provide HIV testing themselves, but to improve access to statutory services.

This is in line with what most non-government groups working in AIDS recommend – testing requires rigorous laboratory standards and procedures as well as highly trained staff. Instead, high-quality counselling and support is offered to both HIV-negative and positive individuals, which is not usually within the capacity of statutory sector workers.

Nel: So what do you feel is the future for the sex worker rights movement, given the range of responses to the epidemic?

Cheryl: The prostitutes' rights movement grew out of women's liberation two decades ago. Many of the leaders were from the women's movement and made important theoretical connections in terms of linking sex work with women's subordination, introducing the idea of the right for women to work, equating sex work with marriage, and challenging the stigma attached to selling sex.

Then came the radical feminism of the 1970s and 1980s – women such as Robin Morgan and Andrea Dworkin who see all prostitutes as exploited sex slaves. I think this has left people confused, perhaps especially feminists and the left. In the USA, for example, there is still a very powerful abolitionist movement, with roots in both radical feminism and in Christian fundamentalism. Increasingly we are seeing this philosophy expressed by international human rights bodies.

One of the ugliest moments in these developments has been the alliance of state agencies with feminism, heavily influenced by the fundamentalists. Perceiving exploitation outside marriage or loving relationships goes hand-in-hand with declaring that marriage is the proper and only place for sex. It's no coincidence that much of the so-called protecting legislation arising from these alliances has ended up penalizing sex workers as well as clients. British kerb-crawling legislation extends the criminalization to men as well as women, when what's needed is to remove the farcical criminal law. The legislation backfires in a way similar to the condom law in Australia mentioned earlier. Its principle is similar to the one dominating the 1994 age of consent debate in Britain for gay men – young men are protected by making them into criminals.

During the last few years, two factors have had major influences on prostitutes' rights activism. The HIV epidemic has led to alliances between gay men and sex workers (some of them men too). They are both labelled risk groups – cores of infection – and clearly need to protect themselves against the accusations and assumptions. This alliance led to many of the original feminist leaders leaving. In parallel, the sex-workers' rights movement has moved away from the women's movement, leaving behind the victim ideology. We lost some key activists, but gained others.

There is exciting potential for alliances within AIDS activism, and with the sex-positive and queer ethos of the late 1980s in the USA and elsewhere. For example, there's a 'sex-work positive' sub-group within ACT-UP in New York. Activists in many countries have been successful in raising awareness and changing attitudes to sex work. Recently the organizers of an AIDS conference reported that it was very difficult to get researchers to present their sex-work studies because of fears of being shouted down by prostitute activists. Wonderful – they should be shamed into silence!

I find it interesting that within current human rights discourse, attention is on the 'natural' and visible conditions that are historically linked with discrimination and prejudice – focusing on what people are and what they have no choice about: for example, their ethnicity and gender. While of course these issues are fundamental, this type of formula can lead to constructing a very disempowering role for people as passive victims, with no control over their lives unless rescued by others.

I see some parallels happening in gay rights activism. The marginalization of men who have sex with men – the denial of their very existence – is appalling. But I think that gay rights movements have stressed the naturalness of same sex desire, of being exclusively homosexual, much more in the past few years, in order to fit in with current human rights concerns.

I feel that some human rights campaigners – much influenced by radical feminism – feel the need to put sex workers into a similar position, defining them as people who are forced into selling sex with no choice or freedom in order to justify a sympathetic position towards prostitutes. But we shouldn't let ourselves be convinced that all sex workers are victims, acting without choice. If you leave out slavery at one end and being a film star at the other, most of us don't choose our occupation. Work is a necessity. Industrial rights are therefore a human right and improving these are where the focus should be.

I think for prostitutes, in developed countries at least, the way forward is to further an understanding of prostitution as work and fight for workers' rights. Historically the state has never supported workers' health issues – labour is expendable, and it has been the role of labour organizations to achieve rights to health and safety at work. The state has never been interested in prostitute welfare, and the terrain is a very problematic one to negotiate. In some Australian states, where prostitution is legal and most women (and men) work in brothels, rights organizations are remaining independent of the state by forming unions funded by members' contributions. This avoids the problem of the unelected activist negotiating terms and conditions. It's early days for that idea but I think it's a very exciting possible new direction for prostitutes' rights organizations, especially in developed countries. In developing countries, the answer is – of course – development.

I'm currently working on a conference for representatives from organizations throughout Europe who are providing health promotion and/or clinical services to sex workers, including STD clinics, welfare agencies, researchers or people involved in resourcing or planning health services that might reach sex workers. The idea is to expose people who are setting up services to the experiences of established sex-worker organizations such as Hydra in Berlin and the Red Thread, and look at ways of adapting the lessons learned to further develop their own work. But that's another story.

Note

Cheryl Overs currently works as a consultant on sexual health and prostitution, and co-ordinates the Sex Work Projects Network. She was a founder member of the Australian Prostitutes Collective and the International Committee on Prostitutes' Rights.

REVIEWS

Out of the Shadows: Women, Resistance and Politics in South America

Jo Fisher

Latin American Bureau: London 1993
ISBN 0 906156 77 7 £7.99 Pbk

Out of the Shadows, Jo Fisher's book on women and politics in South America, is a testament to South American women's tenacity in the face of severe hardship and oppression. It is the latest of the excellent series of publications by the Latin American Bureau on contemporary issues in South and Central America. The author spent two years researching the book, travelling in Uruguay, Paraguay, Argentina and Chile. The political women of the region have radicalized the traditional roles assigned to women by societies in which machismo is still a dominant ideology. They turned the roles associated with nurturing and home-making around and literally brought them out into the streets. In this way, they have given a very public, collective voice to their private, individual sorrows. This exemplifies the process described by bell hooks: 'Speaking becomes both a way to engage in active self-transformation and a rite of passage where one moves from being object to being subject. Only as subjects can we speak. As objects we remain voice-less – our beings defined and interpreted by others' (hooks, 1989: 63).

Maxine Molyneux, in her discussion of the Nicaraguan revolution and women's interests, differentiates between two types of women's interests – strategic gender interests and practical gender interests. The former is a deductive scheme in which 'ethical and theoretical criteria assist in the formulation of strategic objectives to overcome women's subordination' (1985: 232–3). The social actors in this case are highly politically aware individuals. In the latter type of political action, the everyday realities come first and the achievement of particular strategic goals are not really a priority. The types of action in Fisher's book usually fall into the latter category. She documents forms of activity initiated by the women themselves, those who are directly involved, designed to improve conditions in the 'here-and-now'. Consequently, the worse the conditions, the more likely it is that action will take place. The question as to why strategic gender interests do not usually inform South American women's political action may indicate that these astute women's perception of feminist theory may not be the most positive.

Fisher documents the negative image that the political women of South America had about Western

feminism and feminists. Her interviewees believed that these were
culture- and class-bound in their
analysis of women's issues. This is a
product of the dominant image of
Western feminism as white, North
American and middle class. The
dominant stream within North
American feminism is based on a
very individualistic model, with the
collective basis of feminist thought
being pushed to the background.
South American women in general
cannot relate to this mode of thinking because for them, the empowerment of the whole community comes
first. Thomson (1986) found that
women in El Salvador distrusted
Western feminism because it contra-
dicted their Catholic, often conservative views on the family and women's
roles. Also, the pronatalism of the
male revolutionary rhetoric led Sal-
vadorean women to aspire to producing more 'sons for the revolution'.
This also indicates lack of inter-
action and debate between feminists
of different national and political
backgrounds. Feminism of the 1980s
and early 1990s has witnessed the
expression of new concerns, particularly by non-Western feminists.
These concerns are those of differences between women in the world,
assumptions of a common global
agenda and potential 'colonization' of
one group of feminists by another
(see Mohanty, 1984). It is clear that
there exists a need for the clear
articulation and appreciation of local
and regional identities within feminist thinking. I believe that it is a
testament to the openness of the
women's movement that these issues
are addressed at all, and that potential problems and divisions are not
ignored, as in some other contemporary social movements.

The example of one particular
group, the 'Mothers of the Disappeared', is indeed an inspiring
one. The amazing courage demonstrated by this group was a force too
strong even for the brutal armies of
Pinochet and other military dic-
tators. This group began in Chile in
the 1970s but spread right throughout South and Central America.
Groups of women whose husbands,
partners and sons had been 'disappeared' by the army engaged in
very dangerous public political activity, despite the 'disappearance' of
some of their leaders by the authorities. They thus instigated and institutionalized a form of political organization that was initially perceived
by the public as 'soft' and un-
threatening. However, they were actually responsible, perhaps more
than any other group, for the raising
of awareness internationally about
repression in South and Central
America. Another effect of women's
autonomous organization in South
America and the resulting rising tide
of articulate voices was the realiz-
ation by many women that many of
the international organizations that
were meant to be progressive were
instead very male-dominated and
did not serve the interests of women.
Thus their own initiatives enabled
them to criticize the actions of
others.

Another example of an apparently benign but actually very subversive activity which is discussed by
Fisher was the production and sale of
'arpilleras', the tapestries which
documented the women's lives and
forms of political action. They became instruments for spreading
knowledge internationally and, consequently, their distribution was
prohibited by the authorities. The
'arpilleras', above all, demonstrated
the very real power of symbols. The
depictions of apparently mundane
everyday activities like shopping,
sewing and cooking were a very
touching reminder of the disruption
of ordinary people's lives by political
repression. Another example of this
symbolic power is the liaison between a women's folk group from
Chile with the Amnesty International tour in which Sting, among
others, participated. This folk group
performed a Chilean folk dance and

one of the women danced on stage alone, effectively evoking the loneliness of their lives without their 'disappeared' partners.

This book shows that, when the state does not provide for the people, the burden falls upon women to maintain the community. Moser (1992), in her research in Ecuador, found this to be the case and deemed that women exercised a 'triple role' – that of home-makers, workers in the workplace and participants in community politics. As this process continues, however, women's increased articulation of their needs and their visibility in the public domain begins to perpetuate itself, thus enabling new definitions of what is appropriate behaviour for women to emerge. The book is also a testament to the diversity of women's experience and necessary political strategies, from the communal kitchens and Mothers of the Disappeared in Chile to the struggle to include women's concerns in Uruguay's trade union movement and Paraguay's peasant movement.

South America's women's movement has very effectively challenged the patriarchal nature of formal politics, both left and right, and has literally 'given a voice' to some of the most oppressed members of South American society. A challenge for the future is how to forge unity and solidarity among the many groups in question, in order to build an even stronger movement from the diverse groups documented in this important and invigorating book. South American women and feminists can reach out beyond their local worlds to others' local worlds and feminists can then, in this way, reach a new definition of the 'local' and forge global links on the anvil of diversity.

Ethel Crowley

References

CAIPORA WOMEN'S GROUP (1993) *Women in Brazil* London: Latin American Bureau.

hooks, bell (1989) *Talking Back: Thinking Feminist, Thinking Black* London: Sheba Feminist Publishers.

MOHANTY, C. T. (1984) 'Under Western eyes: feminist scholarship and colonial discourses' *Boundary* Vol. 2, No. 12: 333–58.

MOLYNEUX, M. (1985) 'Mobilization without emancipation? Women's interests, the state and revolution in Nicaragua' *Feminist Studies* Vol. 11, No. 2, Summer: 227–54.

MOSER, C. (1992) 'Adjustment policies from below: low-income women, time and triple role in Guayaquil, Ecuador' in Afshar, H. and Dennis, C. editors, *Women and Adjustment Policies in the Third World* Basingstoke; Macmillan: 87–116.

Accommodating Protest: Working Women, the New Veiling and Change in Cairo

Arlene Elowe Macleod

Columbia University Press: New York 1991
ISBN 0 231 07281 3 £9.50 Pbk

The aftermath of the 1967 and 1973 wars with Israel created a propitious environment for a new movement, voluntarily initiated by women: it is the veiling movement. By the early 1980s it became an overwhelming fact of life, almost the norm on Cairo streets. According to Macleod, the veiling was spurred largely by Islamic groups in universities, but later gained considerable appeal and was adopted by a broader spectrum of women. This veiling has raised many questions as to its symbolism and implications: if the veil is a symbolic action, what exactly does it symbolize? Are women supporting a return to traditional patterns of inequality by reviving this 'powerful symbol of women's subordination'?

Macleod attempts to answer these questions by venturing into very thorny areas. She studies how class interacts with gender, and notes that the problems women face in Egypt are also problems of poverty and not purely of gender inequity. The Cairenne society is a society where people are acutely class conscious, and have a 'strong sense both of hierarchy and of their place in this social and economic ranking system'. It is also a society where, in the midst of modernization and commercialism which result in confusion as well as the loss of the sense of identity, there is an increased interest in praying, and in the return to God, in the hope of a better future. But the problem is that theological debates and interpretations are impregnated with state politics which consecrate women's inferior position in the hierarchy.

Macleod's findings are the result of a five-year study in which she interviewed Egyptian women from the lower-middle-class stratum. The book discusses the dilemma of women in the midst of the turmoil of a changing Cairo: women leaving their traditionally accepted roles of mothers and wives as they are pushed into the workforce through economic pressure. Tragically, these women are not looked upon as dignified workers, but are rather blamed for leaving their homes and abandoning their 'traditional' images and identity. So how do these women react?

Despite the existence of a feminist movement in Egypt, feminism as an ideology has not reached these classes. Thus while society's changes force these women to join the workforce, the gender ideology remains static, continuing to demand that a woman's place is at home. As the author suggests, 'the economic ethos and gender requirements clash', placing women in an impasse. The *higab*, in such a context, serves as a moderate resolution to women's con-

flicts and dilemmas. It is a statement which creates a 'new self-image, offering in symbolic fashion a partial resolution of the pressures women experience at the intersection of competing subcultural ideologies'.

Cairo's lower-middle-class women do not work for the intrinsic value of work; Macleod rightly observes that this value is an upper-class prerogative. These women fund their family's basic needs from their earnings, and their entrance into the workforce is not a choice made for self-development or bliss, but a 'hard fact of life'. Unlike Western women, they do not attempt to seek individualistic emancipation, autonomy and self-sufficiency, but are rather attempting to focus on fulfilling basic family needs. Nevertheless, work offers these women a considerable amount of security and mobility which is otherwise denied them. Disenchanted with the economic and moral power of their work, they therefore look forward to the day when they leave it, without losing the gains they have acquired, basically mobility.

Macleod asserts that Egyptian women are not, as the West perceives, 'victims of an oppressive cultural milieu with its ultimate symbol the veil', but rather, they are strong and confident in their behaviour, 're-sourceful in manipulating their situation': they struggle, but it is their special mode of struggle. The veil, according to Macleod, is political protest with the only means available to these women: it is not a stereotypical revolt, but rather a struggle which involves an 'ambivalent mixture of both resistance and acquiescence, protest and accommodation'.

One very important observation the author makes is that the movement is not a return to the veil, but rather a new veiling – one which represents a part of an ambiguous political struggle she appropriately terms 'accommodating protest'. The new veil is a sort of fashion statement as well as a 'values' statement.

It is a selective return to roots and to a set of values which women feel the need to re-emphasize, and it serves to resolve women's inner conflict. Women who take to the veil, therefore, do not attempt to challenge their previous roles as mothers and wives, and work does not form a disruption from their main duties or an infringement of their values. Rather, the veil emboldens them, and emphasizes their austerity, functioning as a 'bridge, an alleviation, a kind of balance for these women, compensating for their otherwise inappropriate behaviour', whether this 'inappropriateness' is education or work. Women, therefore, have made a statement about their ability to work, and still feel proper Muslim women: they 'feel more at peace with society, their reputation becomes more secure, and their freedom of movement remains assured'.

There is one major problem which Macleod points out: these women, in their attempts to accommodate, are selective in their return to roots and in their approach to cultural values. But this return will be taken up by others without such selection, eventually subduing the protest, while emphasizing accommodation only. Such resistance then is accompanied by acquiescence. It is an acquiescence that may eventually run amok by 'inadvertently strengthening the inequalities they would like to escape'.

Marlyn Tadros

Subject to Others: British Women Writers and Colonial Slavery 1670–1834
Moira Ferguson
Routledge: New York/London 1992
ISBN 0 415 90476 5 $19.95/£12.99 Pbk
ISBN 0 415 90475 7 $55/£40 Hbk

Women Against Slavery: The British Campaigns 1780–1870
Clare Midgley
Routledge: New York/London 1992
ISBN 0 415 06669 7 $69.95/£37.50 Hbk

In 1824 Elizabeth Heyrick – a Leicester-born Quaker and 'the foremost female anti-slavery pamphleteer' of her generation – argued that 'slavery is not an abstract question, to be settled between the Government and the Planters – it is a question in which we are *all* implicated'. Heyrick's words signal her keen awareness that white British women were not exempt from the moral consequences of colonial slavery. It was precisely this sense of personal moral obligation which she believed legitimated those claims to action in the public sphere made by mostly middle-class anti-slavery women on behalf of slaves. Her biography, together with those of Mary Prince and other Black women enslaved in the name of 'civilization', is crucial for understanding the uses to which white women put both the metaphor of bondage *and* the material realities of black slavery in order to forge a national political identity for themselves in pre- and early Victorian Britain. As both of these studies make clear, without Black women's own persistent quest for liberty, white women's philanthropy and indeed their early identification with Britain's 'civilizing mission' would have had an almost unimaginably different justification. What Midgley and Ferguson together require, then, is that we not simply re-materialize women's historical contributions to anti-slavery, but also critically examine what Ann Curthoys calls our presumption of women's 'historical innocence' (Curthoys, 1993: 174).

In the broadest sense these books address the mainstream historical establishment, which has either neglected or marginalized women's role – black and white – in the abolition of slavery. To borrow bell hooks's term, they also 'talk back' (hooks, 1990: 207–11) to established historians of women and of feminism who have been insufficiently attentive to the historical intersections of race and gender politics in the West and, until recently, particularly in Britain. Vulnerable to appeals about the un-Christian nature of slavery because of the ways in which evangelical discourse positioned them, bourgeois white women throughout Georgian Britain took up the cause of men and particularly of women slaves with tremendous fervour. They set up their own anti-slavery societies through which they carried on a wide range of activities related to the anti-slavery project, including boycotting sugar; petitioning Parliament over slavery and the apprenticeship system; producing 'physical propaganda' like workbags to sell for the cause; and writing, writing, writing – pamphlets, plays, poetry, speeches, cheap repository tracts. Slavery was undoubtedly one of the chief idioms through which white women's political, cultural and national identities were articulated in this period, with Black men and women serving as the 'subjects' through whom they claimed their own socio-political subjectivities. That white women in Britain saw this as natural, unproblematic and foundational to their own quest for legitimating work in the public sphere is borne out in all of their ideological productions. One of the constitutive effects of white women's preoccupation with anti-slavery is that while they pressed for immediate abolition, they gave an unmistakably racist cast to attendant discourses about [white] female emancipation. Anti-slavery rhetoric moreover imagined emancipation inside the framework of the bourgeois English family – a formulation which shaped the tradition of female emancipation in Britain as much around maternalist imperatives as ethnocentrist ones.

White women's often sentimentalized convictions of racial and cultural superiority did not go unchallenged by Black women and men, who resisted both while slaves and – also through their writings – once 'in freedom'. Grace Jones, Mary Prince and Ellen and William Craft figure in such narratives not only as self-reflexive agents in the movement for abolition, but as self-conscious disrupters of the discourses which white women worked to create about them. The ways in which Midgley and Ferguson juxtapose the public discourses of white and black women from the same historical moment suggests that these women's histories are not separate and distinct, but were (and are) simultaneously constitutive. Such an approach will be instructive to historians of women and feminism – for whom the struggle to understand their own implications in historically racist cultures remains a painful one on all sides, and to whom histories which put at risk triumphalist accounts of Western women's movements are presumably welcome.

Midgley is more tentative than Ferguson about the relationships of British women who opposed slavery on the one hand, and Victorian feminists on the other, and rightly so. Her leap from the decline in anti-slavery activity in the 1840s to the women of the Ladies' National Association in the 1880s is the weakest link in an otherwise admirably rigorous and analytically rich book. This is not because later feminist women did not appropriate people of colour as their special imperial burden, but because there are distinctions to be made between early Victorian slavery and late Victorian imperialism – distinctions which are elided in both studies. Ferguson, for her part, insists on linkages between 'anti-slavery protest in prose and poetry by Anglo-Saxon female authors' and modern feminism from the start. Without much attempt to define feminism's historical specificities over a considerable time period, such a claim ends up being impressionistic rather than thoroughly substantiated. This, together with very problematic notions of 'voice' and 'speaking subjects', weakens the critique which Ferguson wishes to make of the impact of slavery on feminist discourses. Bringing historical subjects 'to voice' is a worrisome project, reproducing as it were the ventriloquism which white women historically deployed in order to 'liberate' Black women and, not incidentally, themselves. The ramifications of that particular emancipatory impulse – with its embedded-

ness in imperialist assumptions about who is properly a historical 'subject' and why – are still with us. Those who wish to scrutinize white women's complicity in the histories of slavery, imperialism and racism more generally must, I think, admit that speaking, like the act of writing history itself, is always already incapable of being innocent of the material conditions which make it not simply possible, but audible as well.

Antoinette Burton

References

CURTHOYS, Ann (1993) 'Identity crisis: colonialism, nation and gender in Australian history' *Gender and History* Vol. 5, No. 2, Spring.
hooks, bell (1990) 'Talking back' in Anzaldua, Gloria, *Making Face, Making Soul* San Francisco: Aunt Lute Press.

Racially Mixed People in America
Edited by Maria P. P. Root
Sage: California 1992
ISBN 0 8039 4102 1 £19.50 Pbk
ISBN 0 8039 4101 3 £42.50 Hbk

In *Titus Andronicus*, the queen has a mixed-race child who is described by the nurse as a 'joyless, dismal, black and sorrowful issue'. The black father of the child retorts thus: 'Coal black is better than another hue in that it scorns to bear another hue.' In 1772, Edward Long, a plantation and slave owner was appalled at the fact that English blood was being 'contaminated' by black men who were producing children with 'lower class women in England'. The paradigms for discussing the issue of mixed race were thus laid out centuries back by racist societies on both sides of the Atlantic. Through the years, researchers, journalists, politicians, carers and society in general have continued to be bound by these paradigms. Mixed-race people are a problem, have insurmountable problems or, extraordinarily, are ex-

pected to provide a nice coffee-coloured solution to all our problems in time.

This book, which is a collection of writings by diverse contributors – 'innovative nonconformists', according to the editor, Maria P. P. Root – has taken on the huge task of dismantling these constructs not by providing alternative realities which only help to maintain the framework, but by exposing the foundations on which the debate has hitherto been built. As Root puts it: 'The authors repeatedly and independently break with the characterization of a racially mixed person relegated to a marginal, anomic existence as they offer multidimensional theories as contexts within which to examine multiracial phenomenology.' For this reason alone, the book well deserves to be read, especially now, as around the world nationalistic fervour, ethnic cleansing, and a re-emergence of the violent quest for racial and ethnic purity gathers momentum.

It is also an extremely important book because of the demographic changes that are transforming the Western world. In the US, non-white migration and a bi-racial baby boom are creating a deep panic in the dominant white Anglo-Saxon world, and new enemies are daily being created, within and globally, in a bid to recreate the racial order of previous times. Questions of a national identity are increasingly assuming a new significance and complexity and a cowboy view of the world is proving to be hopelessly inadequate – and dangerous. As the editor says: 'The increasing presence of multiracial people necessitates that we as a nation ask ourselves questions about our identity: Who are we? How do we see ourselves? Who are we in relation to one another?'

We have to remember how threatening such an analysis must be in a country which only finally abolished laws against miscegenation in 1967, where the insane 'one drop' rule which said that having a single drop of non-white blood made you Black was rigorously enforced and where the most terrible exploitation of Black and native Americans was justified on the grounds of racial inferiority. It is also a country which, like the UK, continues this ignoble racist tradition through more subtle methods.

This political context and the historical antecedents which the book describes make fascinating reading but what gives the writing extra energy is the fact that most of the contributors have personal experiences of what it means to be mixed race. You don't feel you are being voyeuristic or anthropological and the controlled passion and fury lifts much of the writing above the awful academic babble that hides meaning in so many serious American books, including, in part, this one. One example is this moving assertion by one of the writers, Philip Tajitsu Nash: 'Each of us pays the price of racial and cultural stereotypes every day of our lives. We either buy into them and live

with their insidious effects or stand up to them and risk the wrath of those who benefit from them. Multicultural people have a special role to play in combating stereotypes. When we are around, athletic ability cannot be deduced by kinkiness of hair, math aptitude cannot be gleaned from the shape of the eyes'.

Some of the most interesting chapters in the book are those which deal with the issue of the personal identity of mixed-race people; how this has always been defined by society, how this has meant a denial of the inner identity of the individuals and a criminal simplification of the complexities and ambiguities that such identities have to embrace.

There is also some fascinating evidence provided that bi-racial people are more cognitively flexible and less dogmatic than monoracial people and often better adjusted.

Another important issue that is raised by a couple of contributors is the danger of assimilation of minority communities into a powerful and overwhelming society with a pathological drive to control and homogenize the world. This is a question that Jewish communities across the diaspora are now asking themselves as marrying out becomes commonplace and one that is worrying the African-American and Afro-Caribbean communities in the US and Britain. The rise of Black separatism and antagonism towards 'sellouts' is a by-product of that anxiety. More was needed on this in the book; in some ways it is merely touched upon.

The taboo subject of 'passing' is better handled. This is the phenomenon by which bi-racial adults who can pass for white do so sometimes to the end of their lives, often as a practical mechanism in order to avoid the negative experiences of being Black.

But by far the most significant chapter in the book for me was by Christine Iijima Hall, herself half Black and half Japanese who through her research not only challenges the conclusions reached by academics like Stonequist (1937) and his followers that mixed-race individuals were marginal, ill-adjusted people, but goes on to show that bi-racialism and bi-culturalism made them 'strong people with diverse and positive perspectives on life', better able to function in the multifarious world we all inhabit now.

Yasmin Alibhai-Brown

Reference

STONEQUIST, E. V. (1937) *The Marginal Man: A Study in Personality and Culture Conflict* New York: Russell & Russell.

Finding Our Way: Rethinking Ecofeminist Politics
Janet Biehl

Black Rose Books: Montreal/New York
1993
ISBN 0 921689 78 0 £11.99 Pbk
ISBN 0 921689 79 0 £23.00 Hbk

Nowhere in the world of contemporary theory is there richer ground for leg-pulling than the realm of ecofeminist writing. For some people to be Green is to be truly green and if you want to save the world through espousing the ecofeminist line then you better get used to being accused of political naivety. Ever since Mary Daly acknowledged the help of a spider in the writing of her vast Wickedary I have had a problem with the web of ideas that has spun from ecofeminism. Is she serious? is the question uppermost in my mind when reading anything which falls into the ecofeminist canon. Biehl's work is more respectful in that it does assume the seriousness of ecofeminist theory but respect does not result in a gentle critique. There are no cheap jokes or jibes here but Biehl's view is unambiguous. Ecofeminists have got it wrong.

Biehl analyses the works of a range of feminist writers and theorists which are, for the purposes of this book, lumped together under the umbrella title of ecofeminists. Charlotte Spretnak, Carolyn Merchant and Starhawk are three of those whose work, Biehl concludes, takes us along a path 'toward a narrow parochialism, primitivism, and irrationalism that will ultimately mystify and support the status quo rather than transcend it'.

Biehl's merciless attack on ecofeminist theory begins with an exposé of the lack of theoretical rigour in key ecofeminist texts. Facts, she alleges, are valued if they support the ecofeminist world-view, disregarded if they do not. In her view, far from being a radical force for social change, ecofeminism has largely become an exercise in personal transformation. Biehl also highlights the irony of a discourse which while focusing on religion as a locus of patriarchal power seems to be creating 'a religion in its own right' breeding its own hierarchy of shamanesses and priestesses.

Biehl draws on anthropological and archaeological research to back up her criticisms of ecofeminist writing. In response to those ecofeminist writers who suggest that worship of a goddess in some way facilitates a desired non-patriarchal society, Biehl points to some obvious historical exceptions and then asks the obvious questions. Did the worship of a goddess orchestrate early social relations? Or did the social relations in the cultures themselves produce the goddess? This line of questioning leads to a key issue – the role of myth. Ecofeminists, Biehl argues, appear to believe that swapping from god to goddess, in effect changing the content of myths from 'bad ones' to 'good ones' would change social reality.

Many readers would see this as

the critical point in Biehl's analysis and hope for more exploration of the cultural role of myth. They will be disappointed. Biehl is clearly not interested in taking the poststructuralist route via Barthes, preferring instead to organize her criticism of ecofeminist theory from the lane marked 'social ecology'. Biehl uses Murray Bookchin's 'dialectical naturalism' as an alternative model for defining nature and argues that this theoretical concept allows for the possibility of what all eco-theorists appear to want – a different and less damaging relationship between humanity and the natural world.

Unfortunately, from the moment at which she names her preferred way of theorizing the world Biehl's work loses its critical edge. In reproducing Bookchin's arguments explanation comes perilously close to exultation. Dialectical naturalism, she explains, is an holistic approach which looks at the world as a whole from a developmental perspective. It is a theory of progress which posits a necessary passage from a state of 'potentiality' to that of full development which, in the case of individuals allows for the ultimate destination of self-actualization. One example given is the development of the individual from a state of childhood to a 'fuller more differentiated being'. What this example does not address is the vast debate around the issue of just where the boundaries lie between childhood and adulthood and just what it means to be a 'fuller more differentiated being'.

In fact, the theory of dialectical naturalism seems little more than greenspeak for personal growth. There is an unnerving similarity between Biehl's enthusiastic espousal of Bookchin's theory and the work of ecofeminist writers. Both share a fervent belief in one key set of ideas and while it is often satisfying to be taken in an obvious direction by an author with a set destination in mind, there is a lot to be said for the theory flirt. An author who has not quite settled on a complete explanation for everything but who was willing to engage with a range of ideas may have produced a more satisfying critique of ecofeminist politics.

To be fair, Biehl's project is to rethink rather than just demolish ecofeminism and this she does. Her ultimate desire is clearly stated: to see the elimination of capitalism and the nation-state and the restructuring of society into decentralized, cooperative communities. For Biehl the problem with ecofeminists is not what they aim to do but the way that they do it.

Shelagh Young

Getting Smart: Feminist Research and Pedagogy With/In the Postmodern

Patti Lather

Routledge: New York/London 1991
ISBN 0 415 90377 7 £35.00 Hbk

Research on gender inequality in education and postmodernism has never really clicked. The emphasis on improvement and action in educational research and the orientation of research on the individual learning and development processes of teachers and pupils appear to be at odds with postmodernism. The line of argument inspired by postmodernism of 'gender as a social construction', which has proved fruitful in other areas of women's studies, has scarcely produced any research on gender and educational issues (ten Dam and Volman, 1991). The few exceptions concern small-scale research projects (e.g. Davies, 1989). Patti Lather's *Getting Smart* qua theme really gets to the heart of the matter. Lather tries to make a connexion between feminism, postmodernism and critical educational theory and considers the consequences of such a connexion for research and teaching. In our work we try to apply postmodern insights to research into education and gender inequality. Especially the criticisms that postmodernism precludes questions of improvement, and that it conceptually excludes agency of women and men, are bothering us. It is against this background that we have read *Getting Smart*.

Lather defines postmodernism as a discourse in which knowledge is continually seen in relation to power, in which the subject is no longer central and in which totalizing explanations are broken with. The relationship between feminism and postmodernism is one of love and hate. According to Lather, postmodern thinking in women's studies results in the paradoxical situation that, on the one hand, a 'feminine' subjectivity is increasingly sought which can liberalize the masculine concept of rationality while, on the other hand, the new, scarcely established 'feminine' identity is already being deconstructed. Lather concurs with others within women's studies who have pointed out the danger of political nominalism in the postmodern: does the subject's room for action not disappear with the (coherent) self, and does a well-defined category 'woman' or 'gender' not remove the possibility for political action? (Young-Bruehl, 1987; Tress, 1988; Alcoff, 1989) At the same time, there are attractive sides to postmodernism. According to Lather, it instructs feminists to bring dominant discourses up for discussion and to avoid dogmatism and reductionism themselves.

Lather does not only consider the question of the significance of postmodernism for feminism, she also turns the question upside down in her argument that feminism is the 'quantum physica' of postmodernism. First, it is within feminism that the relationship between theory and practice has been researched most creatively. Second, 'action' and 'sub-jectivity' are continually pointed out within the feminine discourse as essential elements for social change. Finally, feminism has a tradition of self-reflection, which Lather considers essential to prevent new discourses of truth. This all means that feminism is pre-eminently suitable for politicizing postmodernism. Following this introduction, the implications of this politicized postmodernism are explored for educational research and teaching.

In spite of the exciting questions raised in *Getting Smart* and the sympathetic approach, we were disappointed by the book from this point on. The next four chapters which are about research are full of repetition. Lather also takes the principle of intertexuality extremely literally; large parts of the book consist of citations strung together. The way in which the questions she raises are dealt with is also not very satisfactory.

The research advocated by Lather strongly resembles the action research of the seventies. According to the author, research must produce emancipatory knowledge that will enable the oppressed to understand and change their own reality (p. 53). Not only the research product is important but also the research process. In this process there must be an element of reciprocity between the researcher(s) and the researched, as well as an interchange between theory and empiricism. The research process must persuade the researched to reorientate themselves on their reality to such an extent that they are able to change ('catalytic validity'). The analysis of the researcher must go further than the experience of the researched without withholding subjectivity from them.

There are, however, a number of problems in connexion with the idea of reciprocity that are not discussed in the book. Are research results not valid, for example, when the researched do not subscribe to the interpretation of the researcher?

That Lather emphasizes the socially constructed, historically embedded and value-related character of knowledge is new compared to action research. The result of research should not be a new, 'true' story. This raises certain questions for researchers, like: can I develop meanings when processing empirical data, instead of restricting them, how can I produce multi-voiced, multi-centred texts, and how can I deconstruct how my own longings as emancipatory researcher give form to the text?

The author answers these questions in the last chapter of *Getting Smart* by means of an example. In this chapter, Lather shows how she tries to put into practice in teaching and research the principles explained earlier. She presents the results here of research on the resistance of students in an introductory women's studies course. The research data was collected over a period of three years from interviews with students, research reports, extracts from those students' diaries and from notes made by the researcher herself. The central theme of the research is, in fact, the problem with which Lather sees herself confronted as a teacher: the conflict between the desire to instil certain perceptions into students and the fear of forcing these perceptions on them.

Lather has produced a 'multi-voiced text' about her research. Instead of presenting her findings in one report, she tells four different stories about her data. The development undergone by Lather in recent years is evident in these stories: from a neo-Marxist, feminist researcher who questions, preferably by means of action research, why people resist or shut themselves off from 'good' perceptions of their own situation in life; to someone who is aware of the difficulties involved in understanding knowledge as the representation of reality, who is aware of the role of the researcher in the production of meaning and of the power attached

to every categorization. She calls the first story 'realistic'. It assumes that by using an adequate research method it is possible to know the reality. The second story is the 'critical' story that in particular takes note of the underlying power structures. The third story is titled 'deconstructive'. It puts the unsaid and the unsayable in texts to the fore and explains its own constitution. The last account is the 'reflexive'. It brings the narrator back into the story with her desires and life history. Unfortunately it remains unclear what the relationship is between the four stories. Do they form a hierarchy? Are all four ultimately necessary? Lather of course does not end her book with an unequivocal position or conclusion. She closes with a postscript, an epilogue, an afterword and a coda which summarize what the book is about in four different ways.

Our disappointment is maybe particularly connected to the problems which are raised by weaving together three traditions of thinking – Marxism, feminism and postmodernism; problems which are sometimes pointed out by Lather, but scarcely made any clearer, let alone solved. She calls her argument first and foremost post-Marxism. It is 'Marxist' in the sense that the struggle for liberation is the central issue and 'post' because this is not, and cannot be, the only argument. In the second place, Lather sees her position as post-feminist. She calls for research that would correct the invisibility and distortion of women's experiences with a view to eliminating the unequal position of women (p. 71). The prefix 'post' serves again to avoid totalizing narratives. The 'post' element undoubtedly refers to the third tradition of thinking, the postmodern one. In several places it is doubtful how 'post' the approach proposed by Lather really is. The Marxist element does seem to be dominant given that Lather talks about oppression, liberation and emancipation, and she struggles with the concept of 'false awareness'. The 'experiences, desires and needs of women' are also regularly and heedlessly presented as unequivocal and recognizable factualities. In our opinion the interesting question of the possibilities and impossibilities of 'agency' and 'change' within a postmodern framework merit discussion in greater detail.

Getting Smart is above all a quest by Lather the academic and teacher through reams of literature about postmodernism, feminism and pedagogy for an explanation for her ambivalent attitude towards the postmodern. As a result of this quest the author, according to what she herself says, sees perspectives for 'those who want their intellectual involvement to be able to play a role in the struggle for social justice'. With her book, Lather has stressed yet again that it is important to think about this subject. She has not shown us perspectives for our actual work, in which we want to make use

of the postmodern's intellectual power to attract in research that contributes to fairer education.

Geert ten Dam and Monique Volman

References

ALCOFF, L. (1989) 'Cultural feminism versus poststructuralism: the identity crisis in feminist theory', in MALSON, R., O'BARR, J., WESTPHAL-WIHL, S. and WYER, M., editors, *Feminist Theory in Practice and Process*. Chicago and London: University of Chicago Press: 295–326.

DAVIES, D. (1989) 'The discursive production of the male/female dualism in school settings' *Oxford Review of Education* 15: 229–42.

TEN DAM, G. T. M. and VOLMAN, M. L. L. (1991) 'Conceptualizing gender differences in educational research: the case of The Netherlands' *British Journal of Sociology of Education* 12: 309–21.

TRESS, D. (1988) 'Comments on Flax's "Postmodernism and gender relations in feminist theory"' *Signs* 14: 196–200.

YOUNG-BRUEHL, E. (1987) 'The education of women as philosophers' *Signs* 12: 207–21.

'Race', Gender and the Education of Teachers
Edited by Iram Siraj-Blatchford
Open University Press: Buckingham
1993
ISBN 0 335 19017 0 £12.99 Pbk

With so much work published on issues of equality in education generally, it is surprising that this is the first collection to be devoted entirely to teacher education. The stated aim of the book is 'a very practical introduction to the specific issues of concern to teacher educators'. It is divided into three sections. The first section sets out to present a holistic view of 'race' and gender issues in teacher education considered in their wider educational context. The second section is chiefly concerned with the experiences of students and the final section examines policy, strategy and action required to promote equality in and through teacher education. The book is aimed

at teacher educators and students and serves as a good introduction for those coming to the issues for the first time. It is also a useful text in presenting the current debate in a context where teacher education is being politically structured to take place largely in and under the control of schools.

The changes occurring in teacher education parallel those taking place in the school sector. The removal of powers from teacher education institutions themselves and their delegation to schools combined with increased central government direction over the nature and content of courses follows the delegation of school policy from local authorities to school governing bodies and the introduction of the National Curriculum. These political changes are consciously intended to eliminate the promotion of equality under an ideology of choice and standards. In this context the pursuit of equality in and through education is having to be fundamentally re-thought.

The book reflects the emergence of anti-oppressive (anti-sexist and anti-racist) perspectives on 'race' and gender inequality. The articles seek to take a holistic view of inequality, though issues related to sexuality and disability are not directly addressed. The section which examines the experiences of black and female students in teacher education is a particular strength of the book. The articles demonstrate how racism and sexism impinge on students' experience, motivation and achievement and how this may condition their expectations and practices in schools. For example, the article by Anne Flintoff examines gender relations in physical education courses in an initial teacher-training institution. She shows how strongly gendered interactions between students lead to the devaluing and undermining of women's contributions. The article points to the need to challenge such oppressive behaviour and attitudes if they are not to be exported into schools and transmitted to pupils. Similarly, in the first section of the book the article by Iram Siraj-Blatchford draws on her own research on the experiences of Black students in teacher education to show that racism from fellow students, lecturers and during teaching practice is a common experience for these students and significantly shapes their hopes and aspirations. The book highlights repeatedly the need for further research in this area if action is to be taken to ensure that Black and women students have a positive experience of teacher education and if they are to fulfil their potential in their chosen career. It is also clear that unless racism and sexism in the institutions themselves is challenged they will simply reproduce and help to sustain the culture of oppression and inequality in schools.

The final section of the book considers strategies to promote equality in the political context in which teacher educators now find themselves. All of the articles deal in different ways with a context in which the control over policy is increasingly fragmented and where it is more difficult to place equality issues on a central agenda. The article by Pratap Deshpande and Nargis Rashid on in-service education for teachers suggests the need to place equality issues on a broader quality agenda as a strategy to enable local authorities to raise issues of equality in schools. In their article John Clay and Rosalyn George argue that the shift to school-based initial teacher education and the modularization of initial teacher-education courses threatens to erode the study of equality issues as a core element of courses. While they recognize the limitations of a 'permeation' model, where the responsibility for dealing with equality issues is devolved to individual modules and courses, they are forced to concede that this may be the only way forward. 'Permeation' is only likely to be effective where it is carefully planned and where there is substantial and a sustained staff development programme to ensure that lecturers are able to deliver appropriately. A more radical strategy explored in this article is the need to empower students and staff to question and challenge oppression within the institutions themselves. They propose the creation of an open forum on social justice where staff and students can share experience and ideas and support each other.

In a context where, across the whole of Europe, racism including racist murders are on the rise, where women are scapegoated as lone parents for all the ills in society and where governments create an ethos in which the far right is able to flourish, the struggle for equality has never been more crucial. The book illustrates, using teacher education as an example, the limits and possibilities of such a struggle.

Samidha Garg

Shaping up to Womanhood: Gender and Girls' Physical Education
Sheila Scraton
Open University Press: Buckingham 1992
ISBN 0 335 09693 X £11.99 Pbk

Research in Physical Education and Sport: Exploring Alternative Visions
Edited by Andrew C. Sparkes
Falmer Press: London 1992
ISBN 0 750 70075 0 £15.95 Pbk
ISBN 0 750 70074 2 £40.00 Hbk

These books are a welcome contribution to the field of sport and physical education.

Sheila Scraton's work provides a much-needed insight into the relationship between physical education and gender, a topic often neglected both in research on gender and education and by feminism in general. The focus on physical education during adolescence raises many questions concerning the relationship between educational practice and ideologies of gender, femininity and sexuality.

Girls' physical education was slow to develop in the late nineteenth century. The emphasis was primarily on gentle exercise such as callisthenics. However, gradually a wider variety of sport was introduced, first in public schools and then in state schools. Physical education was shaped by ideologies of biological capacity, the need for women to develop the feminine qualities of grace and poise and the requirements of motherhood. Women were warned that vigorous exercise could be damaging and interfere with reproduction.

Many of these themes can still be identified today. Interviews with Physical Education teachers and advisers revealed a belief in natural differences between men and women. Boys were described as stronger and willing to 'launch themselves', while girls were seen to be more suited to gymnastics. Sports such as rugby and football were perceived to be particularly unsuitable for girls. Ideologies of the wife and mother role were not challenged and in practice had a significant impact on the ability/freedom of girls and female physical-education teachers to fully participate in sport.

In practice, physical education is more commonly taught as a single-sex subject in the early years of secondary schooling with mixed lessons introduced from the fourth year onwards. Mixed-sex teaching has the potential to challenge traditional views of sex differences by encouraging boys and girls to work together. In reality the situation is more complex. Girls wishing to play football in mixed groups may find it difficult to integrate into such groups due to a lack of previous training and negative ideas concerning their abilities. One of the main aims of physical education was to maintain standards of behaviour and appearance. This meant that girls and boys were often treated differently. Girls are encouraged to look good and behave like young ladies.

Ideologies of gender difference, femininity and sexuality are deeply ingrained in the policies, priorities and day-to-day practices of schools. They do not simply exist in the minds of individual teachers. Many schools attempt to encourage girls by providing activities which further emphasize femininity and looking good. Sheila suggests a more positive approach should include initiatives to ensure female-only space is available for girls to develop their confidence through collectivity. In addition girls should also be encouraged to take control of their own bodies.

Tackling inequality involves challenging existing ideologies, promoting an awareness of gender issues and encouraging change in physical education policy and practice. This book will go some way to doing just that.

The Sparkes book confidently tackles the current issues surrounding research in sport and physical education. Rather than being a research manual, the book explores the influence of theoretical traditions and the personal meanings that researchers bring to the research process. It is refreshing to find articles using a phenomenological approach, discourse analysis and life histories.

Sherry Woods uses phenomenological interviewing technique to explore the experiences of lesbian physical-education teachers. Participants were asked to reflect on their experiences and they commented on issues such as openness, the split between their professional lives as teachers and their personal lives as lesbians and strategies adopted to avoid disclosing their lesbian identities. This research is located within a critical framework which is concerned to challenge the homophobia and heterosexism within education. As such the article is vital in breaking the traditional silence regarding lesbian lives.

There are also articles on discourse analysis in education by Gill Clarke and on feminist research by Sheila Scraton and Anne Flintoff.

The book is well informed and accessible. Each chapter makes a distinctive contribution to this discussion of research paradigms and methods. As such it is essential reading for anyone interested in sport and physical-education research.

Jackie Davis

Full Circles: Geographies of Women Over the Life Course
Edited by Cindi Katz and Janice Monk

London: Routledge 1993
ISBN 0 415 07562 9 £12.99 Pbk
ISBN 0 415 07552 1 £40.00 Hbk

Different Places, Different Voices: Gender and Development in Africa, Asia and Latin America
Edited by Janet Momsen and Vivian Kinnaird

London: Routledge 1993
ISBN 0 415 67563 7 £12.99 Pbk
ISBN 0 415 07538 6 £40.00 Hbk

Feminist geography: the combination of these two words too often still occasions surprised reactions, among feminists and among geographers, despite the growing body of exciting feminist work being done under the disciplinary auspices of geography. A great deal of this work is, undeservedly, little known beyond the disciplinary boundaries.

However, the establishment of a new series by Routledge under the general heading of *International Studies of Women and Place*, edited by Janice Monk and Janet Townsend, should begin to attract the wider attention that this body of scholarship deserves, not least for the eye-catching stylish covers to the first volumes.

The first two books in the series, *Full Circles* and *Different Places, Different Voices*, are both similar and different in their focus, emphasis and the range of contributors. Both are sets of collected essays that take as their central theme the commonalities and differences in the everyday experiences and coping strategies of women who are widely separated by geographical distance and by socio-economic circumstances – both their own and those of the nation-state in which they live. Each collection has a useful editorial introduction that situates the following chapters in the context of both specifically geographical scholarship and in feminist literature more broadly, thus ensuring that the curious reader from whatever place she starts has a guide through the text. *Full Circles* also has a welcome editorial conclusion, although attempting to summarize the intervening mass of fascinating detail proved a daunting task. The editors' discussion of the relationship between different geographical scales, from the local to the global, is very helpful and, indeed, might be the place to start for those who have not a clue about what geographers are interested in these days.

The books are also similar in that each individual chapter is based, in the main, on detailed case studies and periods of field work engaged in by the authors. Herein also lies a significant difference between the two texts. *Different Places, Different Voices* includes papers by women living and working in the 'Third World', from urban and rural Africa, Asia and Latin America, although the work of Western feminists is also included, whereas the contributors to *Full Circles* are all Western women, working in the US, the UK and (a sole contributor) in France. In the former collection, the focus is specifically on the 'less developed' world; in the latter, case studies from France, Australia and the US provide a vivid contrast to those from the Caribbean, Colombia and the Sudan. Only in the chapter drawing on research in the Sudan, however, are the lives of women in rural areas in that country compared with those of women in US cities. I should have liked to have seen more comparative analyses as they seem to me to be the most successful way of uncovering the particular significance of location and of place in women's daily struggles. I also longed for more self-conscious reflection of what the collision of different worlds in a specific place meant for all the women involved – whether the observed or the observers. How 'out of place' did the women from the West feel in the villages they studied, and

what are the implications for the stories and conclusions reported in these two books?

The main difference between the collections is the particular emphasis on changes over the life course in *Full Circles*. Thus time and space are the twin focuses of this text compared with the singular focus on the difference that place makes in *Different Places*. In the former collection, the chapters reveal the enormous variation of experiences among women of the same chronological age, as well as differences in household and family circumstances, labour-market participation and levels of economic security at different stages in the life cycle. Many of the contributors focus on the 'middle years' – on women with or without children, in and out of the labour market. There are papers about the combination of home and work in the USA, in rural areas in the Caribbean and urban France, as well as the child-care strategies that enable or disallow the combination of paid work and childrearing, whether through state or informal provision of care. While many of these questions have been discussed at some length by feminists the comparisons that are permitted by the juxtaposition of papers dealing with different places are fascinating. There are also interesting chapters about parts of everyday life that have not been written about so frequently, outside biography and autobiography, that is. Thus the consequences of old age in West Virginia and childhood in the US and the Sudan are examined. The editors suggest that the papers were ordered thematically. In fact, I found it difficult to distinguish what the themes were and one or two chapters seemed oddly misplaced to me; for example questions about the journey to work were raised in chapters 2 and 3 as well in 11.

Although *Different Places* does not aim to explicitly address women's changing experiences throughout the life course, turning to it after *Full Circles* reinforces the point of the editors of the former collection that it is almost axiomatic that it is adult women in their 'prime' who should be the subjects of feminist research. In this collection, the chapters are ordered by continent rather than thematically. In rapid succession the lives of adult women in urban, but mainly rural areas in Africa, Asia and Latin America are examined. Getting by as traders, agricultural labourers, factory workers, wives, daughters and political activists, these women combine stoicism and courage. For most of the women – a snap shot of whose lives is captured here – life is a constant round of drudgery and, in the main, submission to male authority, whether father, husband, boss or village elder.

The parallels and differences between women living in different places, let alone different nations or continents, are left to speak for themselves. Instead of attempting such a task, the editors have chosen to preface each major section of *Different Places* with a short introduction to feminist geographical work in the higher education institutions of that continent. This decision does rather betray the origins of the volume in an international conference but it also provides a fascinating glimpse into the preoccupations of scholars working in different places. Thus, among the African contributors environmental questions loomed largest; in South Asia issues about linking work and home, whereas the impact of modernization in general and of migration in particular was the primary focus of the papers about Latin America. For 'Western' readers it is also a salutary reminder of the specificity of their/ our concerns. The impact of these introductory pieces is to make the authors of the papers in *Different Places* seem more anxious than those in *Full Circles* (only one, Janet Townsend, appears in both) about their disciplinary location. There is something of a tendency to produce papers that conform to a particular model of how to do and present geographical research and the dominance of positivist methodologies within the discipline in many parts of the world is revealed. Greater reflection on the links with other feminist scholarship, in development studies and anthropology most obviously, might have led to more methodological variety and, perhaps, greater theoretical sophistication.

Both these books, however, provide stimulating insights into the variety and diversity of women's lives across the globe, raising important questions about the significance of place and location for women's lives. Thus, they help in beginning to address a set of questions that are increasingly urgent as global capital and nationalist politics are disrupting the interrelationships between place, identity and lifetime opportunities, often with appalling consequences. How does place matter to women? A number of questions might be useful to keep in mind when reading the multiple case studies in both collections. How is a woman's sense of herself, her identity and community membership attached to a particular place, or piece of territory? How is it affected, altered and reconstituted by migration and/or proletarianization? What about women who are 'between' places? Where is 'home' for migrants? It seems to me that unless detailed comparative studies are undertaken of how place, meaning and identity are constructed and reconstructed, the particular significance of place is hard to uncover. Both these texts provide a useful beginning to attempts to answer some of these questions.

Linda McDowell

Unsettling Relations: The University as a Site of Feminist Struggles
Himani Bannerji, Linda Carty, Kari Delhi, Susan Heald and Kate McKenna
Toronto: Women's Press 1991
ISBN 0 88961 160 2 £6.95 Pbk

Unsettling Relations: The University as a Site of Feminist Struggles is a collection of challenging and readable essays by five women, each of whom is involved in feminist politics and academic teaching/research. As its title suggests, the book is concerned with the university as a set of social relations which are involved in the production of power and privilege, together with feminist struggles to resist and change them. Framed in this general way, the book is located intellectually within the now quite long history of feminist critique of the academy as a male-dominated, liberal and middle-class preserve. Not surprisingly, therefore, some important parts of its conceptual framework are drawn from previously well-known feminist work – particularly that of the feminist sociologist Dorothy Smith. Two features are worth noting here: one is the notion that academic knowledge production is always inscribed within social and cultural relations of ruling. The second is the conviction that authentic (rather than simply 'academic') knowledge is intimately connected with – although not a direct reflection of – our bodily, sensuous and practical experiences in daily life.

Where the book is quite distinctive is in the sustained, detailed and critical attention it pays to the powers and privileges which are to be found, and which must be challenged, in the social relations of *feminist* pedagogy and research. Here, the authors' starting point is in more recent critiques of the way that many women have been socially positioned as 'other' and as 'different' by a white, middle-class, heterosexual and able-bodied hegemony in feminist knowledge. As one of the contributors to the volume has written previously, such practices have produced 'silences or absences, creating gaps and fissures through which non-white women, for example, disappear from the social surface' (Bannerji, 1987: 11). A further aim of *Unsettling Relations*, therefore, is to write the experiences of many previously neglected women into analyses of feminist academic relations. In order to achieve this, the introduction describes how each contributor to the volume has been enjoined to centre 'race' and class as well as gender, and to reflexively include a history of her own personal experiences of social positioning, within her chapter.

Following a brief 'introduction' to the background and aims of the book, a number of the main themes are developed in the first chapter by Linda Carty. Her own experiences of racism in education are used to illustrate the history of black people's marginalization in academic knowledge including feminist theory, given the construction of whiteness as a 'neutral' reference point. Kari Delhi explores how her whiteness has positioned her in relations of power over other women, and argues that white middle-class women must resist the comforts and seductions of university as 'home'. The third chapter by Himani Bannerji poses the question of why feminist research and pedagogy has been unable to validate non-white women's experiences, subjectivities and direct agency. She then answers this question by providing a critical account of feminist epistemologies (essentialist, politics of difference and Marxist/socialist), and by arguing for a 'reflexive and relational social analysis which incorporates in it a theory of agency and direct representation based on our experience' (p. 94). One important benefit of this approach is that it works out a political position within which racist social practices can be identified and challenged by all women 'without substitution, guilt and condescension' (p. 96).

The final two chapters are more centrally concerned with the subject positions of women as learner and teacher. Kate McKenna describes instances recorded in ethnographic field-work notes of her experiences on returning to university as a mature student of women's studies, to demonstrate how social relations and modes of (sometimes self-) regulation can limit feminist learning and knowing. Susan Heald's chapter brings the book to an end with an overview of liberal humanist and poststructuralist theories of subjectivity, together with a reflection on the various intersecting and often contradictory discourses which constructed a pathway for her own social development. She suggests that women in academic life need to learn how to protect themselves, by understanding how 'non-normalcy' makes participation difficult, and elaborates on this by referring to one of her chosen tactics of concealing her lesbian sexuality and difficulties with hearing in the classroom. However, she recognizes that deconstructing the otherwise apparently unitary category 'white women' is also vital, since comparisons across many dimensions of difference are necessary if we are fully to understand the way relations of oppression and domination are maintained.

This book deserves to be read widely. It is successful as an example of a collaboration between feminist teachers/researchers, addressing important and at times controversial issues coherently but without obliterating differences of views. A number of the contributors remark honestly how they experienced difficulties with writing in the personal (Linda Carty because she did not want to present a false picture of a 'personal debacle' (p. 33), and Kari Delhi because she doubted the motives of white feminists writing personal

'confessionals' (p. 51) and was wary of engaging in self-indulgence) – comments which I found useful. Nevertheless, each writer does, at least to some degree, manage to reflexively incorporate the particularities of the social positioning of her own biography within wider social and political analyses of racism, dominance and subordination, and the production of marginality and otherness in academic life. Consequently it testifies to the possibility of transforming feminist research, by putting important political, ethical and epistemological principles into practice more fully.

If I had to express reservations, one would be that the authors have not reflected fully on the position, role and value of institutions of higher education and learning in the context of wider historical and contemporary political relations and change. As a white woman with a permanent academic position, I recognize that my own interests and privileges are implicated here. However, while it is important that feminist academicians reflect critically on our own social relations and practices, this must not be at the expense of devaluing – both personally and politically – our daily lives as teachers and researchers and the academic work that we do. Bannerji and her colleagues are correct to point out that we must be accountable to our political affiliations beyond the university in our academic work and relations. But equally, we must acknowledge, as feminist researchers, the complexity of the relationship between our politics and our teaching and research, which is bound up with the practical effectivity of meaningful symbols, words and ideas. Also, speaking personally, I have come to believe that we have a special responsibility as the incumbents of institutions of learning to speak out for the right to do intellectual work which can promise no direct practical or instrumental benefit. Active protection of this 'privilege' is particularly important in many places at the present time, given widespread capitulation to the view that 'education' is no more than a training in skills that will prove useful in the production of markets, goods and wealth.

The latter point also leads me to resist, in part, the criticism many of the authors make of the way that feminist studies within the university may function as 'home'. I can agree that there is a need to undermine those social relationships which function as a bastion of middle-class privilege. I can also appreciate the well-chosen metaphor which alerts us that, together with the comforts offered by an academic 'home', such an environment can threaten to limit us through the imposition of obligations, conventions and ties. However, having entered university as a young, working-class woman, and later located myself within feminist studies (particularly as fashioned by 'standpoint science'), my experience is that I have needed the sense of security, confidence and (temporarily fixed) identity they have afforded me in my struggle to find a personal and politi-

cal voice. I would, therefore, tend to agree with the suggestion in Susan Heald's chapter that it may be necessary to construct a new 'home', based upon changed and firmer foundations, to support the activities of feminist academic research.

This book could certainly be recommended as useful reading on postgraduate and even some undergraduate courses that are informed by the principles of feminist pedagogy and research. The compelling accounts of personal struggles with academic institutions and practices also make it a potentially useful resource for Ph.D. students, as a support through difficult times in their research. I shall recommend to my students that it is read alongside articles such as Angela MacRobbie's one on the politics of feminist research in *Feminist Review* No. 12.

Karen Henwood

Reference

BANNERJI H. (1987) Introducing Racism: Notes Towards an Anti-Racist Feminism *Resources for Feminist Research/ Documentation sur la recherche feministe* Vol 16, No. 1.

Feminist Epistemologies
Edited by Linda Alcoff and Elizabeth Potter

London: Routledge 1993
ISBN 0 415 90451 X £12.99 Pbk
ISBN 0 415 90450 1 £35.00 Hbk

You might say that the problems of feminist epistemology are the problems of a political project hoist by its own petard. It's one of the very basic tenets of feminism that propositions commonly presented as 'objective' knowledge are all too often highly value-laden assertions which both arise from and perpetuate situations of domination and oppression: this tenet has been seen to apply not just to assertions of 'knowledge' about the inferiority of women made by medical, scientific, academic and

other establishments throughout history, but also, more recently, to 'knowledge' claims made by feminists themselves which have arisen from and perpetuated forms of domination within feminism and between women along axes of race, class, age, ability and difference. The epistemological problem which emerges from this long, fierce and often painful history now is: if, as feminism has claimed, assertions of 'knowledge' are so often both producers and guarantors of domination and power, how can feminism itself legitimately claim to be a site of 'knowledge' about the oppression of women or, indeed, about anything at all? And if feminism *cannot* make such a claim, how can it continue as a political project for the liberation of women from what it says it *knows* to be injustice and oppression?

The essays in this collection represent a variety of 'takes', from a number of different angles, on this striking problem: having destabilized, if not destroyed, the 'objectivity' of dominant establishment 'knowledge', feminist thought is in search of some stable epistemological ground(s) of its own. The result is a lively and eclectic book which manages both to provide an overview of a certain section of the feminist debate on epistemology as it currently stands and at the same time to make a fresh contribution to that debate. I say a 'certain section' because, as the editors state in their introduction, the essays here come from a particular area of feminist academia – from what the editors call 'the uneasy alliance of feminism and philosophy'. This restriction gives the collection coherence and focus without, however, producing homogeneity or narrowness of interest. As the editors warn, different readers will have different reactions to the collection: some of the issues presented and approaches taken will seem obvious and even 'old hat' to feminists but new and disconcerting to 'mainstream' philosophers, and vice versa. I certainly found this to be the case, and although I consider this to be far more of a strength than a weakness for the collection as a whole – both in terms of the eclecticism and heterogeneity I have already mentioned, and as an illuminating example of interdisciplinarity in action – the effects of that mix of 'feminist' and 'mainstream' in some cases is not always to feminism's benefit.

For example, four of the eleven essays in this collection develop, in various ways, the view that knowledge is produced by communities rather than individuals, a view which departs from the traditional philosophical approach to epistemology and which the four authors here claim have various advantages for feminist epistemology. However,

while some of these essays present arguments which are both intellectually persuasive and politically insightful – particularly that by Elizabeth Potter, who combines a deft use of Wittgenstein to feminist ends with a startling revelation of the hidden agenda of sexual politics behind that most 'objective' item of scientific knowledge, Boyle's Law of Gases – others, in elaborating community-based epistemologies into coherent philosophical accounts, seem to lose sight of that function of *power* in traditional knowledge claims which makes epistemology an issue for feminism in the first place. Appealing to debate between 'epistemological communities', or to 'public standards', as a means for settling conflicting knowledge claims (as suggested in this collection by Lynn Hankinson Nelson and Helen E. Longino respectively) takes little account of the very real power that dominant 'epistemological communities' – which, after all, include both government agencies and multinational 'scientific' corporations – wield over those many other epistemological communities (not just women) whom they oppress.

The other epistemological debates which appear in the collection include the epistemological status of non-propositional knowledge – 'knowing who' or 'knowing how' rather than 'knowing that' – and the attribution of epistemic privilege to socially marginalized groups, an attribution perhaps most famously made by standpoint epistemology, which is set out here in a new essay by Sandra Harding. Harding's essay is accompanied by a critical reply from Bat-Ami Bar On which is fine and sharp-edged both politically and intellectually and which is for me the highlight of the collection, with implications not just for standpoint epistemology but for all those feminisms which make use of the tropes of 'margin' and 'centre' in their analyses of oppression, tropes which are now common but which, according to Bar On, are philosophically and politically questionable.

The questions of feminist epistemology are crucial to feminism, both theory and practice, and rescuing feminism from epistemological nihilism is one of the most urgent tasks now facing feminist thought. This collection presents an engaging and informative picture of how that task is progressing in a number of directions, with the breakthroughs and the difficulties in that progress, and will be of very great interest, use and relevance to all readers concerned with the thorny question of what feminists know.

Merl Storr

Shifting Scenes: Interviews on Women, Writing and Politics in Post-68 France
Edited by Alice A. Jardine and Anne M. Menke
New York: Columbia University Press 1993
ISBN 0 231 06773 9 $16.50/£9.50 Pbk

Three Steps on the Ladder of Writing
Hélène Cixous; Translated by Sarah Cornell and Susan Sellers
New York: Columbia University Press 1993
ISBN 0 231 07658 4 £13.50 Hbk

Shifting Scenes is a collection of interviews with fifteen French women writers and theorists including Hélène Cixous, Marguerite Duras, Luce Irigaray, Monique Wittig and Christiane Rochefort. The interviews were conducted and introduced by Alice A. Jardine and Anne M. Menke, who work in Modern Languages departments at Harvard and Swarthmore College respectively. The 'America meets France' dimension of this work is perhaps its keystone, and is one of the major themes of the introduction, where the editors refer to their own, albeit ambivalent, complicity with the American desire to revise the French canon, and their interviewees' shared desire to question the relevance of their 'American' questions. The publication of this book in America is in itself an expression of the cultural gap which has perhaps become its major subject, for it is unlikely that such an anthology would have attracted equivalent institutional support in Paris. We are therefore presented here with the paradox of the existence of a canon of contemporary French women writers in American universities and of the almost complete absence of any equivalent in France, coupled with the questioning of the value and meaning of such a phenomenon by many of the writers themselves. Jardine and Menke make it perfectly clear that their choice of writers is very much related to their perceived significance in American academic circles, and, along with the nature of the questions posed, this seems to suggest that the Paris/New York axis rather than 'post-68 France' is the real cultural context for this work.

The sense of witnessing the encounter of alien cultures is compounded by the fact that the editors' concerns as women working within the academic institution are not necessarily those of the French writers, many of whom, whether by choice or as a result of politically motivated exclusion, are very much outside it. This encounter is presented in the form of interviews in an attempt to avoid the 'third-person pronouns, past-tenses, and "fixing" of narratives' characteristic of 'History'. The final text is none the less a literary production rather than an attempt to record the original social events. It is immediately obvious to the reader that these polished, complete sentences bear only a distant relationship to spoken language and it is no surprise to discover that most of the writers took advantage of the opportunity to rewrite the text and to review the translation, while some responded in written form from the outset. The same set of five questions is repeated for each interview, and a final question is designed to address the particular interests of the individual writer. While in some cases, such as that of Kristeva, the format seems to allow the writer to express her fundamental concerns, for others it may have operated as a constraint. Consistency and the opportunity to make comparisons are the advantages of this approach, but allowing the writers the possibility of setting their own agenda might have significantly shifted the focus, and produced more varied and illuminating texts.

The tight framework used in these interviews, combined with the high level of textual control exerted perhaps makes the claim that this is 'Discourse' rather than 'History' slightly disingenuous; the reader is sometimes left wondering, given the editors' rejection of biographical auteurism and questioning of the canon, exactly how these texts should be read and what status is being claimed for them. They are clearly not neutral contributions to the great feminist debates of our time, but have emerged from a specific institutional context, a series of social/professional encounters and considerable textual reworking. Perhaps more analysis of this largely effaced process would have been revealing, and would have avoided the danger of these interviews being perceived as transparent crystallizations of particular writers' ideas.

The interview form does none the less allow the often controversial issues to emerge as unresolved questions, rather than locking them into a linear argument, and the very

widely varying positions taken here on questions such as the relationship between biological gender and writing, or between feminism and psychoanalysis, do both contribute to these debates and militate against the use of such oversimplifying categories as 'French feminism'.

In reading *Three Steps on the Ladder of Writing*, by Hélène Cixous, we enter a very different domain, for the focus here is more on the nature of creativity in a universal sense than on the politics of literary criticism and production in the late twentieth century. This is the translated text of three lectures, given by Cixous at the University of California, Irvine, in May 1990, and entitled 'The School of the Dead', 'The School of Dreams' and 'The School of Roots'. Cixous combines her own reflections on the process of writing with detailed readings of passages from writers with whom she has a long-established affinity, such as Clarice Lispector from Brazil, the Russian poet Tsvetaeva, Genet and Kafka. The range of cultures and periods represented by these and other writers enriches Cixous' text as well as echoing her own multicultural background. As a Jewish woman, born in Algeria, of a German-speaking mother, Cixous is both immersed in, and outside, French language and culture, and thus particularly well-qualified to undertake the journey to a foreign country which she describes in 'The School of the Dead' as a necessary stage in the process of reading as well as writing. It is partly in this sense that she sees writing and death as inextricably linked, for the writer must sacrifice the familiar, the intimate circle, and be prepared both to gain from the experience of loss, and to uncover painful and violent truth. 'The School of Roots' develops the theme of exile, of the search for a deeper level of meaning, from a position of cultural rootlessness and marginalization, which Cixous sees as women's place in patriarchal society.

'The School of Dreams' takes up

again the symbol of the ladder which opens the book, but this time we see Jacob's ladder, rather than the letter 'H', and writing is compared to the angels climbing down the ladder into the depths. The metaphor of journey inwards is only partly accurate since dreams efface the journey: we are simply and suddenly in a place combining 'extreme familiarity with extreme strangeness'. One of the most fascinating dream pieces which Cixous presents here describes a woman who leaves the battle with dirt and disorder in 'the numerous great rooms of the university' and finds herself in a church in front of an iron chest, which beneath her hands begin to blossom with colour, with

'star flowers'. When she leaves her creation momentarily she returns to find the images have been covered over by a painter who has used a brush and box of colours to produce an abstract image, 'à la Braque'. Cixous warns us against the interpretation of dreams, but this poetic exploration of the relationship between writing, the body and gender transcends what Cixous refers to as 'sterile debates' on nature and culture and leads to the evocative parallel between writing and flowering/taking root which forms part of Cixous' 'attempt to conclude'.

Lyn Thomas

A Dozen Lips
Eavan Boland, Clodagh Corcoran, Carol Coulter, Gretchen Fitzgerald, Maureen Gaffney, Trudy Hayes, Edna Longley, Gerardine Meaney, Ruth Riddick, Helena Sheehan, Ethna Viney and Margaret Ward
Dublin: Attic Press 1994
ISBN 1 85594 060 4 £16.99

According to Maeve Kneafsey at Attic Press, Ireland's feminist publishing house, LIP pamphlets were originally conceived of as a space for women to engage with contemporary and often contentious issues. Attic decided that, in contradistinction to book-length manuscripts, the pamphlets would each pursue one substantial discussion, eschewing the traditional dictum to provide 'both sides' of an argument. Additionally, the pamphlets recalled the interesting prominence the word *lip* itself holds in Irish culture. As Ailbhe Smyth, Director of Women's Studies at University College Dublin and editor at Attic Press has said in another context, many women remember mothers admonishing their

daughters not to give them any lip, not to 'talk back'. *A Dozen Lips*, one of Attic's most recent publications, combines twelve pamphlets which taken collectively do not argue but rather 'talk back' to one another in the most productive sense, while simultaneously suggesting the trajectory of feminist thought in contemporary Ireland.

Although each pamphlet in the collection has much to contribute, the first and last indicate the whole. Clodagh Corcoran's 'Pornography: the new terrorism', originally published in 1989, begins the discussion and Gretchen Fitzgerald's 1992 'Repulsing racism: reflections on racism and the Irish' concludes it. Corcoran recounts her experience viewing pornography and uses this as a call for women to recognize (anti)pornography as a civil rights issue. Her pamphlet belies its early inception within Ireland's women's movement both in its failure to be self-reflective about the fact that perhaps not all women would be ready to see pornography as a civil rights issue – women in Northern Ireland, for example, might contend that adequate housing is a more immediate civil rights issue than is pornography; northern women might also suggest that they are dealing with a more profound 'terrorism' than that mentioned in the author's title – and also in her reliance on theorists and activists in the United States and United Kingdom for her analysis. Corcoran's essay is peppered with the oft-quoted 'pornography is the theory; rape is the practice', and she cites the 1986 US Attorney General's Commission on Pornography as that which established links between pornography and violence against women. One might wonder how Corcoran would respond to recent theorists such as Carol Vance and others who have suggested the inherently flawed nature of the Meese Commission and who maintain that sexually explicit material might be differently contextualized by lesbians.

Corcoran's essay does become particularly interesting, however, when she discusses the specificity of the Irish women's experience: 'Irish social standards and Irish legislation have never embodied principles and behaviours that respect the sexual rights of women' (p. 18). She notes the constitution along with contemporary issues in Ireland (i.e., the Kerry Babies Tribunal), and contends that for Irish women 'the sexual colonisation of our bodies has been enshrined in male-dominated legislation and legislators' (p. 18). This portion of Corcoran's discussion is important but still does not adequately relate pornography to legislation in Ireland. She would perhaps have been wiser to highlight the implications of this country's treatment of women and its parallel inability to contend with female sexuality itself. Finally, Corcoran castigates women who collaborate with the enemy – 'women defending pornography symbolise the internalisation of male oppression' (p. 20) – rather than explore Ireland's inability to recognize the range of female sexualities, an inability which is resonant in *A Dozen Lips'* lack of attention to lesbianism.

Gretchen Fitzgerald's essay is significant both for its self-consciousness about feminisms in Ireland and its ability to suggest the direction the women's movement might take. Fitzgerald too begins by recounting her experience; yet hers is a much more self-conscious exploration, as she examines the effects of racism upon a woman of colour on a world-wide scale and then in a specifically Irish context. Fitzgerald provides a genealogy of racism and finally suggests how she defines it: 'For me, the term racism denotes the relations of power by which one group dominates another because of ethnic or cultural differences. Racism is reinforced and combined with other forms of prejudice and discrimination based on class, gender and religion' (p. 252). Next she contends that the argument that the Irish are not racist simply because they have been exploited and oppressed is not a credible one: 'Experiencing racism does not prevent one being racist oneself' (p. 253). Importantly, she traces Ireland's role as a missionary people and connects this to contemporary development work. Although she applauds what she sees as an evolving sense of enlightenment on the part of development workers – noting her distress when she initially arrived in Ireland only to find schoolchildren 'buying' (sponsoring) black babies – she maintains that charity and development work are still conceptually flawed. This is the import not only of Fitzgerald's contribution to *A Dozen Lips*, but also of the collection as a whole: she discusses an oft-hidden issue – racism in Ireland – and aligns it with the institutional powers within Ireland itself.

Fitzgerald's exploration of (racist) institutions in Ireland extends from Irish legislation (or lack thereof), to immigration law; to the media and education ('The prevailing ethos in primary, secondary and third level schools and colleges is as inherently racist as it is sexist.' p. 262); to the European Community

('Harmonisation of policies in relation to freedom of movement has
become a contentious issue.' p. 264);
and, finally, to feminism in Ireland.
About this she has much to say: 'The
women's movement in Ireland has
scarcely begun to address these
issues [racism in institutionalized
settings]. For me, the divisions
which have characterised the politics of feminism in relation to black
women first need to be recognised
and then overcome' (p. 267). This
suggestion, which reminds one of the
path of women's movements in other
countries, is given a specifically geo-
political twist, as Fitzgerald establishes the specificity of what this
means for an Irish context: 'Thus, in
Ireland, Traveller and black women
need to ally with settled white
women to achieve a solidarity and
strength in order to win collective
battles' (p. 267). It is significant that
Fitzgerald's essay concludes the
collection.

Yet in between Corcoran's pamphlet and Fitzgerald's, there are
other works which provocatively respond to one another and suggest the
direction of the women's movement
and feminist theory in Ireland. In
'Sex and nation: women in Irish
culture and politics' (1991), Gerardine Meaney talks back to Edna Longley's 1990 'From Cathleen to
anorexia: the breakdown of
Irelands'. Both women seek to address the tensions between feminism
and nationalism, republicanism and
unionism. Longley compares Irish
nationalism to bad poetry and notes
that political images (employed by
both) eventually exhaust themselves: 'I think this happens at the
juncture where the image women-
Ireland-muse [an equation which
harkens back to Eavan Boland's
pamphlet in the collection] meets
contemporary Irish women. There, I
believe, the breakdown of nationalist
ideology becomes particularly clear'
(p. 176). Like the anorexic Cathleen
(Ni Houlihan) of Longley's title, the
nationalist dream too has 'declined

into a destructive neurosis' (p. 102).
Although her title implies the importance of women to and in her essay,
Longley's proclivity to talk less about
women and more about males associated with nationalism, unionism and
workers parties is correctly taken to
task by Gerardine Meaney. Although
Longley discusses male authors and
politicians to contextualize her
analysis and to suggest the extent to
which all of these men are implicated
in an exploration of women and
nationalism, her critique leads her to
make statements such as the following: 'but at least unionism does not
appropriate the image of woman or
hide its aggressions behind our
skirts' (p. 177). The problem might
well be less who's appropriating
whom, and more who gets lost in the
rustle of fine garments.

Carol Coulter's 1990 'Ireland:
between the First and Third Worlds'
usefully places any discussion of
Ireland within a colonial context. She
suggests the possibilities for a kind of
nationalism and simultaneously critiques the inconsistencies inherent in
the state, the Republic of Ireland.
Eavan Boland's by now oft-quoted
1989 pamphlet 'A kind of scar: the
woman poet in a national tradition',
examines the problematics for a
woman writer who must find her way
out of the national tradition pre-
scribed for her. Her essay is excellent
and certainly productive for women
writers, but, importantly, Longley
suggests that Boland's poem 'Mise
Eire', which begins Boland's pamphlet, destabilizes the *Mise* but keeps
the *Eire* intact. Margaret Ward in
'The missing sex: putting women into
Irish history' adds a useful genealogy
of women and Irish history. She tells
us some of what we already know: to
date Irish history has usually been a
male and class-based narrative;
nationalist and feminist women have
both fared poorly in written accounts
of history, but it has perhaps been
'easier' to deal with the nationalist
cause; in Irish life, the relegation
of the female exists as much in

academic as in social institutions. Ward's work becomes much more provocative when she outlines what she sees as the future for the study of Irish history. She imagines this future as one concerned not only with gender, class and sex analyses, but also with understanding the way the three are imbricated. She stresses, too, what others have termed a gendered history, one which maintains 'the interrelationships of women and men's lives, using inclusive historical perspectives in order to analyse their experiences' (p. 223). Ward notes that until this new history can take root, women's studies should be on the core syllabus as an 'interim measure' (p. 223). One wonders if yet another LIP pamphlet is needed to address both the use of women's studies as an interim measure and also to assess the work of others who have suggested alternatives to women's inclusion into the mainstream of history.

The remaining pamphlets probe the significance of a theorization of power for sexual politics (Maureen Gaffney (1991), 'Glass slippers and tough bargains: women, men and power'), and the importance of, distant movements and methods (Helena Sheehan (1989), 'Has the red flag fallen? The fate of socialism in the 1990s'). Ethna Viney's 1989 pamphlet 'Ancient wars: sex and

sexuality' provides a helpful history of discussions of sexuality in Ireland and can be usefully read in conjunction with Coulter's pamphlet, as the latter foregrounds the internationalism unavailable in the former. Similarly, Viney's statement that 'the climax of female sexuality is giving birth. . . .' (p. 65) can be interestingly juxtaposed to Ruth Riddick's 1990 pamphlet, 'The right to choose: questions of feminist morality'. Riddick's work is particularly relevant to those interested in learning about the ways in which issues surrounding reproductive rights have galvanized women in the Republic. Readers might remember, however, Longley's suggestion that this very issue (reproductive rights in the south) has had the effect of eliding others (the construction of the nation).

As *A Dozen Lips* indicates, one pamphlet dedicated to an in-depth discussion of a particular concern of Irish women is stimulating and thought-provoking, but a combination of twelve of these documents is truly spectacular. Taken as a whole, the collection suggests the extent to which women in Ireland are talking to one another and at the same time signalling the trajectory in feminist thought in the Republic of Ireland and Northern Ireland.

Megan Sullivan

Crossing the Boundary: Black Women Survive Incest
Melba Wilson
London: Virago 1993
ISBN 1 85381 429 6 £7.99 Pbk

'I am an incest survivor. Let me qualify that – I am black, female and approaching middle age. I have reached a point in my life where I feel that sharing that information may

be useful for those who are also black, female and have survived child sexual abuse'. Thus begins Melba Wilson's introduction to *Crossing the Boundary*. Wilson's aim in writing this book is that it will help her to come 'to terms with the sexual relationship which occurred more than thirty years ago between [her] father and [herself]; and help other Black women who have similar experiences to be able to do the same.'

In Britain very little research

has been carried out on sexual abuse and Black women. To date much of the existing work on this subject has come from America. The available research indicates that the incidence of abuse occurs about as commonly in the Black communities as it does in the white communities. Yet it does not get talked about. Often the reason for not speaking out is the fear of exposing the Black community to stereotypical judgements by white people. Melba Wilson writes from the conviction that the taboo against speaking out must be broken.

In this book Wilson does not aim to produce statistical data on the incidence of sexual abuse in Black communities. She interviewed about twelve – mainly African-Caribbean women. The reader is not told how many Asians were interviewed and how the interviewees were selected. Wilson also includes secondary information – ideas of those who work with Black women survivors, as well as any research on Black women survivors. She challenges theories of the Black family that emerged out of the Euro-American frame of reference. She articulates Black feminist philosophy, principles and theory, creating the framework for a Black feminist understanding of child sexual abuse.

Through careful analysis of the autobiographical and fictional work of Black women writers such as Maya Angelou, Alice Walker, Buchi Emecheta, Joan Riley and Opal Palmer Adisa on incest and the voices of individual women, Wilson challenges the myth that sexual abuse does not happen in the Black communities. The book also raises important issues in relation to the curious anomaly Black women are caught in. On the one hand, sexual abuse is not supposed to exist in Black communities: this brings about a reluctance to raise it as an issue. On the other hand, sexual abuse exists to such an extent that it is almost considered normal by many inside the Black community.

If I have a major criticism, it is the treatment of Black people as a monolithic group. There is a need to explore the similarities and differences between Black women survivors of Asian and African-Caribbean origin. This will further our understanding of the ways in which cultural influences lead to sexual abuse and the implications of incest within the different communities.

The final section provides a useful list of resources which are invaluable for Black women survivors of incest and child sexual abuse.

This book is long overdue. The amount of work published for, by and about Black women is totally negligible and Black women's voices have gone unheard. Melba Wilson gives a voice to Black women survivors of incest and child sexual abuse.

The book will be of interest to a wide audience. It merits extensive readership and debate. It should be able to achieve both, not least because of its accessible and thought-provoking style.

Lena Robinson

Hardship and Health in Women's Lives
Hilary Graham
Hemel Hempstead, Hertfordshire:
Harvester Wheatsheaf 1993
ISBN 0 7450 1265 5 £10.95 Pbk
ISBN 07450 1264 7 £40.00 Hbk

The work of Hilary Graham has consistently provided a persistent and powerful voice on behalf of the overwhelming structural poverty faced by many women raising children in our society and this book is particularly timely in the present climate of 'lone-parent bashing' which is reaching astonishing and totally unacceptable proportions by the present government.

Using sources such as social surveys, official statistics and subjective experiences, Graham graphically sketches out the features of hardship encountered in women's lives, and the subsequent consequences with their own health and that of their children.

The first chapter provides an excellent introduction to the uses and abuses of social science research, by describing both the potential and the limitations of the sources. There is a growing awareness that feminist researchers cannot afford to simply dismiss these methods, that it is important to recognize them while acknowledging their shortcomings and Graham demonstrates how official statistics and large surveys can be made accessible. She then discusses the classification and categorization of complex concepts such as social class and ethnicity, with the inevitable reductionism involved in the collection of data by these methods.

Having stated the shortfalls, Graham then proceeds, chapter by chapter, to blend these sources to provide a vivid illumination of the domestic circumstances and responsibilities of women caring for children. These encompass routes into motherhood, housing, responsibility and caring, paid work, financial management and health status, and show that with careful explanation, the statistics can give stark, hard-hitting messages. For instance, when Graham discusses a table showing the discrepancy in tenure between two-parent and lone-parent families, (24% of the former are in rented accommodation rather than owner occupied as compared to 65% of lone parents, rising to 88% of lone parents with disabled children), she points out that public sector housing is the 'residual' sector, occupied by those households who do not have the income to buy their own home, and who struggle against disadvantage. This may well be stating the obvious, but sadly is very necessary in this climate which substitutes 'scrounging' for 'needing' and vilifies

the lives of women who are already struggling enough.

The accounts of managing money, including the dangerous temptations of consumer credit, portray another side of the story of how well some women do cope. 'Coping' is a central issue in the discussion on the effects on health of the accumulation of disadvantage in these factors and Graham has always treated the thorny issue of the ongoing increase in cigarette- smoking among women on low income with sensitivity, pointing out how it is used as a means of 'getting through' – a strategy which helps as well as hurts (p. 183), although she by no means underplays the potential damage to mothers and children.

Throughout the book, Graham is very careful to emphasize that women are not a homogenous group, that they are differentiated by social class and ethnicity, and that to be non-white and on low income can result in multiple disadvantage (there are three times as many ethnic minority women in temporary homeless accommodation as there are white women, for instance). She shows that women are also disadvantaged by disability (their own or their child's) or by their sexuality. There is, of course, the danger of using statistics in this way to further marginalize or pathologize the lives of the large number of women who do not fit the 'cosy' categories so embedded in the hegemony of our society. However, this book does seem to transcend the trap of depicting women purely as 'social problems'. For instance, when discussing the role of children in the household, Graham highlights the positive aspects such as the emotional support children give their mothers, which does not necessarily damage their development but may enrich it. The use of the qualitative material is essential in this process as the inclusion of women's own voices illustrates the complexities of their situations and the richness of their lives despite the hardship, and Graham's tone ultimately demonstrates admiration rather than condescension: 'Mothers emerge from the patchwork of their lives as survivors. They are not the powerless victims of oppression but are agents of their lives, actively engaged in caring for health and struggling against hardship' (p. 202). No doubt this book will be criticized for regurgitation of the same old material or of overstating the case by those who continually suppress the gendered voice in inequality but it provides a powerfully concise and highly accessible resource, not only in academic terms, but in the political struggle against the oppression of women.

Gillian Bendelow

NOTICEBOARD

We're Counting on Equality

Many organizations now have an Equal Opportunities Policy but how well is it working? A comprehensive monitoring scheme is essential for ensuring that equality is a reality in the workplace. This guide provides information on:

- undertaking a workplace audit;
- anti-discrimination laws and the implications for monitoring;
- monitoring barriers to equality;
- issues to consider when monitoring discrimination on the grounds of sex, race, disability, sexuality, HIV/AIDS and age.

Available from City Centre, 32/35 Featherstone Street, London, EC-1Y 8QX, 071 608 1338, price £12.50.

Calls for Papers

'Anniversary conference: Mary Wollstonecraft in Sweden 1795–1995' Uddevalla, Sweden, 2–6 September 1995

Call for papers and/or preliminary registration.

This international conference is to commemorate the 200th anniversary of Mary Wollstonecraft's journey to Scandinavia in 1795 later immortalized in her *Letters*. Our aim is to bring together scholars from different disciplines who are working in fields related to Wollstonecraft's main concerns understood in a broad sense. Conference strands are: 1. Romanticism and Gender; 2. Feminist Thought; 3. Revolution: Women and Gender; 4. Travel Writing. We would also welcome suggestions for panels (two to three papers, a chair and a commentator). Delegates will also have an opportunity of visiting places seen by Wollstonecraft and there will be entertainments and lectures for the public.

Abstracts (1 page) and/or preliminary notice of participation by 1 December 1994. Enquiries to Prof. Catherine Sandbach-Dahlström, Dept of English, Stockholm Univ. S 106 91 Stockholm, Sweden. Fax. 46 8 159667 Email dahlstrc@engelska.su.se.

Women in Central and Eastern Europe Vol. 15, No.4, Fall 1995.

CWS/cf's Fall 1995 issue is committed to an exploration of the lives of Women in Central and Eastern Europe in a global context. The changes of 1989 had a profound impact on women's lives in Central and Eastern Europe. On the one hand the relaxation of the one-party system favoured the emergence of new autonomous women's organizations. On the other hand, benefits that were taken for granted by women during state socialism are no longer guaranteed under the new Central and Eastern European regimes. The issue will focus on women's experiences in the former Soviet Union, the former Czechoslovakia, the former Yugoslavia, the former German Democratic Republic, Poland, Hungary, Romania, Albania and Bulgaria since 1989. We are seeking articles from feminist scholars and grass-roots activists in Central and Eastern Europe as well as from Western contributors who do research on women's issues in Central and Eastern Europe or have extensive co-operative contact with Central and East European women's groups. Authors who have not previously published in Western publications are encouraged to submit manuscripts.

Invited are essays, research reports, true stories, poetry, cartoons, drawings and other artwork which addresses the experiences of women living in Central and Eastern Europe. Deadline: 15 December 1994.

Canadian Woman Studies, 212 Founders College, York University, 4700 Keele Street, North York, Ont. M3J 1P3 (416) 736–5356 Fax (416) 736–5700 (indicate extension 55356).

Thamyris

Contributions are invited now for the second volume (2 issues) of *Thamyris*, the forthcoming new journal on *Mythmaking from Past to Present*.

The journal's special issue of 1995 is devoted to mythmaking on gay and lesbian sexualities, homosocial arrangements and masquerades representing myths from different ethnic backgrounds, historical periods and geographical locations.

Of interest are contributions exploring interconnexions between gender-biased concepts, sexual orientation and/or ethnicity. A variety of disciplinary and interdisciplinary approaches is sought to stimulate challenging debates. The journal intends crossing cultural as well as continental frontiers and participating in international discussions on the topic of mythmaking. All periods are covered.

The deadlines for submissions are: Vol. 2, No. 1, special issue (Spring 1995) 1 February 1995; and Vol. 2, No. 2 (Autumn 1995) 1 August 1995.

A *Notice to Contributors* and any further information are available on request.

Requests, proposals and manuscripts should be sent to the editors: Jan Best & Nanny de Vries, Najade Press, P.O. Box 75933, 1070 AX Amsterdam, The Netherlands.

Woman/Time/Space

There will be an Interdisciplinary Conference at the Centre for Women's Studies, Lancaster University, on 'Women/Time/Space', on Saturday, 25 March 1995. Papers are invited on such topics as: Memory; Nostalgia; Raced and sexualised space/time; Gendered use of time; Periodization; Tradition; Custom; Life Cycles; Generations; Kinship; Inheritance; Routines; Work time/space; Housing; Turning points; Agoraphobia/claustrophobia; Architecture; Public space; Domestic space/time; Cities; Landscape; Leisure; Urban/rural; Institutional space/time; Transport; Travel; Tourism; Outer space/inner space; Imagined futures; Utopias; Fantastic time/space; Nationalism; Regionalism; Globalization; Staging; Chronotopes; Visual space; Technology; Cyberspace; Sacred time/space; Virtual reality. Please send proposals with one-page abstracts to the Conference Organizers, Women/Time/Space, Centre for Women's Studies, Cartmel College, Lancaster University, Lancaster, LA1 4YL, by December 15th, 1994.

Lesbian Review of Books

A new quarterly, *The Lesbian Review of Books*, will begin publication in August 1994. *The Review* will feature books by, about, and for lesbians. It will offer review essays on authors, genres, topics, and contemporary issues, as well as reviews of individual books in the areas of history, literature, poetry, drama, film, psychology, erotica, spirituality, science-fiction, biography, and ethics. A regular feature in each issue will be reviews of the latest in lesbian fiction and lesbian mysteries. Early issues will contain review essays on contemporary lesbian poetry. Latina lesbian writing, the lesbian mystery, lesbian children's literature, and the current state of the coming-out story.

Subscriptions are $10/year or $18/two years. *The Review* will be published in August, November, February, and May. For a sample copy of the August issue, send $2.50. Subscriptions, *The Lesbian Review of Books*, P.O. Box 6369, Altadena CA 91003.

The Review also seeks reviewers. Send your name, address, and areas of interest to Loralee MacPike, Editor, at the address above.

Feminist Review

Since its founding in 1979 **Feminist Review** has been the major Women's Studies journal in Britain. **Feminist Review** is committed to presenting the best of contemporary feminist analysis, always informed by an awareness of changing political issues. The journal is edited by a collective of women based in London, with the help of women and groups from all over the United Kingdom.

● WHY NOT SUBSCRIBE? MAKE SURE OF YOUR COPY

All subscriptions run in calendar years. The issues for 1994 are Nos. 46, 47 and 48. You will save over £5 pa on the single copy price.

● SUBSCRIPTION RATES, 1994 (3 issues)

Individual Subscriptions

UK/EEC	£22
Overseas	£30
North America	$40

A number of reduced cost (£15.50 per year: UK only) subscriptions are available for readers experiencing financial hardship, e.g. unemployed, student, low-paid. If you'd like to be considered for a reduced subscription, please write to the Collective, c/o the Feminist Review office, 52 Featherstone Street, London EC1Y 8RT.

Institutional Subscriptions		**Single Issues**	
UK	£62	UK	£8.99
Overseas	£68	North America	$12.95
North America	$100		

☐ Please send me one year's subscription to **Feminist Review**

☐ Please send me_____copies of back issue no._____

METHOD OF PAYMENT

☐ I enclose a cheque/international money order to the value of_____ made payable to Routledge Journals

☐ Please charge my Access/Visa/American Express/Diners Club account

Account no. ☐☐☐☐☐☐☐☐☐☐☐☐☐☐☐☐☐☐

Expiry date_____ Signature_____

If the address below is different from the registered address of your credit card, please give your registered address separately.

PLEASE USE BLOCK CAPITALS

Name_____

Address_____

_____

_____Postcode_____

☐ Please send me a Routledge Journals Catalogue

☐ Please send me a Routledge Gender and Women's Studies Catalogue

Please return this form with payment to:
Trevina White, Routledge Journals, Cheriton House, North Way, Andover, Hants SP10 5BE

BACK ISSUES

19 The Female Nude in the work of Suzanne Valadon, **Betterton**. Refuges for Battered Women, **Pahl**. Thin is the Feminist Issue, **Diamond**. New Portraits for Old, **Martin & Spence**.

20 Prisonhouses, **Steedman**. Ethnocentrism and Socialist Feminism, **Barrett & McIntosh**. What Do Women Want? **Rowbotham**. Women's Equality and the European Community, **Hoskyns**. Feminism and the Popular Novel of the 1890s, **Clarke**.

21 Going Private: The Implications of Privatization for Women's Work, **Coyle**. A Girl Needs to Get Street-wise: Magazines for the 1980s, **Winship**. Family Reform in Socialist States: The Hidden Agenda, **Molyneux**. Sexual Segregation in the Pottery Industry, **Sarsby**.

22 Interior Portraits: Women, Physiology and the Male Artist, **Pointon**. The Control of Women's Labour: The Case of Homeworking, **Allen & Wolkowitz**. Homeworking: Time for Change, **Cockpit Gallery & Londonwide Homeworking Group**. Feminism and Ideology: The Terms of Women's Stereotypes, **Seiter**. Feedback: Feminism and Racism, **Ramazanoglu, Kazi, Lees, Safia Mirza**.

23 SOCIALIST-FEMINISM: OUT OF THE BLUE
Feminism and Class Politics: A Round-Table Discussion, **Barrett, Campbell, Philips, Weir & Wilson**. Upsetting an Applecart: Difference, Desire and Lesbian Sadomasochism, **Ardill & O'Sullivan**. Armagh and Feminist Strategy, **Loughran**. Transforming Socialist-Feminism: The Challenge of Racism, **Bhavnani & Coulson**. Socialist-Feminists and Greenham, **Finch & Hackney Greenham Groups**. Socialist-Feminism and the Labour Party: Some Experiences from Leeds, **Perrigo**. Some Political Implications of Women's Involvement in the Miners' Strike, 1984–85, **Rowbotham & McCrindle**. Sisterhood: Political Solidarity Between Women, **Hooks**. European Forum of Socialist-Feminists, **Lees & McIntosh**. Report from Nairobi, **Hendessi**.

24 Women Workers in New Industries in Britain, **Glucksmann**. The Relationship of Women to Pornography, **Bower**. The Sex Discrimination Act 1975, **Atkins**. The Star Persona of Katharine Hepburn, **Thumim**.

25 Difference: A Special Third World Women Issue, **Minh-ha**. Melanie Klein, Psychoanalysis and Feminism, **Sayers**. Rethinking Feminist Attitudes Towards Mothering, **Gieve**. EEOC v. Sears, Roebuck and Company: A Personal Account, **Kessler-Harris**. Poems, **Wood**. Academic Feminism and the Process of De-radicalization, **Currie & Kazi**. A Lover's Distance: A Photoessay, **Boffin**.

26 Resisting Amnesia: Feminism, Painting and Post-Modernism, **Lee**. The Concept of Difference, **Barrett**. The Weary Sons of Freud, **Clément**. Short Story, **Cole**. Taking the Lid Off: Socialist Feminism in Oxford, **Collette**. For and Against the European Left: Socialist Feminists Get Organized, **Benn**. Women and the State: A Conference of Feminist Activists, **Weir**.

27 WOMEN, FEMINISM AND THE THIRD TERM: Women and Income Maintenance, **Lister**. Women in the Public Sector, **Phillips**. Can Feminism Survive a Third Term?, **Loach**. Sex in Schools, **Wolpe**. Carers and the Careless, **Doyal**. Interview with Diane Abbott, **Segal**. The Problem With No Name: Re-reading Friedan, **Bowlby**. Second Thoughts on the Second Wave, **Rosenfelt & Stacey**. Nazi Feminists?, **Gordon**.

Paradoxes of Gender

Judith Lorber

In this innovative book, a well-known feminist and sociologist challenges our most basic assumptions about gender. Judith Lorber argues that gender is wholly a product of socialisation, subject to human agency, organisation, and interpretation, and that it is a social institution comparable to the economy, the family, and religion in its significance and consequences. Calling into question the inevitability and necessity of gender, she envisions a society structured for equality, where no gender, racial, ethnic, or social class group is allowed to monopolise positions of power. *448pp. £20.00*

New in Cloth and Paper

Women and Politics Worldwide

Edited by Barbara J. Nelson and Najma Chowdhury

This important collection of essays is the first to analyse the complexities of women's political participation on a cross-national scale and from a feminist perspective. The book surveys forty-three countries, chosen to represent a variety of political systems, regions, and levels of economic development, to examine the extent of women's participation in political and economic decisions, women's political goals in different countries, and their potential to mobilise for change. *832pp. Cloth £35.00 Paper £17.95*

Representations of Motherhood

Edited by Donna Bassin, Margaret Honey, and Meryle Mahrer Kaplan

Offering new perspectives on motherhood, distinguished contributors from a variety of fields look at the conflicting positions on motherhood within the feminist movement; draw on psychoanalysis to grapple with mothers' profoundly ambivalent feelings toward their children; discuss how advances in medicine influence the meaning of motherhood; and examine how representations of mothers in art, film, literature, the social and behavioural sciences, and historical writing have affected women. *304pp. Illus. £20.00*

Sisters of the Brush

Women's Artistic Culture in Late Nineteenth-Century Paris
Tamar Garb

The Union of Women Painters and Sculptors was founded in Paris in 1881 to represent the interests of women artists and to facilitate the exhibition of their work. This lively and informative book traces the history of the first fifteen years of the organisation and places it in the context of the Paris art world and the development of feminism in the late nineteenth century. *224pp. 62 illus. £35.00*

Yale University Press • 23 Pond Street • London NW3 2PN

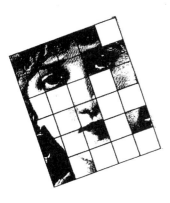

Second to None

A Documentary
History of American
Women
Volume I: From the
16th Century to 1865
Volume II: From 1865
to the Present
Edited by Ruth Barnes
Moynihan, Cynthia
Russett, and Laurie
Crumpacker

Volume I opens with a
Navajo origin myth
and presents Native
American, Hispanic,
African, and Euro-
American women from
the sixteenth century
through the Civil War.
Volume II ranges from
a tract by Elizabeth
Cady Stanton to the
testimony of Anita Hill.
Volume I
£42.75 HB, £19.00 PB
Volume II
£42.75 HB, £19.00 PB

We the Women

Career Firsts of
19th-Century America
Madeleine B. Stern
Wood engravings by
John De Pol
£11.95 PB

Feminisms of the Belle Epoque

A Historical and
Literary Anthology
Edited by Jennifer
Waelti-Walters and
Steven C. Hause
Texts translated by Jette
Kjaer, Lydia Willis, and
Jennifer Waelti-Walters

Chosen from newspa-
pers, speeches, novels,
political tracts, and the
like, these selections
portray the range of
feminist response to
the prevailing social
situation of women—
from the generally
meliorist position of
the Christian feminists
to the radical stances of
socialist and utopian
feminists.
£40.00 HB, £15.95 PB

Women, Elections, and Representation

Second Edition,
Revised
R. Darcy, Susan Welch,
and Janet Clark

The authors examine
women candidates and
candidacies in the
United States and
several other demo-
cratic nations. Their
careful analysis reveals
that male voters and
political elites are not
the barriers to women's
election that common
wisdom suggests.
£32.95 HB, £11.95 HB

Durkheim and Women

Jennifer M. Lehmann

i"Lehmann makes the
topic of Durkheim's
theorizing in relation to
women central to the
vital question of the
relationship of
capitalism and of liberal
social thought to
patriarchy. Lehmann's
work raises this issue in
a clear and perspica-
cious way."
—Roslyn W. Bologh
£28.50 HB

Gender and the Academic Experience

Berkeley Women
Sociologists
Edited by Kathryn P.
Meadow Orlans and
Ruth A. Wallace

With Berkeley as the
backdrop, sixteen
women describe their
marginal status in a
department and a
profession then
dominated by men.
Beginning with the first
woman graduate in
1952, each woman
constructs a personal
memoir of her
educational experience.
£32.95 HB, £13.95 PB

University of Nebraska Press c/o Academic and University
Publishers Group · 1 Gower Street London WC1E 6HA

House / Garden / Nation

Space, Gender, and Ethnicity in
Post-Colonial Latin American
Literatures by Women

Ileana Rodríquez

Translated by Robert Carr with the author

Focusing on the nation as garden, hacienda,
or plantation, Rodríquez shows us five Centro-
Caribbean women writers debating the
predicament of women under nation formation
from within the confines of marriage and home.
272pp, £15.95 pb, £47.50hb

Sex Workers and Sex Work

Anne McClintock, editor

Protesting the stigmatized public image of sex
workers as hapless victims, the contributors to
this volume debate the politics of female
representation and agency and claim a place
for sex workers at the feminist front line.
260pp, 33 illustrations, £7.50 pb

Feminism and Postmodernism

**Margaret Ferguson and
Jennifer Wicke, editors**

This collection of essays explores the
significant agreements and tensions between
contemporary feminists and postmodern
theories and practices. Contributors include
Toril Moi, Linda Nicholson, Andrew Ross,
Marjorie Garber, and David Simpson.
304pp, £14.95 pb, £32.95 hb

Maternal Fictions

Stendhal, Sand, Rachilde, and Bataille

Maryline Lukacher

Maternal Fictions offers a complex
psychological portrait of Stendhal, Sand,
Rachilde, and Bataille, writers who managed
at once to challenge patriarchal authority
and at the same time attempt to return to
the maternal.
192pp, £14.95pb, £32.95hb

Duke University Press ● c/o AUPG, 1 Gower Street, London WC1E 6HA